The Amazing Power of Music

Unless otherwise specified, all Scriptures are taken from the King James Version of the Holy Bible.

THE AMAZING POWER OF MUSIC
© 2009 by Dr. Jack W. Wheaton

Printed in the United States of America

ISBN 1-933641-32-0

The Amazing Power of Music

Dr. Jack W. Wheaton

Left to right: Jung Ho Pac (conductor, San Diego Symphony), Jack Wheaton and Jeanne Wheaton.

I would like to dedicate this book to my wife, Jeanne. Without her constant encouragement and help, this book would have never been completed.

Contents

Beginnings

The Power of Music 10

Why This Book? 13

Music and Science

How the Brain Perceives Music................................ 18

The Learning Process and Music 42

Adrenaline—Hormone of Fear 51

The Fight–or–Flight Response................................. 58

Breath Control.. 65

Music Therapy... 71

Noise Pollution 79

Recent Scientific Discoveries................................ 86

Power of Music Updates 101

Music and Society

I Am Music 108

Seven Basic Human Emotions...................................110

Advertising 115

Music for Cinema and Television Drama 122

A Brief History of Rock 'n Roll 129

Music and Religion

New Age Music 138

Quotes. 147

Rock Music in the Church 152

The Nuts and Bolts of Music

The Seven Parts of Music. 177

Rhythm. 186

Form 204

Melody 213

Countermelody 220

Harmony 223

Texture. 232

Style 235

Musical Instruments 239

The Future

The Future of Music. 245

Bibliography. 252

Beginnings

Chapter 1

The Power of Music

Music is the most powerful of all art forms. Why? Because the auditory signal that is triggered by music is inducted through the mid-brain, the hypothalamus, the area of the brain that scientists tell us interprets, expresses, and feels emotion.

Because music bypasses the critical brain—the cerebral cortex—we cannot censor or prevent our bodies and/or emotions from reacting to music. We not only "hear" music, our entire body "feels" music.

Music effects all the involuntary systems of the body—circulation, respiration, secretion of hormones, and other substances like adrenaline from the seven glands that are part of the endocrine gland system. Science has conclusively proven that *music is a language of emotions and cannot be censored.* Our body and our emotions will react to music, whether we like the sounds we are hearing or not.

Like so many things about our environment and ourselves, the ancient Greek philosophers (400–200 B.C.) were extremely aware of the power of music and the individuals' ability to censor his or her reaction to it. Plato saw the potential dangers of the misuse of music in society in his famous quote, "I care not what you teach in your schools and universities, but let me teach music and I will control your society!" (*The Republic,* Plato, p. 343).

There has never been a successful religious, social, or political movement without music leading the way. "Yankee Doodle" was first, and then during the Civil War, "The Battle Hymn of the Republic." The French Revolution was lead by marchers singing "The Marseilles" (now their national anthem). "The Internationale" inspired the Communist Revolution. Who can forget Hitler's Storm Troopers marching and singing "Deutchland uber Alles" on their way to conquering Europe in the 1930s and '40s?

Music is the universal language. Music can be understood and felt by all of humanity. You don't have to be Russian or speak Russian to enjoy Tchaikovsky, or Italian to enjoy Puccini, or American to enjoy the music of Gershwin. Although there are some musical styles that are more difficult to relate to—the music of the Far East, tribal Africa, and the Middle East—we can still sense the emotional content in most instances and react pleasurably to it.

Music is part of all of life's celebrations—birth, weddings, anniversaries, graduations, military service, college, national holidays, and even death. Music is always there to comfort, console, inspire, lift up, entertain, and bring joy and reflection. Music can bring an instant tear to the eye, or a smile. Music can trigger long-buried memories. None of life's major events are celebrated without music; all are made more meaningful by music.

The practitioners of music are more than artists; they are alchemists as well. They change people, places, and things. They help to make life bearable; they aid in advancing the causes of freedom; and can actually aid in the cure of several types of severe psychosis. Recent studies show that they can also aid in healing certain diseases, as well as minimize emotional and physical pain.

On a more practical level, music can help restore order with an unruly crowd, stimulate crop growth, increase animal production (i.e., milk and eggs), help memorization, unify a body of believers, citizens or friends, or even help control enemies of the state.

Recently the United States was attacked by a handful of fanatics who not only killed over three thousand people, but also managed to destroy one of our proudest landmarks, the Twin Towers in New York City. They brought a chill of fear and anxiety into the living room of every American home. What was one of the most important ingredients in expressing our grief, our shock, our outrage, our fear, and most of all our unity in pledging to fight together? Music.

Music not only eased our grief over 9/11, music unified us in our determination to preserve our wonderful way of life and our free society. "God Bless America," that wonderful, patriotic song of Irving Berlin, sums up all that is good and wonderful about our country. We all hope and pray that God will continue to bless America and our music—a product of a free society—and will help bring freedom to the rest of the world as well. Thelonius Monk, the great modern jazz pianist–composer, was once asked to define the essence of jazz. His response was, "Jazz is freedom." Then he added, "Think about it!"

Chapter 2

Why This Book?

I've spent my life playing, writing, conducting, and teaching music. I've enjoyed every minute of it. I believe music is one of the most powerful forces in the universe. However, like other forces, fire for instance, we sense it can be helpful or harmful. We need to learn more about music—its ability to inspire, heal, or harm. Today we have the scientific tools to really understand the amazing *power of music.*

How many musicians, conductors, composers, singers, and lyricists really understand the power of the media through which they work? The answer: very few. Our society today, particularly parents, law enforcement agencies, and the government, are becoming increasingly concerned about the physical, emotional, and cultural damage certain styles of music can have on a society. *Not all music is good for your health.*

Today, experts estimate that as much as 28 percent of our young population could suffer some kind of hearing loss, largely due to the uncontrolled volume of contemporary pop music (LA Times, 11/85). Scientists and medical practitioners are just beginning to discover that nervous and immune systems can be weakened by the overstimulation of the endocrine gland system, particularly the adrenal glands, due to triggering of our natural defense mechanism built into our subconscious minds called the "fight–or–flight" response. *Loud, repetitive music triggers this defense mechanism.*

Because of this response, sound is being researched as a possible military weapon. Batons that project a high–frequency sound within a small cone parameter can cause excruciating pain but no lasting damage, and may replace the electric Taser® and guns as a more practical ways of controlling crowds and unruly prisoners. Low-frequency sound waves can paralyze communications on the battlefields of tomorrow, cause disorientation and illness to the enemy, and may replace more harmful means like poison gas and current weapons of mass destruction. The government is actually developing a sound gun that can project a low-frequency wave along a laser beam that could someday knock an airplane out of the sky.

Others are becoming increasingly concerned about the growing amount of anarchistic, immoral standards of the lyrics of many of the so-called "pop" songs of today. While we have come a long way in championing women's rights in our society, you would never know it if you listened carefully to the lyrics of some of the rock, rap, gangsta rap, and hip-hop music of today that is being recorded and marketed to naïve teenagers by socially irresponsible cable television channels (MTV, VH1, Fuse) and record companies. Do we really want fourth graders calling women the degrading names found in these lyrics? Do we really want to teach our kids the joys of "killing a cop" through the lyrics of gangsta rap?

A famous historian once said that civilization is always just one generation removed from barbarism. It is the responsibility of the generation that is in power at the moment to monitor these creative outlets that can and often do misuse the power of music and weaken our society in the process. We need to teach children, parents, and communities the importance of preserving the foundations of a healthy society.

The naïveté on the part of our culture today regarding the dangers of unmonitored pop music and its potential negative effects on individuals and society as a whole is dangerous. *Freedom is not license!* A free society must be a responsible society. Setting standards in these areas of creative endeavor is not artistic censorship; it is self-preservation. No society can last long when its very foundations of morality are under attack. The irresponsible television and record companies may not be the ones who threw the bomb, but they are certainly the ones *who lit the fuse.*

Positive Power of Music

Now for the good news. We have created a whole new post–World War II era field of music therapy. Music can heal as well as harm. Iowa State University has led the country in research regarding music's effects on livestock and plants. It's not uncommon today to drive across Iowa in the summer and hear music coming from loud-speakers on top of fences being played over cornfields. They have discovered that certain types of music dramatically increase crop yields. Music is being played in barns while cows are being milked and music is piped into chicken ranches to stimulate growth and egg production.

Dramatic and exciting studies are showing how music can help Alzheimer's and Parkinson's disease patients, how music can be used as a mild anesthetic, how music can speed post–operative recovery and healing, and how music can lower blood pressure and reduce cholesterol.

Dramatic advances have been made in realizing that the study of music—particularly at specific ages, ages when the human brain is going through major changes (ages 3 to 5 and 13 to 17)—can increase learning skills, stimulate long–term memory, affect self–worth, and encourage positive motivation. Super–learning—the playing of slow, classical music softly in the background while people study a foreign language or other subject matter—has shown that the use of a specific type and style of music dramatically accelerates the learning curve in both the speed of learning and the retention of knowledge.

We are rediscovering some of the ancient knowledge regarding combining music with light and color for healing and entertainment. Color is nothing but sound rising to a much higher frequency. Someday our symphony orchestras will have a computer that instantly raises the sound vibrations of the orchestra into the color spectrum and then projects those colors and patterns on a giant screen behind the orchestra. When that happens, we will not only "hear" our favorite Beethoven symphony, but we will see it as well.

The research that I have done over the past few years in writing this book has been both enlightening and disturbing. Our failure to recognize the physical, emotional, and cultural dangers of unmonitored pop music is causing increasing chaos and unnecessary harm, particularly to children and young adults. On the other hand, the recent discoveries of music's tremendous abilities to heal are encouraging. Music will always be with us. We need, as individuals and a society, to understand both its strengths and weaknesses—its positive and negative powers—so we can keep music as a centerpiece of life without losing the quality of life in the process.

Years ago I asked a famous African American jazz musician why he had devoted his life to music. I will always remember his answer: *"Because a note never hurt anyone!"* Maybe the notes he was playing never hurt anyone, but today there are styles of music that can cause pain, permanent physical, emotional and psychological damage, and increase the subculture of anarchy. We need to know this and make others aware.

The wonderful, positive healing uses of music also need to be made known—so we can more correctly use this most powerful of art forms in our individual lives and the lives of our families and our nation.

Music and Science

Chapter 3

How the Brain Perceives Music

Childhood music lessons actually enlarge the brain. German researchers found that the brain area used to analyze musical pitch is an average of 25 percent larger in musicians. The younger the musical training begins, the larger the area.

—*Natural,* April 23, 1998

We have made many astounding discoveries in science regarding music over the past 100 years or more. Research into the brain and how it processes sound has given us an exceptional look into our own bodies and how they work. For instance, researchers and anthropologists have discovered that the love of music is a universal feature of the human species found in every culture. Music is also *deeply embedded in multiple structures of the human brain* (Natalie Angier, *New York Times,* January 9, 2009, "Science").

The brain tells us that it is a calculating complex of musical relationships, setting up musical expectations, and detecting violations of these expectations while we listen to music, even if the brain's "owner" doesn't "know" it. Nothing has been done consciously; there is no effort necessary to trigger this process outside of carefully listening to music. These findings show that nature has wired all of us, regardless of musical aptitude, for music (N. M. Weinberger, "What the Brain Tells Us About Music," *Musica* research notes, vol. VII, issue 1, Fall 2000).

Brain scans have revealed that professional musicians have significantly more activity in the part of the brain that controls hearing. "When professionals move their fingers, they are also hearing the music in their heads," says Gabriela Scheler of the University of Tubingen, Germany. She goes on to say that the research findings suggest that professional musicians have "liberated" their minds from worrying about hitting the right notes. As a result, they are able to listen, judge, and control their play, she said. "Presumably this enhances their musical performance" (Seth Hettena, Associated Press, San Diego, November 27, 2001).

Recently an entire set of self-help books for different motor skills (tennis, golf, music, etc.) emerged from the publishing world. The trend started with the widely popular "Inner Game of Tennis" and, later, "The Inner Game of Music." The new information in these books relates to how the reader can transfer the basic kinesthetic (muscle and skeletal movement) activities and necessary reaction skills needed to perform these skills from the cognitive left brain to the intuitive right brain, where the split-second reactions are faster, more spontaneous, and more accurate. The cognitive left hemisphere of the brain, then, is left doing what it does best: monitoring and evaluating the process.

Jascha Heifitz, the world-renowned concert violinist, was once quoted as saying that when he performed, part of him was on stage making the movements necessary to produce the music, while another part was in the audience, evaluating the results. This kind of "split-mindedness" is common, and even necessary to developing advanced musical skills. Playing skills must become intuitive—performed automatically with the correct stimulus-response without premeditated planning on the part of the left hemisphere of the brain. In the Japanese version of Buddhism called "Zen," this is called "no-mindedness." A classic book titled *Zen and the Art of Archery* by Alan Watts defines this process in a way the Western mind can understand and practice.

The wonderful and innovative beginning music training program for young, beginning string and keyboard players called the "Suzuki Method," after its originator, Japanese educator Dr. Shinichi Suzuki, uses these Zen-like concepts to teach children music. Suzuki believed the basic skills of playing the instrument should be taught before teaching the process of reading music. These basic skills should be taught through careful imitation and repetition until the musical response was intuitive, not cognitive.

In the 1970s I had the opportunity to attend a Suzuki demonstration at the Music Educator's National Conference. Dr. Suzuki, though up in years, had flown over from Tokyo to explain and demonstrate his new approach to teaching beginning instrumental music. He brought with him a small group of young violinists, many playing half–sized violins, ages 5 to 9 years of age.

To demonstrate the thoroughness of his teaching methods, Dr. Suzuki, in a live demonstration with these young violinists, would have them begin playing a musical example they had learned in this manner. To prove that their musical performance was intuitive (right brain), not cognitive (left brain), Dr. Suzuki asked the students simple questions, *while they were playing.* He asked them their name, their age, and even asked them simple mathematical equations, like "How much is 3 and 7?" If they could answer these simple questions while playing a simple but demanding piece by Bach or Vivaldi, then the transfer was complete.

Learning to play a musical instrument in this manner, and later practicing and learning new material this way, allows the brain to maximize its potential and involvement and encourages the correct use of the two different hemispheres of the brain in the process. Another advantage of learning a musical instrument this way is that it is fun! It removes a great deal of the anxiety and discomfort involved in trying to do up to five new things simultaneously when learning to play in the old–fashioned way.

The Old–Fashioned Way

There sits the piano. You want to learn to play it. What's involved? Well, when starting to learn to play the piano "the old–fashioned way," you've got five formidable and challenging skills to learn and combine:

1. One needs to know the correct position at the piano: back straight, arms straight out in front of you (not reaching up or down—ad-

just the piano bench to find the correct height), fingers curved, and each finger touching the keys.

2. The notes—Three things you must learn about notes: (a) their names, (b) their recognizable sounds, and (c) how they are written on the musical staff.

3. Next is the rhythm of the piece. Either by rote (imitation) or by reading, a student must learn to count and correctly read or learn basic rhythm patterns.

4. Next comes fingering. Moving the hand up or down the keyboard requires knowledge of fingering.

5. Learning to read music—learning the musical staff and the names of the lines and spaces; learning how to count the written notes and rests; learning about occidentals and key signatures; and learning the difference between the bass clef (left hand) and the treble clef (right hand), and how to put them together.

The frustration that can result in trying to learn and apply these five different skills simultaneously can be overwhelming. Is it any wonder that so many young players do not like to practice, make little progress, and eventually quit, even though they still want to play? New approaches to teaching beginning instruments like the Suzuki and Yamaha approach removes a great deal of frustration from learning and also encourages older would-be pianists to come back and learn how to play this new, fun way!

Not understanding the human brain and how it works has been part of the problem in using old-fashioned methods to teach people how to make music. It's been like trying to put a square peg in a round hole. Until now, the students learned how to play *in spite* of the teaching methods, not because of them. The brain loves to learn. It enjoys learning new skills. It is particularly "happy" when the intuitive (right brain) and cognitive (left brain) skills are being used properly. *Motivation is not a problem when students are using their brains correctly in the study of music.*

Many of the well-known early jazz musicians never learned to "read" music. They learned to play by imitation, "by ear." Many of today's successful rock musicians did the same. Two of the most successful pop musicians of the past century, Paul McCartney and John Lennon of the Beatles, never learned to read music, but look at the songs they wrote! John Lennon's mother said that when he was a teenager learning to play guitar, he would sometimes practice until his hands would bleed and she would have to take his guitar away from him for a while. *That's motivation!*

Learning to Let Go

Centuries ago a Japanese Buddhist monk sat down to ponder the problem of self-defense. As a monk, he was forbidden to use a weapon in self-defense; yet robbers would still attack he and his fellow monks when traveling outside the ashram. This monk began observing wild animals and noticed how these animals would use their bodies to defend themselves. Suddenly this monk realized that his own body could be used as a weapon. From this realization, the martial arts were born: kung fu (China), karate (Okinawa), jujitsu (Japan), and other variations.

This same monk developed a method of teaching the martial arts:

» Define each blow or attack and practice very slowly over and over—slow motion. Concentration moving smoothly and accurately.

» After many repetitions slowly, suddenly make the move or moves *as quickly as possible.* In this second phase, it is important for the student to do this without cognitive thought—"no mindedness." Keep the conscious mind empty, observing.

» Gradually add additional defense and attack moves to your slow practice routine, much like a slow-motion ballet. The collection of these movements into a group is called a *kata.* An advanced martial arts expert may have a daily *kata to practice that is an hour or more in length.*

» In exhibitions, contests, and combat, the martial arts expert enters the fray with the express purpose of keeping his conscious mind above the fray, supervising the overall action but not contemplating the moves. *All the details of the various moves are intuitive and controlled by the right brain.*

Good martial arts teachers, like good music teachers, teach us how to "let go" of our kinesthetic movements and learn to *trust* the right brain to do the detailed work faster, with less effort and more accuracy. Martial arts teachers call this a state of "no mindedness." When engaged in combat, what should the student be thinking of? The answer: *Nothing.* The concentrative mind is there only to supervise and referee. Once this state is achieved, there is a sense of freedom and power that is exhilarating and encouraging. Performing on a musical instrument is a great deal more fun and the results are better, faster, and more long lasting when the student learns to practice in a similar manner: drill slowly and smoothly on isolated difficult passages then attack them up to tempo without cognitive interference. It works. It makes the study of music more fun and it utilizes the human brain correctly in the process

The Brain and Long–Term Memory

Music lessons can improve long-term verbal memory, according to a recent scientific study in Hong Kong, China. Those who know how to play a musical instrument and practice regularly have an advantage over non–musicians. Studying musical notes and scales seems to enlarge a region of the brain called the *left plenum temporal,* which is involved in remembering words.

This research is consistent with previous studies linking music training with an enlarged cerebellum, which forms the bulk of the brain. Scientists at the Beth Israel Medical Center in Boston found that the cerebellum of expert musicians was 5 percent larger than that of people who had not studied music. ("Music Lessons Found to Spur Memory," Reuters, London, *SD Union Tribune,* November 12, 1998).

Brain research today has proven that a person can "grow," i.e., increase brain regions by musical practice. You can shape your own brain according to what you do. Practice makes it easier for involved brain cells to work more efficiently together (ibid., p. 5).

Another recent study supposes that one of the reasons music is so powerful is that melodies can stimulate the same parts of the brain that are stimulated when thinking about food and sex. People can learn how to drive away sadness and fear by using certain styles of music that makes them feel "happy."

Using prescribed music to control false physical hunger is being examined as a possible new method of controlling our weight. We may soon be seeing *The Music Diet* book on the bestseller list, a book that tells us to go play the piano or listen to Mozart for 20 minutes when we are hungry rather than heading for the refrigerator or cookie jar. Previous studies have linked the midbrain, the *ventral striaturn,* and parts of the cortex to sex and food. The new study, according to Dr. Anne Blood, a researcher at Massachusetts Hospital in Charlestown, Massachusetts, clearly shows a similar response in these areas to musical sounds (AP, "Music hath charms for brain parts," September 25, 2001).

Music Therapy

Music therapy is one of the fastest-growing fields in modern medicine. From 1998 to 1999 the job market for music therapists jumped *30 percent.* There have been phenomenal discoveries that indicate the music is more powerful as a healing agent —physical, emotional, and mental—than any of us could have imagined.

"The therapeutic use of music seems to activate different parts of the brain, including networks associated with motor control, memory, emotion, and speech," claims neuroscientist Michael Thaut at Colorado State University. Dr. Thaut is using the close link between music and movement to help people slowed by strokes, cerebral palsy, muscular dystrophy, and Parkinson's disease regain some control of their automatic nervous system (Peter Jaret, "The Healing Power of Music," *Reader's Digest,* September 2001).

Again, recent studies reveal that music can affect levels of various hormones, including *cortisol* (involved in arousal and stress), *testosterone* (aggression and arousal), and *oxytocin* (nurturing behavior), as well as trigger release of the natural opiates known as *endorphins.* Using PET scanners, scientists have shown that the parts of the brain involved in processing emotion seem to light up with activity when a subject hears music (Andrew Dorman, "Music on the Brain," *Time,* June 5, 2000).

A new study of people with Alzheimer's disease found that music helped them sleep better. When the patients played drums or sang along with songs, their *serum melatonin* levels—which influence how well we sleep—skyrocketed by more than 200 percent. "Through music they slept better, and interacted better with others" says Mahendra Kumar of the University of Miami (*USA Weekend,* October 26, 2001).

By adulthood the brain is crisscrossed with more than *100 million neurons,* each reaching out to thousands of others, so that, all told, the brain has more than *100 trillion connections.* It is those connections—more than the number of galaxies in the known universe—that give the brain its unrivaled powers (Sharon Begley, "Your Child's Brain," *Newsweek,* February 19, 1996).

The Brain Is Wired for Music

» Skill: Math and logic
» Learning Window: Birth to 4 years
» What We Know: Circuits for math reside in the brain's cortex, near those for music. Toddlers taught simple concepts, like "one" and "many," do better in math. *Music lessons may help develop spatial skills* (ibid.).

"Music affects the mind in powerful ways: it not only incites passion, belligerence, serenity, or fear, but does so even in people who do not know from experience, for instance, that a particular crescendo means the killer is about to pop out on the movie screen. All in all, says psychologist Isabelle Peretz of the University of Montreal, 'the brain seems to be specialized for music'" (ibid.).

The temporal lobes of the brain, just behind the ears, act as the music center. When neurosurgeons tickle these regions with a probe, patients have been known to hear tunes or lengthy musical compositions so vividly that they ask, "Why is there a phonograph in the operating room" (ibid.).

Although kids who receive music training improve across the board in school due to the "good mood" and attention effects, they dramatically improve in math. There is something specific about music and math. Speculation is that it has something to do with measuring proportion (counting), ratios (intervals), and sequences (rhythm patterns), all of which are essential elements in mathematical reasoning (Martin Gardiner, Brown University, ibid.).

Right and Left Brain

The right brain hemisphere is linked to spontaneity, creativity, and emotion; the left to linear, logical, non-emotion cognition. The greatest musicians are not only masters of technique, but also adept at infusing their playing with emotion. This indicates an equal balance and strength between the hemispheres.

Could the study of music improve a person's balance between logic and emotion? Sigmund Freud, the great father of modern psychology, was very pessimistic before his death. He saw cultures and nations as being either emotionally repressed (left brain) or emotionally out-of-control (right brain). Emotionally repressed cultures can be guilty of extreme cruelty, i.e., Nazi Germany or the Catholic Inquisition. Emotionally out-of-control cultures eventually produce anarchy and revolution. Freud saw no way out of these two extremes.

The political extremes of totalitarianism and anarchy were played out on history's stage with the left-brain excesses of Nazi Germany and the right-brain out-of-control slaughter of millions in Africa's Rwanda. Sigmund Freud, like many brilliant minds before him, anticipated the discoveries of the differences in brain hemisphere activity and how it plays out in history.

Today, the extreme mathematical logic of modern music, like Schoenberg's 12-tone serial composition school represents the extreme left-brain dominance in music. An out-of-control emotion being shrieked into overly loud microphones by poorly train rock musicians represents the extreme right-brain school of music.

The fact that our society has embraced anarchistic music in the form of rock, rap, and hip-hop to such a degree suggests that our society could rapidly move toward political anarchy. Marshal McLuhan, the great Canadian historian–sociologist, once said that the arts are the "radar" of civilization, and generally telegraph social trends anywhere from 25 to 50 years ahead of time. Disrespect for all forms of authority or rules in the 1960s revealed a society sliding toward anarchy.

A dictator who restores order by banning extreme right–brain art always follows. We saw this in Germany in the 1930s. When Hitler came to power he immediately attacked American "jazz" music and modernist painters like Picasso and plays by liberal authors like Brecht, actually outlawing the public performance or display of this type of art. A good film to rent (if you can find it) on this subject is *Swing Kids,* about a group of young people living in the early stages of Nazi Germany, holding illegal dances where they jitterbugged to the American jazz of Benny Goodman, Glenn Miller, and others. These young Germans were resisting the attempts to drive them away from right–brain art and music. The same subject is treated creatively in the popular film *Cabaret,* showing us the struggle between the extreme left and right brain cultures in Berlin of the 1930s.

Rx Music

Emotional balance on an individual and cultural basis will be a much sought–after goal in the future. Schools and doctors will begin treating out–of–balance and troubled teens and citizens with therapeutic music. Extreme, uptight left–brainers will learn to loosen up with jazz and other forms of spontaneous music, while extreme anarchists and emotionally out–of–control individuals will be prescribed Mozart and Bach. Many of today's teenagers, already struggling with their often out–of–control emotions, are throwing gasoline on the fire when they add drugs, alcohol, illicit sex, and loud, anarchistic rock music to the mix. Today's teenagers are tomorrow's citizens. Only emotionally balanced individuals can lead positively and productively into the future.

Because it is so wired into the brain, it is probably the most powerful and fastest way to correct these imbalances without having to use chemical substances (tranquilizers, stimulants) that are potentially dangerous to both the body and the mind.

In October 1995, researchers in Germany reported that listening, singing, or playing music rewires specific neural circuits. The study also revealed that the amount of daily practice did not affect the cortical map as much as the age of the musician when they started music training. Like other circuits formed early in life, the ones for music endure. "Music trains the brain for higher forms of thinking" (ibid.).

The mechanism behind the *Mozart Effect* supposedly reveals that when children exercise cortical neurons by listening to classical music, they are also strengthening circuits used for mathematics. According to researchers at UC Irvine in Irvine, California, music excites the inherent brain patterns and enhances their use in complex reasoning tasks like higher mathematics (ibid.). "Plato once said that music is a more potent instrument than any other for education" (Dr. Frank Vellutino, Prof. of Ed. Psych., State University of New York at Albany).

Because music activates both hemispheres of the brain and the cerebellum, music therapy can now aid in the rehabilitation of stroke and other brain trauma patients who have lost speech capabilities. *Melodic intonation therapy,* where people sing what they want to say to improve fluency of speech, is now a primary method of language rehabilitation (*Music Making and the Brain,* American Music Conference, September 30, 2001).

Speech classes are beginning to use the technique of having their speakers–in–training "sing" their presentations before "speaking" them. Singing the material improves enunciation, pronunciation, articulation, tempo, vocal inflection, and breathing, as well as tone. Sing–speak is the hottest new technique in improving public speaking.

The reason behind the origin and development of opera was for several practical reasons. When the Renaissance, the Age of Reason, broke out in Europe, and particularly in Italy, young students began dusting off old Greek plays by Euripides and others for public performance. Outdoor performances for large audiences made understanding the spoken dialogue difficult (the Italians had not yet mastered the acoustic brilliance of the Greeks, whose amphitheaters were so acoustically sensitive you could hear a sneeze on stage in the back row). As a result, these early attempts to resurrect the brilliant plays of the ancient Greeks were set to music, largely so audiences could hear the dialogue. Naturally, the singers had to be accompanied by musicians to support their voices which added additional drama to the play.

One of the earliest opera composers, Monteverdi composed the music for many of these ancient plays . . . and so opera, one of the greatest of the Western European art forms, was born out of practical necessity. Later opera was divided into "opera buffa" (comic opera) and "opera seri" (serious opera), much as the ancient Greek plays were largely comedies or tragedies.

What does this have to do with music and the brain? Just this: the description of historical events given above illustrates the fact that man was already searching for emotional balance through music. One of the great surprises in scientific research is the confirmation of the fact that we are always exploring, always seeking balance, always looking for ways to maintain physical, emotional, and mental health, on a subconscious as well as a conscious level. Throughout the centuries, music has been there to help mankind adjust to radical changes on man's ecological, political, moral, or spiritual environment, and to reduce stress in our lives.

Archaeologists have discovered playable primitive flutes carved from animal bone that predate the Lescaux cave paintings in southern France. The tone produced by these most ancient of objects is "sweet and mellow" (ibid.).

What does this mean? This means, that as far as we know, all ancient cultures had some form of music and had already developed some early musical instruments. The earliest musical instruments were the voice, the drum, the flute, and some type of stringed instrument. Later, when rare metals were discovered and smelted, particularly brass, they were quickly made into weapons and armor, and later, musical instruments like the trumpet, the trombone, the French horn, and the tuba.

The most popular and probably the oldest musical "scale" in the world of music is the *pentatonic* scale (do–re–me–fa–so–la). It is the most common scale used even today in classical music from the East, particularly China and Japan. It is also the most common scale used by birds and whales. Because there are no half steps in this scale, it is extremely mellow, pleasant, and devoid of tension.

The pentatonic scale is used increasingly to calm agitated patients and raise the spirits of the depressed. Its light, airy notes, without any tension-points, is therapeutic, something the ancient Chinese discovered thousands of years ago.

Male humpback whales spend close to six months of each year doing little else but singing, using rhythms similar to those found in human music and musical phrases of similar length. These whales are capable of vocalizing over a range of seven octaves. Their songs proceed in a stepwise, lilting musical manner rather than careening madly from octave to octave—they also sing "in key" (ibid.).

How the Brain Interprets Sound

First of all, the external ear, called the *pinna*, helps to funnel sound into the ear, where it travels down the *auditory canal* and the vibrations of sound finally strike the *eardrum*. The sound vibrations, now coded and amplified by the eardrum, continue into the three middle-ear bones called the *malleus, incus*, and *stapes*, which react like a tuning fork when struck.

The vibrations continue into the fluid-filled, snail-like *cochlea*, where small hairs called *stereocillia* attached to the *basilar membrane* are moved by the sound waves, not unlike your patio wind chimes, only on a much smaller scale. These microscopic hairs mark the place where sound vibrations are transformed into electrical signals that are processed by the brain.

These tiny hairs can be easily damaged by overexposure to high decibel sound, resulting in a permanent hearing loss called *tinnitus*, which is a constant buzzing in the ear. *Due to the extreme volume of today's music, as well as the increasing noise pollution of our environment, tinnitus has become a raging epidemic among the young.*

The movements of these microscopic hairs send impulses via the *optic nerve* to the brain, which *translates the perceived messages as sound.* The patterns of sound are organized into pitch, rhythm, tone, range, volume, and tempo—which the brain interprets as music. Other sounds are perceived as communication (language), danger (sudden, sharp loud sounds), sounds of nature (birds, running water, etc.), or noise pollution (cars, trucks, machinery, etc.).

There is a special type of protein that our genes produce in the cochlea, the snail-like organ of the inner ear that *marks the last passage of sound waves from the outside world before they are converted into electrical signals that the brain can interpret.* Inside the cochlea are bundles of these microscopic hairs that *are pushed against a membrane as sound waves travel through its fluid-filled chamber exerting pressure.*

These tiny hairs, called *stereocillium,* are arranged in bundles called *stereocillia.* The tip of each hair is bound to the one next to it by a tiny link, somewhat like lights on a Christmas tree. As the entire bundle of hairs bends to the pressure of sound waves, the strings pull at the hairs they are attached to, opening a kind of door on the surface of each hair.

This door is called an *ion channel.* It allows *calcium* and *potassium* ions floating in fluid inside the cochlea to *flow into each hair and down toward connections* (vesicles) *leading to the brain.* The flow of these ions from the cochlea into the brain results in the transformation of sound waves into *electrical signals,* a process called *mechanotransduction.*

"Something has to open this door, and the molecule that does is called *Catherine 23*" (Dr. Mueller, *SD Union Tribune,* Scripps Research, April 19, 2004). Scientists at Scripps Research Center in LaJolla, California, are discovering that certain types of deafness or gradual hearing loss is a result of a lack of or a diminishing supply of this unique and special hormone. This discovery could lead to a form of gene therapy that could eventually cure or reverse deafness or gradual loss of hearing (ibid.).

The processing of sound to the brain is a complex process, involving several steps. *The delicate mechanisms involved in processing sound can be easily damaged.* Our society's chosen ignorance of this fact has resulted in a growing nation of hard-of-hearing, prematurely deaf citizens and millions more plagued by an avoidable, irritating, and often painful condition called "tinnitus." The primary culprit for these permanent disorders is the uncontrollable volume of today's popular music. *Any music played at 90 dB or above on a regular basis is damaging to your health.*

Our Biocomputer

The *Journal of Nature Neuroscience* devoted a special issue to the topic of how the building blocks of music are to be found in speech. And in the August 6, 2003, issue, David Schwartz, Catherine Howe, and Dale Purves of Duke University argue that the *sounds of music and the sounds of language are intricately connected.*

"In a recent lab test, twelve teenagers played the game *Memory.* Four of them listened to rock, four listened to classical, and four did not listen to music at all. Those who listened to rock had the poorest performance by a wide margin. Those who did not listen did OK, but those who listened to classical music kept enhancing their scores" ("Seven Ways to Optimize Your Brain and Your Life," Dr. Daniel Amen, www.brainplace.com).

As we produce more and more sophisticated computers, we are learning more and more about how the human brain works and develops. The human brain is the primary model for all sophisticated computers. In today's exciting world of biotechnology, scientists are moving closer every day to understanding the human brain as they use it as a model. Still, they are light-years away from duplicating this most fascinating of nature's miracles, the human brain.

Science has revealed that we really have three brains, or bio-computers, running our body and mind. The *thalamus,* a small base-ball-sized organ, sits at the very top of our spinal column. This brain, sometimes called the "reptilian" brain, controls our automatic nervous system, which in turn controls all the below-conscious level activities of our body, including heart, lungs, breathing, digestion, glandular secretions, etc. Damage or shock to this brain can bring death within minutes, since it would shut down the necessary signals to the body to keep breathing, etc.

If you reach around to the base of your skull, where it joins your spine, and move your finger slowly up or down until it resides in that small recession that separates the top of the spine from the skull, you are very close to touching the thalamus part of your brain. A danger-ous blow to the back of the head, at the base of the spine (taught in the martial art of karate), can temporarily paralyze because it stuns the thalamus, the master control of our automatic nervous system. This blow is never delivered in competition, because it could cause serious injury or death.

A larger brain, the *hypothalamus,* fits like a catcher's mitt over the smaller thalamus. This brain controls some of the semi–auto-matic systems of the body and, according to scientists, is the likely location of our emotional reactions to external stimuli. This is the part of the brain that receives and interprets all the audio input that enters our ears. In fact, our audio system is hot–wired into this part of the brain. What this means is that music can trigger an emotional response without our higher brain, our cerebral cortex, being in-volved. Now you know why Plato, the well–known Greek philoso-pher, supposedly said in his book *The Republic,* "Let me teach music in your society and I will control its destiny and future."

Our brain's reaction to music is not controllable. All of our invol-untary systems respond in some way to the music we listen to. We feel the emotions being generated by the music, *even if we conscious-ly resist.* That's one of the reasons for the constant war between the teenage and adult generations over music. The older generation wants music that soothes and heals; the younger generation wants music that stimulates and makes us aggressive and full of uncontrol-lable energy.

Recent studies show that both sides need to modify their ex-treme positions for general health. However, the extremely loud, sharply accented screaming music of the extremists in today's pop music are deadly dangerous to both the older and the younger gen-eration, and have strong negative effects on physical and emotional health.

The *cerebral cortex* is the seat of our intellect, our will, our high-er reasoning abilities, the grand achievement of God in designing our bodies. This part of the brain, which fits like a glove over the hypo-thalamus and has two hemispheres, is the *primary* reason man has abilities light–years beyond other primates. Gorillas, monkeys, and chimpanzees have a lot less to work with in this part of the brain.

The cerebral cortex is the most sophisticated and advanced part of the brain, and represents all that we call "human." It truly separates us from all other created beings. This brain is like an air controller in the tower directing traffic in the sky to a safe landing.

The cerebral cortex is the chief administrator and decision-maker in the brain. It monitors and sends a message of suggested response to the sensory inputs coming into the body. **The only thing it cannot do is control our emotional response to music.** By the time the cerebral cortex receives the forwarded information from the cerebellum regarding music, the mid–brain has already triggered an automatic emotional response. The only thing the cerebral cortex can do at this point is to send a signal to the individual (if the music is too loud or offensive) to turn it off or leave the room. We can only change our environment if we can't control it.

One astounding discovery, made at the UCLA Medical Center in the early 1980s, was the discovery of the almost autonomous and independent functioning of the right and left hemispheres of the cerebral cortex, the upper brain. The right hemisphere controls the left side of the body, and vice versa. This discovery has revolutionized teaching methods, psychological counseling, therapy, and sports conditioning, as well as mental health techniques.

Simply put, the right hemisphere is the emotional, spontaneous, improvisational, playful, and "gestalt" (the whole is greater than the sum of its parts) side of our brain. In music, it is the side that controls our ability to improvise or "play by ear." A right–brain biased person learns new material best through listening. Also, this is the part of the brain that stores long–term memory.

Music learned by "rote," or by "ear," will never be forgotten. Like learning to ride a bike, it's always there. Right–brain dominant listeners like repetition, syncopation, sudden musical "surprises," etc. Right–brain dominant listeners are more into "feeling" music than "understanding" it. The form of their music is cyclic rather than evolutionary. Modern jazz, New Age, rock, rap, pop, hip–hop, and most folk music fall into this right–brain dominant group.

The left hemisphere is the linear, logical, non-emotional, legalistic, reasoning side of the brain. In music, this hemisphere controls our ability to read and interpret music. The rich legacy of Western European music is for the most part based upon a left-brain skill, since this music is written down and preserved for future generations to recreate. The process of *reading music* is primarily a left-brain skill.

Humor is not a left-brain skill. With its emphasis on spontaneity and rhythmic delivery, humor definitely falls into the right-brain category. How many German and Japanese comedians can you name (two left-brain dominant cultures)? Left-brain biased students are "serious" and uneasy when music is approached as "fun and games." For listeners, those that favor most mainline instrumental classical music are left-brain dominant. Jazz, rock, the blues, and most pop music is primarily right-brain driven—highly emotional, spontaneous, and seldom written down before being performed.

The foundation of Western civilization, the "logos" upon which our culture rests (Judaic, Greek, Christian) demands in drama, literature, and music that there be a beginning, a logical development, and a meaningful ending. *Logos*" is the root word for "logic." Maintaining logic is definitely a left-brain dominant concept. Our culture, until recently, demanded "meaning" from all its art forms. Today that is not the case, because as a civilization, since the end of World War II, we have been slowly moving toward a more right-brain biased culture.

Music and Memorization

The left brain is the site for all premeditated planning, and contains only short-term memory. All long-term memory is stored in the right brain. Long-term memory of the music they learn by visual means can only be triggered through creative visualization in the student's head. In other words, they memorize music by transferring the visual symbols to their brain and actually eventually "see" these symbols (in their mind's eye) when playing that music without the written page in front of them.

Music is memorized in three different ways: (1) visual memory—as described in the above paragraph; (2) aural memory—remembering the exact pitch and rhythm order of notes; and (3) tactile memory—the remembrance of exact muscle contractions and movements for a particular passage. Top concert performers use all three processes. In case one breaks down, the other two are there to carry on.

To take advantage of their own biocomputer, music students should close their eyes when making music unless they are reading music. Our marvelous biocomputer, the brain, is built in such a manner that when one of the tactile senses is shut down, *the brain automatically makes the other senses more sensitive.* Music students can take advantage of this knowledge to dramatically increase the effectiveness of their practice sessions. Closing your eyes when making music (except when necessary to keep them open to read music) increases the power of the auditory and tactile input, thereby speeding learning and enhancing performing skills and accuracy.

Brainwaves

The brain has four wave patterns or frequencies that it uses to comprehend reality and express itself.

1. **Beta**—the primary wave-frequency associated with conscious deductive reasoning, thinking, digesting information, and formulating opinions, etc.—primarily a left-brain activity.
2. **Alpha**—a conscious state of relaxation; the feeling we have after a cocktail or two or a body massage; a pleasant visual and aural environment . . . in other words, a state of *conscious relaxation*—right-hemisphere dominant.
3. **Theta**—a trancelike state; hypnosis; an extreme drug or alcohol high, sometimes brought on by physical or emotional trauma. The conscious controls have pretty much shut down and the individual can be induced to do silly (or sometimes dangerous) things, *a la* the nightclub hypnotist who makes people do things their conscious minds would resist. This is the state that extremists will use to "brainwash" an enemy, to plant seeds of uncontrollable behavior triggered by key phrases, sights, or sounds, as in the

disturbing movie *The Manchurian Candidate*. **All occult religions use this brainwave to condition their devotees,** to help them shed their "individual" consciousness for something called the "group" consciousness.

4. **Delta**—deep sleep. This is the fourth type of brainwave and only occurs in deep sleep. Those whose sleep patterns are disturbed are often deprived of time in the delta zone, often resulting in fatigue, lack of concentration, and lack of energy.

Mass Hypnosis or Possession?

One may argue over the spiritual roots of demonic possession, but it does occur, and has been recorded in voodoo, santeria, canto doble, and other African–Latin American religions. Music, particularly rhythm, plays a key role in this process. Through the use of repetitive, syncopated rhythms and ritual drugs, like marijuana or peyote, certain "sensitive" individuals, called "shamans" or medicine men (or women), allow outside forces to possess them briefly to share information with spirits "from the other side." According to Harold Courtlander in *A Treasury of Afro–American Folklore,* the process goes something like this:

1. Well-trained drummers play particular rhythms that help set up the hypnotic state, usually a battery of three or more drummers (although a single drum can do the job with the right rhythm).
2. The constant repetition of these rhythms quickly induces a trance state (theta)—a breakdown or surrender of conscious control.
3. At this point, if you accept the occult explanation, the person in the trance is invaded by an "outside" personality that causes them to act, speak, and move in an unusual way, sometimes speaking a foreign language.
4. Others present gifts to the person who is suddenly inhabited by this outside force and ask for advice for the future from the "ancient one" (possessing spirit).

Music and the Theory of Relativity

When Albert Einstein was a child, he was initially considered so unteachable that he could not participate in a traditional school program. He developed his language skills very late. His mother pulled him out of public schools, bought him a violin, enlisted a music teacher, and hired a tutor for his general education. Somehow his avid interest in music and his growing skills on the violin opened up his abilities to think, reason, and communicate.

The rest is history. Whenever stumped while working on a complex mathematical problem, Einstein would grab his violin and play music for a while. He claimed that it never failed to open up the channels of innovative thought that he sought to solve the scientific problem at hand. Today other scientists are learning to balance their left-brain research skills with right-brain escapes into music, dance, art, and drama.

Albert Einstein and the great Viennese violinist Fritz Kreisler were lifelong friends. They would often get together and help each other with their favorite pastime. Einstein's was, as already reported, playing the violin. Kreisler's passion, aside from music, was chess and working mathematical problems. This is a classic case of each person using the skills and friendship of another to help balance their own personalities and skills.

Language and Music

According to Sandra Blakeslee, some scientists think that language and music are two sides of the same intellectual coin. Cellular circuits that recognize language and music are found on both sides of the brain, according to Dr. Jamshjed Bharucha, a psychologist at Dartmouth College in Hanover, New Hampshire.

The left hemisphere also contains regions that specialize exclusively in language, and the right has some regions that exclusively serve musical perception. The explains the strange examples of "idiot savants" who are severely incapacitated in the left brain but have developed extraordinary musical skills via their right hemisphere.

Music has long been called the "language of emotions." Scientists can now confirm this theory. In recent studies, scientists have discovered that listening to music seems to encourage the brain to release endorphins, which in turn elicit emotional responses to the music.

Behavior Modification

Further research in the United Kingdom (Great Britain) reveals that when Mozart was played during science lessons for school children whose behavior was normally very disruptive, these children demonstrated improved concentration. Pulse rate, blood pressure, and body temperature were reduced significantly because the music increased the production of endorphins, which led to a reduction in corticosteroids and adrenaline, slowing the body's metabolism and improving coordination (www.musiced.co.uk/teachers/powerof-music/fom4.html).

A national convenience store chain was having trouble with teenage gangs hanging around outside the store at night in certain urban areas. The stores in question began broadcasting the music of Mozart through loudspeakers. Reportedly the gangs broke up and eventually went home or gathered elsewhere.

There have been instances in theaters and sports events where crowd control was restored by playing "The Star Spangled Banner" (our national anthem). The calming effect of the music often stopped or prevented riots and civil disturbances. A famous American opera star quieted a major rock festival crowd in England by singing the haunting Christian hymn "Amazing Grace" unaccompanied.

On the other hand, rock music, in particular, tends to fire up its audiences to the point where crowd control becomes a problem; hence, the demise of large outdoor rock festivals. The required insurance to put on this type of event is so expensive it is usually cost prohibitive. At the famous Altamonte rock concert outside of San Francisco in the 1960s, featuring the Rolling Stones, an out-of-control fan was fatally stabbed by another out-of-control fan right in front of the stage, even though the stage area was heavily protected by a cordon of Hell's Angels, bikers who were hired to be bodyguards.

It is no accident that our advertising agencies have discovered the power of music and use it often in radio and television ads. On a more ominous note, it is no accident that MTV and the record industry have also discovered that teenagers can be brainwashed, manipulated, and shaped through the power of music to accept values and behavior that is often contradictory to family, nation, and culture.

Music Imagery

"We don't know what triggers musical image," Dr. Robert J. Zatorre said, "but it is very common for people to wake up in the morning with songs running through their heads" (ibid.).

Wolfgang Amadeus Mozart, one of the greatest composers who ever lived and a certified child prodigy, often composed entire works in his head while on long carriage rides from the court of one ruler to another in late eighteenth century Europe. By the time he had arrived, he could begin putting the notes of the now completed work on paper—as fast as he could write!

Teach to Each

For years I've taught students, and in particular keyboard (piano/synthesizer) students, who had a strong bias in one of these two hemispheres. The right–brain dominant student can usually improvise with ease, but has trouble "reading" music. The left–brain dominant student can read anything, but has a hard time improvising "Happy Birthday." My job as a teacher is to help them *integrate these two hemispheres and develop balanced skills in both.*

Left-brain students want everything written down. They want everything to be taught in a linear, logical manner. They hate spontaneity and last–minute changes. Right-brain students want you to tell them, not write it down. They like surprises and changes, and are easily bored if lessons are too linear and predictable.

Because the northern hemisphere of Europe had a severe climate, early settlers had to think and plan ahead or they would never survive the brutal winters. Thinking and planning ahead is a left–brain bias. Of course, along with this is the eventual emphasis on reading as the primary method of learning, with architecture, literature, and written, formal, and somewhat complex music that has a logical beginning, developmental section, and ending. The scientific age we now live in has its roots primarily in the left–brain dominant culture of Western Europe. However, many scientific breakthroughs are a result of right–brain experimentation and spontaneity.

On the other hand, those who lived in monotonous tropical climates, with only a brief rainy season and ample sources of food developed other primary skills. In this environment, *spontaneity* became a greater survival skill than *logic.* As a result, these tribal, usually tropical, cultures emphasized musical improvisation, syncopation, and repetition over the more linear beginning, development, and ending artistic style of their northern neighbors.

We have seen a great coming–together of these two extreme cultural biases in the last century. The tribal music of Africa, Polynesia, Latin America, and Asia, has strongly influenced the classical music of Western Europe, first through Negro spirituals, then gospel, the blues, boogie–woogie, jazz, rock, etc.

Our young favor right–brain dominant music, while most adults are more comfortable with left–brain or a balanced musical diet; hence, the different listening tastes separating today's generations. Most parents are not comfortable in a rock–concert environment. Most teenagers are not comfortable in a classical orchestra environment. Both must learn tolerance and learn to appreciate the best aspects of each group's favorite music.

Summary

Music's ability to affect the human brain and vice versa has become one of the exciting areas of scientific breakthroughs in the past 100 years. We are discovering so many things about music and the brain. We now know that music can stimulate or slow down brain development. We know that some styles of music can increase our aptitudes and abilities in math and the spatial sciences (geometry, trigonometry, etc.). We know that some styles of music can enhance long–term memory, while others can handicap our mental prowess. I believe we are just at the beginning of a new age regarding music and the brain, and the future looks bright and exciting with more great discoveries on the way.

Chapter 4

The Learning Process and Music

A six-month study involving music and reading suggests that music instruction can cause in improvement in reading.
—*Musica Research Notes,* vol. VI, issue 2, Spring 1999

As we move further into the 21st century, we are discovering an increasingly important link between music, the learning process, and the human brain. It has been established, without a doubt by now, that the correct use of the right type of music *can stimulate learning and increase retention levels.*

One of the early developers of new techniques in using music to teach complex subject matter that required a high level of retention, like foreign languages, mathematics, and the basic sciences, was a Bulgarian researcher, Dr. Georgi Lazanov. He developed a technique of teaching, using a relaxed environment, a well-trained teacher, and soft baroque or classical music playing in the background, usually at a relaxed tempo of 60–72 beats per minute. This new method was quickly labeled *Suggestology.* Although still relatively unknown in the United States, it has swept Europe and Asia and is recommended by UNESCO to third-world nations because *studies show that it dramatically accelerates the learning process.*

Correctly using this technique, students found they could learn a new foreign language three to five times faster than with traditional methods. This is how it works:

Apparently the soft classical music playing in the background relaxes the student and distracts the controlling left hemisphere of the brain so that the lesson material bypasses the left brain and goes directly to the right hemisphere, the seat of all long-term memory.

Dr. Lazanov in his book *Suggestology and Outlines of Suggestopedy* suggests that the combining of soft classical music with a comfortable learning environment and a well-modulated and clear speaking voice on the part of the teacher actually (1) automatically regulates and harmonizes breathing and other bodily rhythms, (2) introduces normally unused parts of the brain to the learning process, (3) increases the joy and motivation in learning because it is so stress-free, and (4) automatically synchronizes and balances the right and left hemispheres of the brain.

This dynamic new learning method using music as an essential element was introduced to the United States in the 1970s in the soon-to-be popular book *Superlearning* by Ostrander and Schroeder. Special centers, workshops, and teacher-training institutions sprung up across the country. Sad to say, traditional academia has for the most part resisted this new and scientifically sound teaching method.

The largest music-education organization in the world, the Music Educator's National Conference (offices in Washington, D.C.) has sponsored a lot of research on music and learning in the past 50 years. Some of the discoveries include the discovery that high school students who study music on a regular basis have a higher grade point average, develop faster physically, score higher on SAT tests (UC Irvine), and their listening skills improve faster, a skill which reinforces learning and memory.

The National Coalition for Music Education stated, "Just as there can be no music without learning, no education is complete without music. To this end, we must destroy once and for all the myth that education in music and other arts is an 'expendable extra' or mere 'curricular icing.'" Reflecting that sentiment, the top three nations in the world academically—Hungary, Japan, and the Netherlands—all consider music education to be *essential* to intellectual growth and emotional stability.

Other recent studies have revealed that deep within the brain are white fibers that connect the right and left half of the cerebellum called the *corpus callosum.* These fibers increase in size and number when exposed to quiet classical music. This increase in size increases communication between the two hemispheres of the brain, which increases *learning efficiency.* The optimum ages for exposing children to this kind of music to bring about the results described above is between the ages of 5 and 6 years old and again at puberty (13–16 years of age) ("Music Enhances Learning," www.splashes-fromtheriver.com/music).

The Siemens Foundation, who sponsors the prestigious Siemens Westinghouse Competitions in math, science, and technology, found that 60 to 70 percent of all their regional finalists (high school level) *played musical instruments.*

The possibility that music might increase intelligence and speed learning has for many years dominated the thoughts of those doing research on learning. Schools around the country now argue that by rescuing music programs from budget cuts, *they can boost test scores.* This article goes on to say that most experts now agree that if a link between music and math or science exists, it is *weakest* when a person simply listens to music, and *strongest* when learning an instrument or composing music (Michele Kurtz, *Boston Globe/San Diego Union Tribune,* June 30, 2004).

Music Linked to Reduced Crime

A Texas Commission on Drug and Alcohol Abuse report showed that "secondary students who participated in band or orchestra reported the lowest lifetime and current use of all dangerous substances" (*Houston Chronicle,* January 11, 1998).

Martin Gardiner of Brown University discovered through detailed research over many years involving more than 1,000 residents of Rhode Island—tracking them from birth to age 30—that the greater their involvement in music, the lower the arrest record. *Teens who had music training in their background were less likely to get into trouble than students who didn't.* The study revealed that the greater the involvement in music, the less likely that person would be arrested for a crime (International Foundation for Music Research, *Musica Research Notes,* vol. 7, issue 1, Winter 2000).

Public Support

A 1997 Gallup Survey on American's attitudes toward music revealed the following:

» 90 percent of survey respondents agreed that music should be part of a well-rounded education
» 88 percent felt all schools should offer instrumental music as part of regular curriculum
» 89 percent believe music helps a child's overall intellectual development
» 69 percent believe school music program participation corresponds to better grades and test scores
» 85 percent believe communities should provide financial resources to support these programs

President Bill Clinton in his February 1997 State of the Union address took time to mention the following regarding the importance of music education: "Learning begins in the first days of life. Scientists are now discovering how young children develop emotionally and intellectually from their first days, and how important it is for parents to begin immediately talking, singing, even reading to their infants." In another address entitled "The Gift of Music," he reflected on the powerful effects music had on his own life: "Music to me was and still is representative of everything I like most in life. It's beautiful and fun, but very rigorous. If you wanted to be good you had to work like crazy. It was a real relationship between effort and reward. My musical life experiences were just as important to me, in terms of forming my development as my political experiences or my academic life" (MENC, 1994).

Sadly, this same former president had to be fitted for hearing aids during his second administration due to growing hearing loss as a result of listening to and playing in rock bands (without using earplugs) in his earlier years.

Other research studies, particularly on the long-term effects of rock music on adolescents, reveal that rock music has a negative effect on basic attitudes, drug and alcohol abuse, sexual promiscuity, and that it encourages anti–social behavior. As early as the 1960s the *New York Times* called rock music a "communicable disease."

According to a recent article in *AARP* magazine (for citizens 55 years of age or older), a person can turn a heart-healthy workout into an IQ lift by adding music. According to a recent team study at Ohio State University, cardiac patients that exercised to music did *twice as well* on a test of cognitive ability as those that exercised in silence. Apparently exercise alone causes positive changes in the nervous system, and adding music obviously stimulates different pathways in the brain . . . adding an extra dimension and reason to exercise regularly to music (Melissa Gotthart, *AARP* magazine, July/ August 2004).

Lullabies sung by mothers to their children are quite similar in rhythm, choice of melodic notes, and subject matter, regardless of language, in different countries around the world. Apparently it starts with the mother's voice. The king of "sing–song" speech most mothers use with their children puts the baby in a trance–like state, which then proceeds to rest, relaxation, sleep, or extended periods of extreme happiness (Christin Kenneally, *Songs of Ourselves,* November 2003).

The McIntosh Resolution (HR 226) cites the "growing body of scientific research" that links music education to improved spatial-temporal reasoning and math performance, as well as the growing evidence that music helps keep at–risk students in school and increased SAT scores among music students. If the House and Senate adopt the resolution, it will officially become recognized that *music education enhances intellectual development, fosters artistic and social success, and enriches the academic environment for children of all ages.*

The public school music programs in Japan and Germany are based on the 1940s music programs in American public schools. Their music education programs have gone on to flourish as ours has disappeared. A leading German music educator recently stated, "The leadership of our country, and our people, believe that to survive in the computer age, *you must have music.* Our leaders and people recognize that the creative, productive use of leisure time through all stages of life is and will be of great importance."

The Japanese Ministry of Education stated, "Our goal is to inspire the children's interest and concern for music and to foster, through the study of music appreciation and expression, that will enrich their entire lifetime."

Schools in Germany and Japan meet approximately 240 days a year, compared with 180 days in the United States. The addition of 60 more days to the school calendar offers 30 percent more instructional time. Upon graduation from high school, these students will have received *over three years* more schooling than American students will.

When I was Administrative Director of Jazz Studies at the University of California in Los Angeles, I had the opportunity to meet and plan with the dean of the School of Music at that time, Dr. Larry Livingston. Dr. Livingston pointed out to me (as a conclusion of his meetings with other school of music deans across the country) that increasingly, piano, violin, viola, and cello majors were coming from foreign countries, particularly China, Japan, Germany, and Eastern Europe. Deans of music at major American universities were discovering the average American high school graduate was so poorly prepared in music and so undisciplined when it came to practicing that the primary source of highly talented and highly motivated students, particularly in these highly competitive and demanding music majors, were increasingly coming from outside the United States.

I attended a Music Educator's National Conference in Los Angeles in 1958. The Russians had beaten us in the initial stages of the space race with the launching of their satellite, "Sputnik." The fallout from this international event was felt in the public school curriculum. Schools across the country began dumping their music programs and stepping up their science courses to meet this perceived global threat.

Music educators had left themselves vulnerable to this wholesale dismantling of one of the finest public school music curricula in the world by refusing to justify music education in an already crowded curriculum on *sound, scientific research.* The strategy at the MENC conference that year was not to trot out recent scientific validation for the importance of music in the learning process, but instead to wave the banner with the slogan "Music for Music's Sake!" In other words, music did not need to justify its place in the school curriculum.

Americans are very practical. We will listen to arguments from both sides, but the arguments have to be based on solid research or they will be tossed out in favor of other more pressing priorities. As a result of this "stick–your–head–in–the–sand" philosophy from our major music education organization, MENC, music classes almost disappeared from public schools across American between 1958 and the 1990s. *Music educators had failed to make a case for a strong public school music program in increasingly crowded school curricula.*

Startled by the sudden disappearance of strong music programs across the nation, the National Association of Music Merchants (NAMM) jumped into the fray with the beginnings of solid research studies that showed the scientifically sound basis for including music instruction in the schools. NAMM is made up of businessmen. Businessmen are practical. They knew that the only way to regain the ground lost between 1960 and the year 2000 was to *prove* that music was vital to a well–balanced curriculum and to improving the learning process itself. This they did, with numerous studies, reports, radio and television commercials, etc. MENC and other music education organizations eventually threw out their failed leadership and elected new leaders who began to fight back, *using objective scientific studies as their argument.*

The startling effectiveness of teaching beginning string players via the "Suzuki" method totally changed the approach to teaching youngsters on string instruments. It's rousing success, first in Japan and later in other countries and eventually even the United States, revolutionized the way we teach beginners in playing a stringed instrument.

The success was followed by new methods in other countries. Hungary fielded one of the most comprehensive and successful general music programs from kindergarten through high school in the world, a program developed by their respective native composer, Carl Orff.

Yamaha, a colossus of Japanese manufacturers, introduced a new approach to teaching beginning keyboardists using some of the Suzuki techniques as well as developing electronic keyboard labs that allowed schools to successfully teach beginning, intermediate, and even moderately advanced classes of 20 or more successfully.

The introduction of the computer to education, along with the increasingly sophisticated but reasonably priced electronic instruments (guitar, bass, keyboard, and even wind and percussion) brought about major changes in not only the way we taught beginning musical instruments, but the types of ensemble students would perform with. New performing ensembles included jazz–rock groups, modern vocal groups, keyboard ensembles (EKG=electronic keyboard group), Latin percussion, song writing and arranging, and composition.

While administrative director of the jazz program at USC, in conjunction with Korg Electronic Keyboards, I started an ensemble made up of four synthesizers (electronic keyboards), and a drummer. We called our group *EKG–USC*. We were well received on and off campus. One keyboardist play the melody (or improvised), another play background figures, another play chords, and another play the baseline and/or special effects. We didn't actually need a drummer because of the new, sophisticated electronic drum machines available, but found it more practical to use a live drummer instead.

Today the traditional school orchestras, concert bands, marching bands, and traditional choirs are being challenged or replaced by these new and exciting (to the students) performing ensembles. Because of electronics, music today can be reduced to keyboards, drums, and the human voice. Keyboard labs are among us and our growing phenomenon on school campuses from elementary school through university.

It is hoped that the continuing research into the power of music and its positive effects on us all, when properly used, will propel music back in the school curriculum based on solid research that gives music just as much right to be there as science and mathematics. One of the purposes in writing this book is to continue the struggle to inform community, parents, and students as to why music education is important and why it should be part of any modern school curriculum.

The research I have found in preparing this book and new discoveries I make every day are just the tip of the iceberg. I believe that in the near future we will discover, through scientific studies, that music is more powerful and important than any of us, even those who have devoted their lives to writing, teaching, or performing music, have any idea! *Music has the right to be part of every student's training and life experiences . . . for many reasons.*

Chapter 5
Adrenaline—Hormone of Fear

The human body has its own emergency set of procedures, which have protected us for thousands of years. One of these protective devices is the body–produced hormone called *adrenaline.* Two small glands, the adrenal glands, sit on top of our kidneys. When the brain sends the signal to this gland that danger is present, the gland secretes a miraculous body–produced drug into the bloodstream that gives us extra energy to run or fight and sharpens our survival instincts by making us more alert and aggressive.

The stimulus can be visual, or auditory, or physical. We can see danger, hear danger, or even feel danger. We could be suddenly bumped or bitten. All can trigger this response. Even our powerful imagination can trigger it by visualization (watching a play or movie) or by hearing it (sudden, sharp sounds, like the typical backbeat of a drummer in a rock band). *Regardless of our conscious intent,* the brain interprets these types of sudden, shock–driven stimuli as a potential threat. The minute the brain determines that a potential threat has occurred, a series of emergency procedures are *automatically* triggered. All this happens *below our level of consciousness.*

Once the emergency alarm has been sounded, a sudden rush of unusual physical feelings occur, including (1) the speeding up of our heart rate, (2) a feeling of heat in the stomach, and (3) a feeling of jitteriness or twitching in our muscles. Once the subconscious emergency alarm has been triggered, it may be hard to sit still or stand still. Further aggressive stimuli could trigger strong physical reaction: shouting, shoving, hitting, and biting—a further physical response to dangerous stimuli.

"Dancing" to loud rock music is less a conscious attempt to synchronize bodily movement with the music, as dancers did in the 1920s through the 1950s, than a subconscious reaction to the music itself. Before rock, dancers consciously moved to the music. There were specific steps to specific rhythms. After rock, the music itself dictated the physical reactions, and no attempt was made to consciously synchronize bodily movements to the music. *Each individual's movements are a subconscious reaction to the overly aggressive and threatening stimuli of the music.*

Once the emergency bell has been sounded by the brain, and a vast number of lightning–like signals have been sent to various organs and parts of the body, each individual so affected has a body that is now pulsing with extra energy supplied by the triggering of the bodies' emergency response system. Emotional reactions tend to be extreme and overly sensitive. Individuals find it hard to control extreme reactions to aggressive stimuli.

Today college and professional athletes are using loud rock music to get them up for the game. A favorite relief pitcher for the San Diego Padres always listens to the rock classic "Hell's Bells" by AC/DC at full volume through his headset before striding onto the field and trying to put out the last remaining opposition batters in a close game. You are ready to "fight" or take "flight." Your sense of aggression is heightened as well, and the "threat" factor has been raised to red.

Training

Certain skills call for a controlled use of adrenaline stimulation. For instance, author David Morell in his recent spy thriller *The Protector* explains how special forces in the military use certain repetitive but dangerous exercises to stimulate adrenaline, until the individual begins to feel comfortable with the stimulus and even in some cases begins to crave it. Any law enforcement personnel, firefighters, infantrymen, jet pilots, or professional athletes will tell you that you can easily get "hooked" on this feeling and ignore danger signs unless highly conditioned and trained.

Put a parachute on someone and tell that person to leap out of a plane at 20,000 feet, and he's going to be terrified. It's a potentially life-threatening activity, and one that's totally unfamiliar. But train that person in small increments; teach him how to jump off increasingly high platforms into a swimming pool. Then teach him how to jump from even high platforms wearing a bungee harness that simulates the feel of a parachute. Then show him how to jump from small planes at reasonable altitudes. Gradually increase the size and power of the planes and the height of the jump. By the time he leaps from that plane at 20,000 feet, he's going to feel the same speeding and contraction of the heart, the same burning in the stomach, and the same muscle jitteriness as before.

This time, though, he's *not terrified.* He knows how to minimize the risk, and he's experienced hundreds of similar activities. What he feels instead of fear is the *sharp focus of an athlete ready to spring into action.* His adrenaline is affecting him the same way it always did, but his mind knows how to control it and to appreciate its constructive effects.

Could this be why former President George H. W. Bush recently celebrated his birthday by parachuting out of plane? Was he seeking, one more time, that special "rush" that he felt as president?

Seeking Danger

The accidental (or deliberate) triggering of these emergency feelings occur during and after a rock concert or seeing a "slasher" movie or witnessing gratuitous violence—even when it is pretend on such shows as professional wresting and participant shows like "Survivor." Could it be that our environment is so safe today that we have to deliberately create danger to get in the rush that comes from the body's automatic response?

The speeding of the heart as a result of this artificial stimuli from sudden, loud, sharp sounds (again, like a loud rock band drummer or guitarist) can cause a greater output of blood to reach muscles and prepare them for extreme action. The faster respiration rate causes more oxygen to get to muscles. The *liver receives the emergency signal and quickly creates more glucose, increasing the amount of sugar in the blood.* At the same time, more fatty acids circulate. Both the sugar and the fatty acids become instant fuel, creating greater energy and stamina.

Professional rock musicians, athletes, race car drivers, dancers, military personnel, pilots, emergency rescue teams, and law enforcement personnel are trained to separate personal fear from the adrenaline rush. These professional *rely* on adrenaline. However, there is a danger even when the person realizes the stimulus is not threatening. The subconscious mind moves quickly in emergency situations and sends out these signals before we can consciously shut them down. On one hand, the feeling is exhilarating. On the other, fatigue sets in when the artificially induced "high" decreases and the nervous system has been tested once again unnecessarily. Where there is a "high," there is a compensating "low." After overstimulation, the body and the mind badly need rest.

Unfortunately, you can get addicted to the adrenaline rush. This addiction can be as intense and hard to break as any addiction to alcohol, cocaine, heroin, or methamphetamines. Although there are long period of inactivity in each of the dangerous professions, *even the waiting for danger* and excitement can trigger the rush. Watch the former jocks on television sports shows to see what I mean.

Although long off the playing field, you can still see the rush—raised voices, exaggerated body movements, aggressive reactions to challenges of opinion, etc. Former rock musicians and older rock music fans can even trigger the rush by closing their eyes and seeing and hearing their favorite loud rock songs in their heads. The average Grateful Dead rock fan is over 50 years old today. Still, they flock to the band's concerts and celebrate as if they had just entered adolescence.

Today, millions of teenagers are rock rush addicts, over-stimulating their adrenal glands and their nervous systems to receive the giant rush. That's why there are fewer big rock festivals anymore. The aggression released is often hard to control and can result in riots, antisocial behavior, or waves of destructiveness toward the immediate environment and fellow concert-goers. Once unleashed, especially with large crowds, these extreme rushes that trigger aggression are very hard to control. *Teenagers with chronic behavioral problems at school or home are generally heavily into loud rock music, particularly heavy metal.*

Fear Sells

And have you noticed how loud the volume is today at most motion picture theaters? It is often almost ear–splitting. This is no accident, particularly if the film is aimed at younger viewers. The motion picture industry has combined two powerful emergency–response stimulants in most modern films—*volume* and *violence.*

Audiences caught up in listening to and watching these films get a "rush" and even become addicted to increasingly louder and more violent films. In fact, a new Hollywood entertainment genre has been created called "slasher" films, where some diabolical stalker hunts down and kills in a very dramatic manner many of the characters in the film. Even though the stalker is usually destroyed (or disappears to reappear in a sequel), the damage is done to the bodies of the fans in the theater.

The limited impact of television because of its small screen and analog, tinny–sounding audio quality is over. Today, large high–definition television with digital sound and home–theater speakers can rival the impact of the local movie theater. Reality television has brought about a new "scare" tactic for the viewer, in that the people on the screen are not actors, the situations are real (although controlled and even sometimes simulated), and the viewer can more easily put his or herself in the place of the person dangling over the Grand Canyon from a helicopter, buffeted by scary, loud music.

You would think that the bestselling CDs of music from a film would be Hollywood musicals. Wrong! The bestselling music soundtrack CDs from films is music written for horror and monster films. Why? *Just hearing the music again triggers the original rush from the film.*

Overstimulation of the adrenal glands can have many serious effects on health, particularly later in life. Overstimulation may:

1. Weaken the immune system
2. Weaken the heart

3. Lead to diabetes
4. Damage the nervous system
5. Cause chronic depression, alternating with outbreaks of violent behavior
6. Lead to obesity. The mind wants massive amounts of food to feed the energy levels necessary when "high."
7. Weaken a person's response to real danger due to a slower response

The Enemy Within

There is a positive and negative side to every major change in man's environment. For too long we have enjoyed the positive without dealing with the negative. The uncontrolled use of loud, percussive music in rock, heavy metal, rap, hip–hop, and film soundtracks from violent films, along with the constant emphasis on gratuitous violence in books, television, films, and plays, and the dramatic enhancement of the news, have all contributed to a society that has over–stimulated its "fight–or–flight" instinct that nature built into our bodies as a protective device.

Today we have many in their mid–thirties with burned out nervous systems. They cannot even stand minimal stress. They either flip out, or become violent, or they deaden their interpretation of reality through drugs and alcohol. Today people often fly into destructive rages for minor offenses, bringing tragedy and violence into the home (child and spousal abuse), the work arena, the highway (road rage), and most disturbing of all, into our public schools, colleges, and universities.

A constant in investigating the backgrounds of most students who bring violence to school is an obsession with heavy metal rock music and violent films. The Columbine High School tragedy in Inglewood, Colorado, a few years ago is a good example. The student killers listened to violent music by the hour, and they even emulated the dress (long black overcoats) of the characters in their favorite violent film, *The Matrix*.

This mostly unrecognized danger can weaken the nation as a whole, making it more vulnerable to outside aggressive nations who have not damaged their bodies, minds, and nervous systems in this manner. The slide into gratuitous violence and loud rock music as our primary sources of entertainment and escape can have serious consequences in the political arena as well.

One only has to look to ancient Rome, with its obsession with the gladiatorial spectacles and chariot races that led to its eventual neglect of defending the nation from without and from within. Yes, loud raucous music was part of the spectacle at that time, as it is today.

Summary

It's time to ask the question, "What have we done to ourselves, and was it worth it?" Sadly, most citizens in the new high-tech world are not even aware of the damage, even in their own personal lives, until it is too late. The medical profession has not helped by isolating and defining the original cause of the problem, but instead has doled out tranquilizers and sedatives to mask the symptoms. Its time to begin holding those who manufacture and sell violent music and produce and distribute violent films responsible for the damage they have caused. If an elderly lady can sue McDonalds for millions of dollars for serving hot coffee that she spilled on herself, why can't we sue record companies and film studios for our hearing loss and for the very real damage they have caused to millions?

This major turn to discovering that music, cinema, television, and gratuitous violence can trigger a "rush" began in the 1960s and has increased in volume and intensity every since. So have the figures for teenage violence, suicide, drug use, and descent into the dark underworld of the occult. Is there a correlation? I believe there is, and I believe it is time to address this internal crisis while we still can. Today it is no longer just a matter of opinion. Solid, scientific studies support the contention that irresponsible use of music and violence has had a negative effect on our society as a whole and must be regulated and corrected—or we face more serious problems in the future.

Chapter 6

The Fight–or–Flight Response

Beginning in the late 1950s, American pop music began to crank up the volume, added a heavy whip–like backbeat to the drums, superimposed a throbbing bass line and an ear–splitting scream from the electric guitar, and the most popular and powerful music style in the history of man was unleashed on modern society.

By normal standards, the melodies, rhythms, and lyrics of most rock songs are bland, simplistic, and sometimes insultingly dull and repetitive. What made the music so popular? Rock music accidentally stumbled upon an inner response built into every human being, a response necessary to survive during more primitive and violent times. This physiological response to loud, pulsing rock music is called the fight–or–flight response.

Rock music is not just entertainment, social commentary, teenage rebellion, or sexual fantasy; it is a drug. The loud, repetitive backbeat with the sharp attack on beats 2 and 4 by the drummer triggers the *fight–or–flight* response, causing the brain to send a signal to the adrenal glands, which in turn begin pouring this powerful stimulant into the bloodstream that allowed our ancestors to have extra energy and aggression to either fight or run, but today allows us to get "high" at rock concerts.

According to Dr. Herbert Benson of the Mind-Body Medical Institute at Beth Israel Deaconess Medical Center in Boston, when the fight–or–flight response is triggered, the body cranks out stress hormones such as adrenaline. Such hormones boost blood pressure, dampen the immune system, and over time can damage a variety of body systems.

The primary reasons rock music is the most lucrative and powerful musical style in history, in spite of its almost imbecilic melodies, chords, and lyrics, is its use of volume to trigger this physiological response. As a result, rock music has become a new drug, one that is legal, sold to minors, and invisible to parents and society in general. It is every bit as powerful and addictive as heroin, cocaine, methamphetamine, and marijuana. In some instances, it is even more deadly, because along with all the internal damage done to the body by the overstimulation of the fight–or–flight response over a period of years, the sheer volume of the music is deafening and usually causes permanent hearing loss among rock fans and players, or "tinnitus," a constant ringing in the ears.

Harvard physiologist Walter B. Cannon accidentally discovered the fight–or–flight response at the turn of the century in his research on the endocrine gland system. Dr. Cannon validated something philosophers and mystics have been saying for some time: there is a closer relationship between our bodies and our minds than we realize, and *music and emotions are the bridges between the two.* Harmony or disharmony in one area (the body or the brain) eventually shows up in the other.

Modern man still walks around in a primitive body, one that was equipped to cope with the sudden dangers typical of a more natural environment. To our primitive ancestors, most often sudden danger was communicated to the brain by *repetitive, often syncopated loud noises.* When our auditory nerves convey to the brain the impulses from loud, percussive, repetitive, and often syncopated rhythms, a part of our brain interprets these sounds as "danger" and sends a signal to our endocrine gland system and in particular our adrenal glands (two small glands that sit atop our kidneys). These glands, when triggered, dump a drug not unlike methamphetamine into our bloodstream. Adrenaline is a strong stimulant that gives us extra energy to run, or turn and do battle, or get "high."

This music–induced high can often lead to aggression and violence, since the emotions under these conditions are hard to control and the individual feels incredibly strong and powerful. This "super-man" complex can lead to danger.

The sudden threat of danger also triggers shallow breathing. When this happens, the diaphragm, the sheet of muscle separating the chest cavity from the abdominal cavity (looks like a small pizza), doesn't contract downward sufficiently, so the *lungs never fully expand into the abdomen.* As a result, the lower portions of the lungs, which are filled with small blood vessels that carry oxygen to our cells, hardly receive enough oxygen and the waste matter in the lungs, carbon dioxide, are not completely exhaled and remains in the body to cause fatigue and other more dangerous symptoms *after the adrenaline high wears off.*

In an effort to compensate for this shallow breathing, the brain, our master controlling computer, sends a signal to increase *our heart rate and blood pressure*, forcing our cardiovascular system to work overtime to compensate for shallow breathing. The constant triggering of this response and its accompanying side effects can place a tremendous strain on the heart. Today we have people in their twenties and thirties dying of heart attacks with no previous diagnosis of heart trouble. Remember that the old adage of "take a deep breath" when angry or frightened is a good one.

Triggers

The body's continued reaction to the initial threat conveyed by sudden, sharp, loud sounds is for the brain to trigger the release of even more stress hormones, only adding to the deadly mix. Too much noise or loud music can set off the fight–or–flight response, sometimes increasing blood pressure by as much as 10 percent.

Other ways of triggering the fight–or–flight response including the witnessing of violent acts (real or dramatized, as in cinema or television), or putting ourselves in some type of potential danger (like bungee jumping or riding a rollercoaster). As kids we like the "high" we get from these self-inflicted fight–or–flight response episodes. They pump us up, make us feel "powerful" and aggressive. That's where the elation comes from after surviving a "double–dare" inflicted on us by our friends when we are young.

That is why in the locker rooms of most high school, college, and professional athletes, you will often hear the loudest, most aggressive rock music available (often through headsets, if fellow teammates object). The music deliberately pumps up the players by triggering the fight–or–flight response, so when they reach the playing field they are like wild animals waiting to be let loose in the ancient Roman Coliseum.

This important realization came about when some scientists began to be concerned about the typical "rock 'n roll" personality and the sudden changes from being calm to being highly emotional and agitated. From the 1950s on (even earlier in some jazz and blues styles), this new loud rock music was used increasingly and unknowingly as a self–administered drug. Rock music uses emotional triggers to excite the built–in automatic response.

This system, unknowingly in most instances, has been accidentally or deliberately triggered for centuries in all groups in all cultures. Its more deliberate primitive use was to arouse men to battle, fog the senses and conscience in orgiastic religious ceremonies, and release social tension. It is no accident that Native Americans often danced to loud, repetitive, rhythmic music for hours before going "on the warpath."

Napoleon once said, "All armies need good cooks and good drummers." The armies of the United States, until the past 50 years, have always been accompanied into battle by loud drums, bugles, fifes, and bagpipes. These are some examples of the fight–or–flight response used in earlier times. The bagpipers pumped up the British in the Battle of El Alamein in Algiers in World War II; Glen Miller's music pumped up the pilots in the planes bombing Germany; American GIs rode into battle in Vietnam on helicopters blaring the neo-pagan music of Richard Wagner's "The Ride of the Valkyries," a scene preserved forever in the haunting film *Apocalypse Now.*

However, today's digitally recorded popular music, along with the more sophisticated replay equipment, allows us all to hear music as loud or louder than originally performed. Monster speaker racks at rock concerts generate sounds so loud that they can hard boil an egg in its shell. Cooking time is approximately a minute and a half.

Listening vs. Feeling

For the most part we stopped "listening" to popular music in the 1960s and started "feeling" it instead. Music itself became a drug, with just as strong an effect and potential danger as marijuana, cocaine, methamphetamine, Ecstasy, or heroin. *Teenagers learned that they could get high on their music.* Listen to rock legend guitarist Jimi Hendrix from 1969 article in *Life* magazine: "I can explain everything better through music. You *hypnotize people* to where they go right back to their *natural state,* and when you get people at their weakest point, you can preach into their subconscious *whatever you want to say"* (*Life*, October 3, 1969, p. 4).

Or David Crosby, of Crosby, Stills, Nash, and Young, when he told *Rolling Stone* magazine that through his music he could alter his audience's value systems and, in effect, steal them away from their parents and their parents' social and moral values (Arthur Baker, *Rolling Stone Interview,* 1981).

Or rock legend Eddie Manson who soberly suggested that: "Music is used everywhere to condition the human mind. It can be just as powerful as a drug and much more dangerous, because *nobody takes musical manipulation very seriously"* (Chagall, p. 15).

Eddie was right. Until now, few took music's powerful ability to sway the emotions of mankind, and even act as a habit–forming drug, very seriously. The statistics today on loss of hearing, emotional disorders, tinnitus, and other physical and emotional problems as a by–product of the "if it feels good, do it" culture can no longer be ignored.

So What Happened?

Something changed in the 1960s. Pop music went from being a luxury to a necessity. People stopped listening (critically) and started to "feel" music more. *Millions of young adults have discovered that certain styles of music could have the same effect as getting high on certain drugs.* When combined with drugs, the dosage was often lethal.

In his book *Music, the Brain, and Ecstasy,* Robert Jourdain says: "It is damage to the inner ear that is a horror to any music lover. It is a form of nerve malfunction. A section of the organ of Corti stops working, particularly the higher frequency regions closest to the opening to the middle ear. *Prolonged exposure to loud sounds (like a rock concert) is the prime culprit in this kind of mechanical destruction.* The result is a sort of accelerated aging. Those who think they are 'just fine' after rock concerts may not have to wait till they turn eighty to learn otherwise" (p. 19).

The author goes on: "In the court music of ancient China, orchestras of over 1,000 players were assembled to produce a sound loud enough to supposedly be heard in heaven. Today we do something similar at rock concerts, perhaps more in the spirit of communing with hell" (p. 43).

Many today of the "flower power," "if it feels good, do it" generation of the '60s, we who are the adults of today, are walking around with serious hearing losses, a fried nervous system (burnout of the adrenal glands through overstimulation), a weakened immune system, high blood pressure, and a great susceptibility to strokes, heart attacks, and cancer. That's a heavy price to pay for a style of music, a style so dangerous that someday it will be banned or played only under controlled circumstances.

Wow! That's a load to dump on something as innocent as pop music. You bet it is, but today it can all be verified through careful research. Sadly, much of this research is still ignored and certainly came too late for the walking wounded adult–children of the "flower power" generation. Those who have not watched the Ozzy Osbourne family "interact" on their MTV reality program should watch. The burnout of Ozzy is visible, along with serious deterioration in communication.

The Cure

Make this information available to the public. Today the record industry is a $20 billion a year industry. It does not want anyone messing with it, so be careful who you talk to and where you present your information. The most important thing is to get this information into the hands of parents and teenagers of today.

Like AIDS, this is a public plague that can be checked through abstinence and education. Failure to do so will only cause another generation to be seriously damaged through too much exposure to rock/pop music, along with a "habit" that demands this music 24 hours a day, even in church.

We are just at the beginning of this fight. It is not unlike the discoveries we began to make about the dangers of smoking back in the 1950s and the gradual education of the public since that time. We face the same battle with contemporary pop music. It is a battle we must win. Learn to respect your body and mind. Don't pollute either for temporary thrills that bring permanent disaster. It's not worth it. The fight–or–flight response needs to be respected, not exploited. It is a wonderful part of our built–in defense system that has been systematically abused, raped in a sense, for corporate and individual profit. It is time to bring this unscrupulous exploitation of our children and the general public to a screaming halt!

Chapter 7

Breath Control

Breath control is an essential part of musical training. That is obvious for singers and brass and woodwind players, but what about strings, percussion, and keyboards? Surprisingly, good string, keyboard, and percussion teachers stress breathing as a way of phrasing, a necessary component in making music.

We can last forty days or more without food, several days without water, but we can last a *maximum* of three minutes without air. How quickly we forget the primary fuel that runs our bodies is oxygen—air. No breath, no life. When we are born, the first act in the new world outside the womb is to take a deep breath. *Our first act is to inhale; our last, to exhale.*

When we inhale, we bring into our bodies air rich in oxygen, which is transported from the lungs to the bloodstream to nourish and run our bodies. Our brain is particularly sensitive to the amount of "air" energy we receive. Recent studies in geriatrics indicate that often senility among the elderly can be arrested or even in some cases erased through deep-breathing exercises.

When we are under stress, afraid, or angry, we tend to shallow-breathe. The old adage of "take a deep breath" before doing or saying something that might be regretted later is still good advice. Unknowingly, when our body is in a stress mode (and yes, certain types of music can trigger that stress mode), we tend to *shallow-breathe,* often unknowingly holding our breath.

When we are afraid or angry (anger is a by-product of fear), we shallow-breathe; when we are secure and happy, we breathe more deeply. Could that be one of the reasons for "happy" people living longer than "sad" or "angry" or "frightened" people? It could be, since oxygen feeds not only our brain but also most of the other systems of our body, clear down to our blood cells. Long life? Breathe deep! Singers, those who watch their health and do not drink or use drugs on a regular basis, tend to live longer; so do wind instrument players, and, surprisingly, music conductors.

Breathing effectively is crucial to being in control, feeling balanced, and being able to correctly express ourselves musically and in other personal ways. Babies and animals breathe naturally, totally relaxed, with deep breaths, using their whole bodies when doing so. In today's highly stressed society, most of us have lost the gift of correct breathing—which only adds to our stress and anxiety. Tom Goode of Boulder, Colorado, who started the International Breath Institute, is quoted as saying, "Most people are chest breathers. This type of shallow breathing produces a whole host of physiological symptoms and has been tied to everything from autoimmune diseases to cancer and heart disease" (ibid.)

Shallow breathing also contributes to lack of energy, low resistance to disease, high anxiety, and negative mood swings, which some of us call "the blues." Learning to breathe correctly and taking several deep breaths daily is one of the best health habits you can adopt—and it's easy and quick.

Musical Schizophrenia

Rock music sends out a dual signal: the lyrics often suggest peace, joy, and love, while the music suggests sensuality, danger, anger, and rage. The body will always react to the music first, because the lyrics have to be *intellectually digested* (left brain) *before* they can affect the listener emotionally. By then it's too late; the body has *already* reacted to the style of the music.

Rock music does not belong in worship service. It represents just about everything the church has preached against for centuries. Until the 1950s, there has always been a dividing line between pop music and music suitable for worship. Today that dividing line has been erased and moral and emotional confusion reigns supreme.

Rock music causes shallow breathing because of the volume.

The sharp backbeat triggers the fight–or–flight response, which triggers fear, anger, agitation, and frustration.

When we take a deep breath, the air is warmed slightly, humidified, and filtered through the nose and mouth. The incoming air then travels past the larynx (Adam's apple), and moves through the vocal cords in the throat to the trachea (windpipe). The trachea divides in two—left and right (bronchi)—which then conveys the air to the lungs. The lungs process the air and send it on its way through the bloodstream to all the cells, tissues, bones, and organs in the body. The final stop is the brain, *which needs large amounts of oxygen to function at its full capacity.*

Once processed, the lungs begin to collapse due to the rising pressure from below of the diaphragm muscle, forcing the old, used, stale air out of the lungs (along with waste material we call carbon dioxide). *Exhalation is just as important as inhalation.* Shallow breathing allows stale air to remain in the bottom of the lungs, with waste material that can re–enter the bloodstream and cause trouble.

The lungs absorb the oxygen from our inhalation, which is then filtered into the bloodstream while carbon dioxide, the waste matter in respiration, is removed from the blood through the act of exhaling. Pulmonologist Dr. Laurence Smolley, co–author of *Breathe Right Now* (Norton, 1998) tells us: "If you don't take a deep–enough breath you don't get the benefit of the gas exchange. You're just letting the air go up and down in your conducting airways." In other words, the necessary exchange of oxygen for carbon dioxide is minimized.

When the pizza–shaped diaphragm muscle pushes the viscera (the intestines and internal organs) down to create the necessary vacuum for air to rush into the deep part of the lungs, it massages and stimulates circulation in these internal organs (the heart, liver, stomach, pancreas, gall bladder, spleen, etc.). "It's like having your own internal massage therapist," says Dennis Lewis, author of *The Tao of Natural Breathing* (Mountain Wind, 1996).

This internal massage as a result of regular deep breathing promotes intestinal movement, blood, and lymph flow and the absorption of nutrients. Well-known author and celebrity Martha Stewart is quoted as saying after studying with a breathing specialist, "I can walk more quickly, and I can do many more sit-ups and other exercises than before." Martha has been seeing a breathing specialist for years and credits her new way of breathing to improvements in her well-being: "After a breathing session, I'm reenergized. It releases stress and lets me get through an eighteen-hour day, and that's pretty important."

Exercises

Everyone can benefit from regularly practicing some simple, daily breathing exercises, but musicians, particularly singers and woodwind and brass players, benefit the most, since it is air that drives the sounds they make.

Roberta Peters, the famous Metropolitan Opera soprano, used to train for an upcoming opera role like an athlete training for the Olympics. It was not unusual for her trainer, fortunately a petite 125 pounds, to stand on her stomach while she did her warm-ups on a floor mat in the gym. A less strenuous form of this simple exercise follows:

1. Lie on your back on the floor in a relaxed position.
2. Place a slight weight on your diaphragm (just below the middle of your rib cage or the top of your stomach)—a heavy book or other object.
3. Take a deep, continuous breath (as deep as you can) for five seconds. Hold the breath for five seconds, and then exhale (like you are trying to blow a candle out) for five seconds.
4. Rest briefly and repeat. Do a minimum of ten repetitions. (Warning: do on an empty stomach and stop immediately if nauseous or dizzy.)
5. Gradually increase the length of each process: inhalation, holding, exhalation, i.e., 6-6-6, 7-7-7, etc.

The following exercise is similar to the one above, except it can be done while walking. Be careful that the air you breathe is as fresh as possible. Avoid doing this exercise during smog alerts or near heavy automobile traffic.

1. While walking briskly, inhale for five seconds.
2. Hold the air for five seconds.
3. Exhale for five seconds.
4. Repeat for a maximum of ten times—stop sooner if dizzy or nauseous.
5. Increase the length gradually, i.e., 6-6-6, 7-7-7, etc.
6. Do on an empty stomach.

The final exercise will increase lung capacity and exercise both the diaphragm, which only works during inhalation, and the abdominal muscles, which control exhalation. Note: You might feel some soreness in the rib cage area for a few days. That means that you are stretching the muscles between the ribs because you are taking in such large breaths. That is a good sign! The soreness will go away.

1. Do standing or sitting.
2. Raise your chin by looking toward the ceiling (this opens the throat).
3. Take a *huge* breath, like a drowning man going down for the third time.
4. Hold this breath in the lungs by keeping the lips *tightly shut.*
5. Without letting any air out, quickly *force another* breath on top of the first one.
6. Take a *third breath* the same way.
7. Exhale three times, like you are trying to blow out a candle from across the room. Bend forward and force *all the air* (carbon dioxide) out of the lungs by the end of the third exhalation.
8. Do three repetitions. Do not continue if dizzy or nauseous.

There are many more wonderful exercises for teaching us how to breathe deeply and correctly, but these three are easy to remember and easy to do and will benefit both musicians and non–musicians alike.

Summary

Why a chapter on breathing in a book on music? Because to understand the production of music by voice or wind instrument, we have to understand breathing. Besides, most of us are amateur singers in the shower, and after practicing these exercises we can sing with our mates, join a choir, or just learn to sing more around the house, in the car, at work, wherever. A singing person is a happy, healthy person. Remember, for the singer and woodwind or brass player, *music is a beautiful sound floating on top of a column of air.*

Marie Plette, a Metropolitan Opera star, is quoted as saying, "Breathing is the most important aspect of a singer's technique. You can't control the sounds that you have—you have what God gave you. But breathing does give you control over the amount of sound you can make and also how long you can sustain a pitch."

The power of music is such that we tend to subconsciously adjust our breathing to the rhythm of the music we are listening to. This potential problem is compounded if the music is loud and repetitious. Slow music, deep breathing. Be as careful what you listen to as you are to what you eat, and concentrate on learning how to breathe deeply.

Chapter 8

Music Therapy

Music has the ability to dispel much of the fear and anxiety associated with facing the unknown alone.

—Stevens, 1990

Using musing to heal, physically or emotionally, is not new. We can trace the use of sound in healing back to the Greeks and, even before, to ancient Egypt, The ancients often combined certain styles of music with certain colors and aromas to around the healing forces. Attacking all the sensory inputs at once with the same message is a powerful stimulus to the brain and the body.

In 1 and 2 Samuel of the Old Testament of the Bible, we find that a spirit of depression troubled the ancient Israeli king Saul. Saul sought out the musical skills of a young David, to calm the frantic up–and–downs of his mind. Saul, by the symptoms described in the Bible, was probably a classic case of bipolarity.

Once, during one of the sessions when David was trying to soothe Saul's mind, Saul suddenly threw his spear at David . . . possibly telling him not to play that particular song again, who knows, but it is an example of the early use of music to heal. Unfortunately for Saul, he chose to discontinue his music therapy sessions with David and tried to kill him instead, forcing David to flee from Saul for over three years.

In an article in the *Washington Post* in 1994 titled "Music Therapy" by Rick Weiss, we read, "For millennia, witch doctors and other spiritual healers have used drums, bells, and rattles to chase illness from the body. In ancient Egypt, physician–priests sang their medical scriptures in specific, curative tones. And the Greek mathematician Pythagoras proposed that music might in some patients restore proper balance among the four humors and their associated temperaments."

In *Drumming on the Edge of Magic,* Mickey Hart wrote, "Music has been used for entertainment for so long, people forget it's a powerful medicine."

According to some historians, England's King George I sought out his court composer, George Frederick Handel, to write some soothing music to calm his overactive nervous system and bipolar mind. Handel wrote his famous "Water Music" for this purpose. It is still used today to calm down, cheer up, and help heal burned-out nervous systems and symptoms of depression by music therapists.

The next time you are depressed, sit down and put on the CD of Handel's "Water Music." You will rise refreshed, renewed, and cheered in spirit. We are just rediscovering some of the older effective music therapy compositions for their healing power today.

During the European Renaissance, the first experiments regarding music's effect on the human body were primitive and concerned music's influence on breathing, blood pressure, digestion, and muscular activity (Munro and Mount, 1978).

Music therapy began to emerge as a healing force during and after WWII. Shell-shocked soldiers, sailors, and airmen who had suffered through horrible wartime events often retreated within themselves and became catatonic. Music had a way of bringing them out. The initial implementation of music therapy on a broad basis began after WWII. The war created a new area of medical practice, resulting in the formation of the *National Association for Music Therapy, Inc.*(NAMT).

Today we are witnessing a similar phenomenon of catatonic withdrawal with newly discovered degenerative diseases like Parkinson's and Alzheimer's disease. Some of today's patients suffering from these degenerative diseases, as well as normal old-age symptoms, can sometimes reach a low point where they often cannot communicate or recognize anyone. In most of these extreme situations, the patient can still recognize and respond to their favorite music.

Music has been a great help in reducing stress and helping to heal the autoimmune system. Harpists are now being hired to play in hospital nursery wards (or recorded harp music is piped in). Harp music calms babies and helps to slow and stabilize their respiratory and heart rates. The harp has one of the purest sounds in music, because the sound from the plucked string of the harp enters the atmosphere with little adjustment. Consequently, the overtones are purer and more healing than other instruments. The same can be said for flute and acoustic guitar.

Music is also now a part of pre–op, surgery, and post–op recovery. Many doctors today have their favorite recordings to listen to while engaged in surgery. Usually the music is soft, soothing, and classical. The perception of pain appears to be altered by music. Concentrating on pleasant imagery induced by music seems to focus our attention away from post-operative pain. Music is being used in post–op recovery and in the days following surgery to modify pain, which allows the doctors to cut back on potentially dangerous pain-killers in the form of prescribed medicine (Jacqueline Manning, RGN, *British Journal of Theatre Nursing,* vol. 7, No. 3, June 1997). Chronic pain is also now being treated with music. Somehow, pleasant music alleviates pain. Burn patients are encouraged to sing when their dressings are being changed for the same reason. Physical therapy is more effective when accompanied by well–chosen music.

Terminally ill patients are increasingly being transferred from hospitals or homes to hospices. Well–trained staff members help those who are terminally ill to (a) accept their situation, (b) learn to be as comfortable as possible under the circumstances, and (c) prepare them for death through carefully chosen music and professional counseling. According to Mary Rykov, MA, MTA, in the May/June 1998 issue of *The American Journal of Hospice and Palliative Care,* "Music's ability to reduce stress, create relaxation, and stimulate pleasant associative memories is now an important part of any hospice program." Today, many hospices have music therapists on staff, or have access to musicians specially trained for this sensitive treatment, usually harpists, violinists, cellists, flautists, or acoustic guitarists.

Music has also been very helpful in treating Alzheimer's patients. Music can trigger old memories, and memory is one of the keys to personal identity, understanding who we are. Some catatonic Alzheimer's patients can only communicate or respond positively when one of their favorite songs is heard. "Music gives them a window of time to come out of the confusion," said Alicia Ann Clair, director of music therapy at the University of Kansas in Lawrence. "Rhythm provides structure and security. It's anxiety reducing. We found very early that people who bump into others and wander around will easily sit still for 30 minutes with some music. Among patients in their 60s on up, music from the Big Band era often stirs up pleasant memories and can improve alertness and cooperation" (ibid.).

Those children affected by autism or attention deficit disorder (ADD) respond well to music, and their learning disabilities improve dramatically. Many autistic children who have totally withdrawn can be brought back to life with familiar, favorite old songs, like "Oh, Susanna," "How Great Thou Art," and in the case of one German–American patient, "The Blue Danube Waltz" by Johann Strauss. Autistic children respond to music therapy in a dramatic way, particularly by playing instruments and beating rhythms on percussion instruments.

Warning: loud pop–rock music is like poison to the ears of autistic children and those affected by ADD. "Music that is angry, negative and loud—filled with hate and fear—can create imbalance in the body and mind and contribute to degenerative diseases. *Discordant music creates discordant effects in our bodies.* The right kind of music is a powerful catalyst for good health and healing, because it touches the very core of our humanity" (*The Healing Sound of Music,* Findhorn Press, 2000).

Music, properly applied, can relieve stress and anxiety, and aid in concentration and learning. "Singing takes a person's mind off the suffering and soothes tension" (Peter Jaret, *Reader's Digest,* "The Healing Power of Music" September 2001). Humming softly or singing before a test, lecture, or performance can quiet the nerves, focus the mind, and dramatically improve performance.

Music for Pain

Self-administered music therapy is a growing phenomenon. Sheldon P. Blau, M.D., in his book *How To Get Out of the Hospital Alive*, suggests the following procedures for lessening pain through music:

» Have a CD or MP3 player with headset handy
» Select soft, melodic classical music (preferred) that is as close to your heart rate as you can get, usually 60–72 beats per minute
» Even humming to yourself can relax you and deaden pain
» Practice progressive relaxation (tensing and relaxing various muscle groups in the body) while focusing on your favorite music
» Chances are you'll slip into the "alpha" wave state of the brain, which is the one that induces total relaxation
» Don't try too hard—relax and listen are the keys
» Closing your eyes and imagining a beautiful place will speed the relaxation and lessening of pain
» Take your CD or MP3 player with you whenever you have to undergo treatments that are painful, scary, or frightening, like a CAT scan or MRV

Dr. Bernie Siegel, in his book *Power, Love and Healing*, describes the hospital of the future: "I expect hospitals will in the future use closed-circuit television in patient's rooms to provide pre-operative preparation, meditation, therapy, healing imagery, healing music, and laughter. Sooner or later they [hospitals] will see that this will help patients heal faster, and reduce hospitalization costs. Wellness is cost-effective."

More Benefits of Music Therapy

According to Sara Altshul, in an article titled "Drum Up Your Immunity" in the June 2001 edition of *Prevention* magazine, "Researchers from the Mind–Body Wellness Center in Meadville, PA, and the Center for Neuroimmunology at the Loma Linda University School of Medicine in California, measured the results of monitoring 11 people in 6 groups. The group that was part of a group drumming class *showed increased immune activity.* Drum therapy is already practiced in the USA as a supportive treatment for a variety of diseases, including cancer, cardiovascular disease, chronic lung disease, diabetes, and asthma."

ABCNews.com for July 10, 2002, reported: "A recent study funded by Congress of more than 25,000 children ages 9–17 shows that *music was the main force that kept them off dangerous recreational drugs,* a stronger and more effective help than family or sports. After music, family and sports came friendship, dancing, computers, and biking."

Playing the piano relieves stress for senior citizens, according to research coming out of Miami. Seniors who took 20 weeks of keyboard lessons expressed less stress at the end than at the beginning, according to music therapist Frederick Times. A control group showed no change in stress reduction. Decreased stress may in turn boost immune systems and improve health. According to Mahendra Kumar, a University of Miami professor of psychiatry and one of the researchers, "While music has benefits for listeners and players of all ages, it may have particular resonance for those in their later years of their life. As people age, their stress levels rise and they lose neurons, making them more prone to psychological complications like depression and anxiety. *Anything that can knock those stress levels back may boost the immune system and stave off disease"* (*San Diego Union Tribune,* April 24, 1999).

A follow–up study of these senior citizens revealed startling decreases in anxiety, depression, and loneliness. Participants showed a 92 percent increase in human growth hormone (HGHO), which positively affects the aging process, which often shows up in low energy levels, wrinkling, osteoporosis, sexual dysfunction, decreased muscle mass, and increased levels of aches and pains. "When people have success with music, boredom is relieved and efforts are directed toward personal productivity and pleasurable results. Seniors experienced positive emotional results and reported generally that they felt better after taking the keyboard classes" (Karl Bruhn and Kim Simmons, "Music Making and Wellness," National Association of Music Merchant's Convention, Anaheim, California, January 20, 2001).

Mood Adjustment

According to ethnomusicologist Elizabeth Miles, different styles of music can create an instant attitude or mood adjustment. She recommends the following:

» To energize: Latin salsa, swing, jazz, black gospel (rhythmic, moves to a fast beat)
» To relax: Gregorian changes (simple and soothing; no strong rhythm patterns or distracting harmony)
» To uplift: Beethoven's "Ode to Joy" (9th Symphony), Irving Berlin's "God Bless America," Handel's "Hallelujah Chorus" from *The Messiah,* "We Are the World," etc. (uplifts our spirits by appealing to our humanity, our religious beliefs, etc.).
» To cleanse: Tchaikovsky's "Piano Concerto" or "Overture" from *Romeo and Juliet* (pounding, stormy, and tragic—the perfect music to cry to)
» To focus: Vivaldi's *Four Seasons* (good for concentration, since the slower sections of the composition are optimal for deep concentration and the faster sections prevent mental fatigue)

—Dana Nourie, *Family Circle,* June 2, 2000

Music Therapy Today

Today there are more than 6,000 registered music therapists (RMTs) in the United States, and more than 80 undergraduate and graduate degree programs in our colleges and universities. In addition, there are 165 clinical internship/training sites.

The baccalaureate degree in music therapy requires coursework in music therapy; psychology; music; biological, social, and behavioral sciences; disabling conditions; and general studies. The degree programs also include fieldwork in community or campus clinics. After graduation, a student must serve a six–month internship in an approved facility to be eligible to take the exams to become a board–certified music therapist.

But research also reveals that music therapy only works if the person listening is "in tune" with the music and the process, i.e., not resisting or criticizing the procedure. The therapeutic effect is lessened when patients are angry, resistant, distracted, critical, or too analytical (Bonny and Savary, 1973).

Summary

I believe that the rediscovery of the healing power of music has been one of the major medical breakthroughs of this century, on par with the cure for polio and the discovery and unraveling of the DNA molecule. *We are just beginning to discover the incredible power of music as a tool in healing.*

I also believe that certain types of music can cause serious harm—mentally and physically, and in some cases can contribute to an early death. The uncontrolled saturation of our modern environment with harsh sounds and dangerous music has created a nation with frazzled nervous systems, a weak immune system, and damaged hearing. The inability to handle stress is another by–product of listening to years of loud music that prematurely fries our immune systems, as well as damages our hearing.

Music therapy must soon take on the commercial music industry, much as professional medicine had to eventually take on the tobacco industry in this country. Failure to do so—or postponing the inevitable—will only result in more tired, deaf, weak, and stressed-out citizens way before their time. Now is the time to do something about it.

Chapter 9

Noise Pollution

The United States lists *noise pollution* as one of the major unsolved problems in today's industrial–electronic age. The World Health Organization is beginning to investigate the health-damaging effects of increasing environmental encroachment of the *unfiltered environmental sound.* A recent statement from one of the reports argued that high-decibel noise or sound *"must be recognized as a major threat to human well-being"* (Dr. Alice H. Suter, *Noise and Its Effects,* www.nonoise.org). The author would argue that unnoticed low–frequency sound waves (below normal hearing range) might be even more potentially dangerous to mankind.

As more of the earth's population shifts from rural to urban areas, the proximity of millions living close together escalates the noise pollution problem. High density urban environments can generate noise levels up to *1,000 times more intense than those commonly found in rural settings.* Fortunately, our brain perceives these increased noise differences on an eightfold basis rather than the actual figures (Jackelyn Frost, CSW, "Is Sound Getting On Your Nerves?," *Allegro* magazine, April 2001).

> One in five teenagers [in Great Britain] have already done permanent damage to their hearing. . . . Ears need sixteen hours to recover from two hours exposure to 90–100 decibel sound.
> —Trick McNair, BBC's "Ask the Dr.," April 14, 2004

Certain styles of contemporary music— rock, rap, hip–hop, etc.— are often played at intolerable levels to those who are sensitive to sound. Scientists tell us that sound approaches the pain threshold somewhere between 90 and 120 dB. Walls of loudspeakers at a major rock concert can generate over 120 dB—a dangerous level that can cause permanent midrange hearing loss, as well as other damaging health effects. Discotheques and rock concerts usually generate a sound signal around 103.4 dB. This high-level sound production can be particularly dangerous if you are a sitting close to the speakers or are using a headset. High decibel sounds through a headset are more damaging because the sound waves are driven into the ear in a closed, tight pattern and there are no extraneous sounds to modify the intensity of the signal reaching the ears through a headset.

Those who use music as a "drug," however unknowingly, are reluctant to turn down the sound. *Most avid loud pop/rock music fans are unaware that the music works like a drug (stimulant) when played at these volume levels.* Rock and pop music fans are even more reluctant to admit it that they are "hooked" on the music—but not aesthetically, but physically. As a result, the *Los Angeles Times* of September 4, 1995, estimated that as many as 28 percent of rock fans in Los Angeles County could be suffering some degree of permanent hearing loss.

Individuals exposed repeatedly to high decibel sound tend to become more aggressive, irritable, anxious, or depressed. The triggering of the "fight–or–flight" response by the repeated sharp beats of the drummer causes individuals to become restless, aggressive, and difficult to control; hence the demise of the large outdoor rock festival—the insurance is too high for the promoters because of the difficulty in controlling a large crowd in this state of emotional arousal.

According to clinical psychologist Bart Billings, Ph.D., in his book *Feeling the Music Can Be Dangerous to Your Health,* "Long–term exposure to excessive levels of High-Intensity Low Frequency (HI/LF) sound waves (through the highly amplified electric bass) and the new type of HI/LF amplifiers and speakers available today can be physically harmful, even causing complications that could lead to death."

According to experts, this new type of loudspeaker raises the ante of potential damage to the listener when music is played through them at high decibel levels. The acoustic signal is literally shot from these speakers in a tighter pattern than traditional speakers, impacting our delicate listening device we call "ears" more severely. Imagine a very powerful fireman's hose. Now imagine sound coming out of it instead of water. *Not only are our ears at risk by damage to our inner organs and nervous system is a distinct possibility.*

According to Dr. William Glasser in the *Positive Addiction,* the stress placed on the body by a traditional rock concert is similar to the stress of jogging, which produces a "runner's high." The elevated feelings from jogging a (usually after running continuously for 20 to 30 minutes) are a result of endorphins released by the brain into the bloodstream to counteract the buildup of discomforting pain in the body. Someone asked a leading rock artist what was the first thing that he had to do to "turn on" an audience. His answer: *make them hurt* (feel pain due to the extreme volume)!

It has been reported that crews that work the decks on aircraft carriers who are surrounded constantly by high decibel noise from takeoffs and landings, as well as the catapult itself, have to wear protective clothes and earphones. The fatigue, spatial disorientation, and confusion created by long–term exposure to this environment can actually cause crew members to walk off the deck of the aircraft carrier without knowing it.

Law enforcement is re-examining traffic accidents where loud music played in the car prior to the accident was a factor. A recent study by the University of Sydney in Sydney, Australia, reveals that exposure to loud rock music in a car while driving *can slow reaction time.*

It is commonly accepted that attendance at a rock concert will leave the participants and spectators extremely fatigued. The next day rock technicians—sound, lighting, etc.—are notorious for being "spaced out." In most instances they are not on drugs (they couldn't do their job if they were), but instead they are manifesting the mental and physiological symptoms of noise fatigue.

A Spanish scientist, Dr. Castello Branco, MD, has been experimenting in his laboratory with high–decibel sound for some time. His research shows that chronic exposure to high-decibel sound (90 dB and up) can produce visual problems, epilepsy, stroke, depression, neurological deficiencies, psychic disturbances, anxiety, hostility, and central nervous system lesions. *These are not opinions or theories, but hard scientific facts!*

The human body is an amazing machine. We are constantly in a state of "homeostasis," which means unconsciously our body and mind are always adjusting to the changes in our immediate environment. This protective mechanism has helped our species survive for thousands of years. However, there is a downside. This system can be artificially manipulated and stimulated through drugs, alcohol, and music.

The rate at which the human heart beats at rest is approximately 72 beats per minute. The heartbeat is not even. There is a long separation between the first beat and the second—boom . . . . boom/boom . . . . . . boom/boom, etc. The low–frequency sound of the rock bass player at this tempo will cause the body to try to adapt to the rock beat. If the tempo of that beat is gradually increased, the beat of the heart will follow. In other words, *something causes the human system to lock into low–frequency sound generators and try to adjust to them.* Some scientists believe it goes back to the womb, where the fetus locks onto the beat of the mother's heart and tries to synchronize with it.

Graphic Violence and Loud Music

Musical soundtracks composed for video games start the background music at slower speeds, with the same heart rhythm (boom . . . boom/boom, etc.) and gradually increasing the tempo—something the body will try to keep up with, resulting in increased attention, anxiety, and aggression. All this is done to attract and hold the player or players in the game and make it more "real."

Increasingly, film soundtracks are using the same techniques of an increased heartbeat, particularly in the more graphically violent films. When this type of manipulation occurs, especially when combined with graphic violence, *the body goes into a survival mode* and an accelerated sense of reality, tension, anger, fear, and muscle contraction occurs.

Stress and Sound Pollution

Chronic sound or noise pollution reduces our ability to handle stress. Studies reveal a weakening of our immune systems as well, making us more receptive to bacteria and viruses that invade our bodies. Loud music or loud noise quickly raises our pulse rate and blood pressure and can cause an increase in stomach acid and/or acid reflux. Stress-related conditions could possibly develop such as ulcers, shingles, and high blood pressure (*American Medical Journal*, vol. 20, May 2001).

Chronic noise puts an individual's body into a continuous state of high arousal which can lead to over- or underproduction of important brain and body chemicals, including (1) neurotransmitters, (2) hormones, and (3) other vital substances. The brain *always* interprets loud, sudden sharp sounds as a dangerous threat to our well-being. To deliberately "trigger" the subconscious responses to loud music to experience the "rush" and/or the "thrill" is a dangerous experiment.

Triggering these emergency responses can also interfere with normal sleeping habits, particularly the necessary REM deep sleep we all need to feel rested. It is no accident that in the Middle Ages, many of the monasteries and convents were silent; devotees spoke as little as possible. Many sought the silence as an anecdote to the noise of a more normal environment. Today retreats, spas, and earplugs or headsets that totally block out sound are becoming more common in fighting the battle against loud noise and music.

Stand Up for Your Rights

We should do everything we can to protect our audio environment—in the home, in the car, at work, at play, at church, at meetings, and at social functions. *We are not to sacrifice our physical and mental health on the altar of powerhouse volume.*

We should refuse to eat in a restaurant with extremely loud music. We should refuse to buy merchandise from a store that pipes in loud music. Refuse to submit to earsplitting entertainment, no matter how popular. Carry earplugs and use them when ever the audio level becomes uncomfortable, even in the movie theater where the sound levels have gradually increased to dangerous levels of 90 dB and above. Resist noise pollution in the home, the business environment, the church, the country club, etc. Join organizations that are dedicated to making our society aware of the dangers of noise pollution.

Nothing is more discouraging than to seek to commune with nature today by walking on the beach or climbing a mountain, only to be met with a portable boombox carried by a pop music junkie who can't leave his musical "fix" at home. If he or she screams for their "rights," we should tell them to listen to their body–punishing and brain–numbing "music" through a headset. Like cigarette smoking, if you want to kill yourself, be our guest . . . but in the meantime, *keep your smoke out of my face and your loud music out of my ears.* Check the Internet for noise–pollution organizations and get their literature. It's time we brought back some audio control to our environment.

Negative Effect on the Sound–Sensitive

Overexposure to continuous loud music or noise (80 dB and above) can have a negative impact on memory, attention, and retention span, as well as academic achievement, particularly in the area of reading skills. Sound–sensitive people can become depressed, anxious, angry, or generally upset and disturbed by loud noise. Mozart, the genius composer, was once asked what his favorite music was. His reply: "Silence." He reportedly fainted the first time he heard a trombone. Many musicians and others are what scientists would call "sound–sensitive." Lab sounds are magnified in their hearing and become acutely painful or distressful long before they bother others.

Musicians make their living listening to and producing sound. In the process, most acoustic–instrument musicians develop an unusually sensitive reaction to uncontrolled sound in their environments. Leonard Bernstein, the great American composer/pianist/conductor, was reputedly unable to eat in a restaurant that had live or synthetic music playing during dinner. It wasn't so much the volume as it was that his analytical mind got caught up in analyzing the music and lost touch with the conversation of his dinner companions.

It is estimated that up to 60 percent of those elected to the Rock and Roll Hall of Fame in Cleveland, Ohio, have suffered some form of permanent hearing loss. Many are almost totally deaf, like Peter Townsend of the popular British rock group *The Who.* Don't sacrifice your body or your mind on the altar of loud music. Turn the volume down or stop listening. Find an environment that is quieter. Carry earplugs and use them. Refuse to be intimidated by sound–bullies who litter your audio environment with their trash.

Chapter 10

Recent Scientific Discoveries

The ear is not only for hearing; the ear is designed to energize the brain and the body.

—Dr. Alfred Tomatis, French ear specialist

Music and color can be expressed in terms of vibration. When color is translated into music vibrations, the harmonies of color are *40 octaves higher than an ear can here.* A piano stands about seven octaves. If the piano keyboard could be expanded another 50 octaves higher, the keys that play these higher octaves would produce color rather than audible sound (D. G. Campbell, *Introduction to the Musical Brain,* Aspen Publications, 1985).

> A hippie at heart, Carlos Santana has long championed music as a potent force for creating positive vibrations that—as this veteran of the 1969 Woodstock festival puts it—*"can change your molecular structure."*
>
> —George Varga, music critic, *San Diego Union Tribune,*
> Sunday, May 30, 2004

We live in the age of science. There have been more scientific discoveries in the last 100 years than all the previous periods of history together. Alvin Toffler, author of the popular book *Future Shock,* gives us this example. If you took the accumulated knowledge of mankind from ancient antiquity to the year 1900 and gave it a graphic representation of one foot, then all the accumulated new knowledge from 1900 to 1950 would be *three feet high.* But here is the mind-blower: if you took all our accumulated new discoveries from 1950 to the present it would be (in comparison) *taller than the Washington Monument.*

Music Research

Recent discoveries in music therapy research have been exciting. Some of the discoveries are actually rediscoveries, harkening back to more ancient times when the early Egyptian and Greek civilizations used music therapeutically for physical and mental healing. In addition to the positive discoveries being made today, some disturbing facts have been unearthed as well. Scientist today definitely know that certain styles of music can make you well or make you sick. Music can put you into man "altered state of consciousness" (without you knowing it). Music can calm or enrage you. And some styles of music can be habit-forming and can cause negative reactions.

Apart from the ear, humans also hear and perceive sound by skin and bone conduction. Other senses, such as sight, smell, and touch, allow perception of an even wider range of vibrations than those sensed by hearing. People are sensitive to sounds in ways that have often not been considered. The human body vibrates from its large structures down to our molecular cells. All have a characteristic vibrational frequency that absorbs and emits sounds. The human body is a system of vibrating atomic particles, acting as a vibratory transformer that gives off and takes in sound.

Our entire body vibrates at a fundamental inaudible frequency of approximately 8 cycles per second when it is in a relaxed state. During relaxed meditation or prayer, the frequency of brain waves produced is also about 8 cycles per second. Moreover, the earth vibrates at this same fundamental frequency. Being in "harmony" with oneself and the universe may be more than a poetic concept (Halpern & Savary, 1985).

Astounding Recent Discoveries

» Heart patients receive the same benefits from listing to 30 minutes of classical music as they did from taking 10 mg of the anti-anxiety medication Valium at a Baltimore hospital.

» Music and relaxation therapy were used together to lower heart rate and blood pressure in patients with heart disease at a Dallas hospital.

» Migraine sufferers are being trained to use music, imagery, and relaxation techniques to reduce the frequency, intensity, and duration of their headaches in a recent California State University study.

» Students who listens to 10 minutes of Mozart prior to taking SATs have higher test scores than students who were not exposed to music (UC Irvine, California).

» People who listened to light classical music for 90 minutes while editing a manuscript increased accuracy by 21 percent in a recent University of Washington study.

» Music's rhythms can affect your heart. The heart tends to speed up and slow down to match the pace of the music that's being listened to at the time.

» Rhythms can also alter our brainwave patterns and stimulate normal breathing.

» Hearing music, our bodies also "feel" the music—to our very bones. The impact of these vibrating sounds on our body can alter our moods and many of our bodily functions, including blood pressure, pulse, temperature, secretion of hormones, and pleasure-producing endorphins.

» Music lingers on in our memory banks like a second language. Just the recollection of a familiar melody can positively affect our automatic nervous system and mood.

» Classical music, particularly the music of Mozart, can calm the listener's mind and body rhythms, improve spatial perception, and promote better and more objective communication of emotions, concepts, and thoughts.

» Musical harmony affects our emotions, helping to release painful memories, angry feelings, and/or boost and improve "happy" feelings (Don Campbell, *Mozart Effect Resource Center*, UC Irvine, California).

» Tibetan monks were recorded chanting the mantra "Ommm." This recording was then played through a resonator plate with sand crystals on top. Within seconds, the sand began to vibrate and form a pattern called the *Sri Yantra,* which is considered in the Hindu belief to be a creation pattern of the universe. The implication is that *for every sound that there is a corresponding shape or pattern that we can see* (Christian Hummel, "Sound: A Key to the End of Pollution and Violence?" *Awareness Magazine,* March/April 2002).

» In a recent study by the U.S. Air Force, a sound pattern was applied to one of two test tubes of nitrogen dioxide, a pollutant found in the atmosphere. To the other tube, nothing was done. When sound was applied to the first tube, *it instantly changed its chemical composition* while the second remained the same (ibid.).

» A similar experiment was conducted over polluted water in Australia. When a specific sound frequency was applied to the sample, it dropped its *E. coli* bacteria to 10 ppm.

» In Auckland, New Zealand; Frankfurt, Germany; and Denver, Colorado, when sound patterns were applied to the geopathic stress zones of the area using harmonizers, the crime rate dropped in those cities from 30 to 50 percent within a few months (ibid.).

» Bird song triggers the blooming mechanism in some plants, according to researcher Dan Carlson. The sounds of frogs, crickets, and other insects perform an important task in that their sounds trigger and may even produce rain for the area (Australian researcher Rodrigo Navarro, ibid.).

» A two-year study done previously at Children's Hospital in Akron, Ohio, shows a trend toward shorter hospital stays for premature babies who listen to classical music (Cheryl Powell, "Hospital uses music to help preemies grow," *San Diego Union Tribune,* January 4, 2003).

» Nurses at neonatal intensive care units nationwide already use soft classical music on a case–by–case basis to help calm and soothe babies (ibid.).

» As early as 1914 music has been used as an anesthetic with doctors and dentists. Today some dentists give their patients the option of music or an injection for pain.

» Classical music helps kids nap. There's something about the soothing sounds and familiar melodies that induces sleep. Story types tend to induce fidgeting, rolling back and forth, lifting their legs, and touching their blankets. Soft classical music stops fidgeting and induces sleep within minutes (Joanna Weiss, "The So-called Mozart Effect," *Boston Globe*).

Below are some of the more startling discoveries regarding music. It is important to know that the human body is in a constant state of homeostasis, trying to adapt to changes in our environment. This has been one of the reasons we have survived; man can adapt to almost any environment given the chance.

» Studies have shown that low–frequency sound pulses (in pop music usually coming from the electric bass) that are near our heart rate zone (72 beats per minute at rest) will cause our bodily system to *lock on* to the bass beat. Video game soundtracks that starts slow then accelerate R&D most popular (Branco Costello, MD).

» Long–term exposure to excessive levels of the new High Intensity Low Frequency (HI/LF) sounds, such as that produced by an extremely loud amplified bass could cause health complications that might be permanent. Rock bands are getting "high" on the endorphins and enkephalins released in their bodies due to the pain and shock of high decibel sound.

» Since sound waves penetrate the body as a whole, cellular structures are now *being damaged through their* [the listener's] *entire body*. Medical professionals have known for years that HI/LF to auditory and balance functions, but for some reason, wider exposure to other body systems has not been emphasized (Bart P. Billings, Ph.D., www.omnisonic.com/bbillings.html).

» Nervous system impulses occur serially and may be described as frequencies. Much the same applies to the active muscle system which is actually *in a state of vibration.* It is in this vibratory field that all the bioelectric, chemical, mechanical, energetic, thermal, structural, kinetic, and dynamic processes take their course (according to Dr. Jenny's research in 1974). Therefore, when the natural course of frequencies and vibrations are altered by external HI/LF sound waves that penetrate the total body system, one can see the potential for a *breakdown in normal body functioning* (ibid., p. 2).

» Because omni-directional speakers diversify the sound (SurroundSound) the body is not as negatively impacted by high decibel sound. Directional speakers, on the other hand, at high volume send a *direct pressure wave that hits the body and moves tissue from front to back, causing discomfort* (cellular damage at HI/LF) (ibid.).

> How do you become successful as a rock band? *Hurt your audience!* [with a loud, distorted bass]. The pain, causing cellular damage results in an adrenaline and endorphins release [to cover the discomfort] causing a person to feel *high.* I remembered a time when I produced a show in conjunction with a major rock group. I remembered the parking lot prior to the show being littered with empty beer and alcohol bottles. I thought to myself that maybe at a *lower level of consciousness* the concert goers were *aware* of the physical pain they were to experience and were preparing for a concert by *anesthetizing themselves with alcohol.*
>
> —Bart B. Billings, *Feeling the Music Can Be Dangerous To Your Health*

Psychologist Dr. William Glasser wrote an important book entitled *Positive Addiction* in 1976. In the book he pointed out that runners receive a "high" approximately 15 to 20 minutes into their run. This high is the release of endorphins into the bloodstream, triggered by a buildup of pain to compensate for the discomfort of the run. Dr. Glasser points out, as a distance runner knows, that this high can be *addictive.* Runners get very upset when their schedule is interfered with and they cannot run daily. This feeling, on a much smaller scale, is not unlike the feeling one gets when withdrawing from addictive drugs or alcohol.

Dr. Billings' research suggests that rock music is *addictive* for the same reasons given above.

In addition to the cellular and neurological damage, loud rock music can also produce *disorientation*. Auto insurance companies are beginning to investigate the possible link between car accidents and powerful in–car audio systems.

Inner ear disturbances due to high decibel levels can also cause balance problems, sudden dizzy spells, and other disturbing and debilitating side effects. I am surprised this research has not hit the college and professional sports enthusiasts and players. Many pro athletes "pump" themselves up before a contest with loud rock music. Could this temporary "fix" in the long run be damaging to their overall health and shorten their careers? Recent research tends to support this theory.

Dr. Billings reports that after sitting for two hours during a rock concert and being struck by high intensity bass waves, he could feel the sound pounding on his body. "I actually felt nauseous at the beginning of the show and somewhat disoriented, but after my body adjusted, the feeling passed." He goes on to tell us that he felt unusually tired the next day: "My body was repairing itself from the trauma done to the cells." He then refers to a newspaper story about a reporter covering an aerobics class that used loud rock music in the background. According to the story, the newspaperman felt tired the next day, not from the exercise (he was in good shape), but *from the pounding of the loud music* (ibid.). Music affects positively and/ or negatively. Music, because it is vibration, penetrates the body, affecting the nervous system, the five senses, the internal organs, and the endocrine gland system, and other lesser–known but necessary systems for complex body to grow, be healthy, and be effective. Loud music negatively affects our subconscious mind, which controls our circulatory, digestive, glandular, and other systems of the body.

August 1992 edition of *Reader's Digest* published an article entitled "Music's Surprising Power to Heal," in which we read: "Music can lower blood pressure, adjust our basal–metabolism, affect our respiratory rates (lessens or increases the stress, depending on the style of music), can increase the body's production of natural endorphins (pain relievers), speed healing, reduce the danger of infections, and balance or imbalance (again, depending on the style of music) the right and left hemispheres of the brain."

"Soft music reduces staff tension in the operating room," says Dr. Clyde L. Nash, Jr., "and also helps relax the patient." (He uses classical music such as Vivaldi and Mozart) (ibid.).

Some studies show that music can lower blood pressure, basal-metabolism and respiration rates, thus lessening physiological responses to stress. Music may help increase production of endorphins and S-IgA (salivary immunoglobulin A) which speeds healing, reduces the danger of infections, and controls the heart rate. Studies indicate that both hemispheres of the brain are involved in processing music. Dr. Sacks explains "the neurological basis of musical responses is robust and may even survive damage to both hemispheres" (ibid.).

Mice and Rock Music

An American high school student, David Merrell, was so convinced that hard rock music is bad for the human brain that he picked up 72 male lab mice, a stopwatch, a 5' × 3' maze, and some CDs to prove his point. David said a group of mice exposed to hard rock music took 30 minutes to get through his maze. The same mice got through the maze in 10 minutes three weeks earlier before being exposed to rock music. "It was like the music dulled their senses," David said. "It shows point-blank that hard rock has a negative effect all around."

David's experiment included three groups of 24 mice: a control group (and no music), a hard rock group, and a classical music group. The mice spent the first week getting adjusted to David's basement. They received measured feedings and 12 hours of light daily. Each mouse navigated the maze to establish a base time of about 10 minutes. David started playing music 10 hours a day. The control group navigated without music. He put each mouse through the maze three times a week for three weeks. The results were startling: "The control group cut five minutes from its original time. The mice that listened to Mozart knocked 8½ minutes off of their time. The hard rock mice didn't even bother to sniff the air to find the trails of the other mice and lost 20 minutes."

David learned to house each mouse in separate quarters. In a previous experiment the preceding year he housed each group together: "I had to cut the project short because all the hard rock mice *killed each other,*" David said. "None of the classical mice or control-group mice do that at all" (Associated Press, February 12, 1995).

Music as a Weapon

According to the March 8, 2005, edition of the *Los Angeles Times,* some troops rotating to Iraq are being trained and issued a new sonic weapon, one that looks like a small satellite dish. The user points the dish toward an unruly or threatening crowd of Iraqis and turns on the sound. A message in Arabic is given to disperse, followed by a shrill, sharp sound that is so uncomfortable all but the most pain-resistant leave the area immediately. The pain, according to researchers, is not unlike "the mother of all migraine headaches." Naturally the troops are protected from the adverse effects of this device.

Law enforcement as well as the Pentagon have been looking for a long time for a safer, more modern way of dealing with riots and illegal gatherings. This new sonic weapon may be part of the answer.

Another new sonic weapon produced by the American Technology Group, San Diego, California, is the *Sonic Pain Stick.* This weapon is excellent for crowd control in small spaces, and possibly even to foil airplane hijackers. When aimed at the culprit it emits a shrill, high-frequency sound within a small radius that can drop anyone to their knees in intense pain.

In the science-fiction movie *Minority Report,* the character played by Tom Cruise introduces a new sound wave weapon that can be set to stun or kill. Unlike the rest of the story, which is set in the future, such a weapon exists today and is being tested by our military and law enforcement (*Village Voice,* April 12, 2004).

According to the July 1997 issue of *U.S. News and World Report,* the United States government has perfected a weapon using low-frequency sound waves. These new, super secret weapons are called *acoustic* or *sonic* weapons. "Sonic weapons can vibrate the insides of humans to stun them, nauseate them, or even liquefy their bowels and reduce them to quivering diarrheic messes," according to a Pentagon briefing. Electromagnetic waves are being used to put to sleep or to heat up (microwave) an enemy. Scientists are experimenting with a sonic cannon that throws a shock wave with enough force to *knock down a man.* The combination of sound waves with a laser beam may someday be able to knock down a plane.

Nazi Germany experimented with sound as a weapon. Using concentration camp prisoners, they exposed them to high decibels of HI/LF sound. They even produced a weapon they use compressed air to project the high density sound (www.omnisonic.com/bbill-ings.html).

Sudden bursts of extremely high volume (90 dB and above) can (a) temporarily destroy hearing, (b) cause mental confusion and disorientation, (c) break down resistance to interrogation, and (d) cause "tinnitus," a painful condition that is usually manifested with a loud ringing or buzzing in ears.

According to Gerr Vassilatos in *The Sonic Weapon of Vladimir Gavreau* (www.borderlands.com/archives/arch/gavreaus.htm), the research of French scientist Vladimir Gavreau in this field has re-vealed some startling discoveries, namely that extremely low–fre-quency vibrations can make a potential enemy ill or even *kill* them. A few seconds of exposure to these dangerous low–frequency sonic sounds create symptoms that come on rapidly and unexpectedly. Their pressure waves impact against the *entire body* in a terrible and inescapable grip. The grip was felt as a pressure which came in from all sides simultaneously, an envelope of death. Next came the pain, dull infrasonic pressure against the eyes and ears. Finally the low-frequency pressure waves begin to impact the environment, causing rooms and buildings to shake like an earthquake.

The physical symptoms lasted for hours after the sound genera-tors were turned off. Eyesight can be affected for days. Internal or-gans—the heart, lungs, stomach, and intestinal cavity—were filled with continual painful spasms for equal time period. According to the scientist engaged in this research, if the sound had not been turned off quickly all the resonant body cavities than absorb this low–frequency acoustic energy would have been torn apart.

Physiology seems to remain paralyzed by infrasound. It causes disruptions resulting in dizziness and nausea. Complete restora-tion can take hours or even days. Prolonged exposure can result in death. Symptoms increase in severity as the frequencies diminish, beginning with 100 dB, which is still in the pre–lethal level. Lethal infrasonic pitch lies in the seven cycle range. Intellectual activity is inhibited, blocked, and *then destroyed.* The action of the medulla is physiologically blocked and its autonomic functions cease.

The Earth acts as a conduit for these low–frequency sounds, allowing them to travel long distances without diminishing their impact. They could be the perfect stealth weapon in war because they cannot be located by a potential enemy without special detecting devices.

In the future robotic tanks equipped with infrastructure generators could sweep an area with deadly infrasound, destroying all enemies within 5 miles. Drone planes could be used to destroy an approaching enemy. A sobering thought is the fact that as of now, *there is no foolproof defense for the system.*

On a less threatening level is the development of a new science called *hypersonic sound* (www.khouse.org/6640/prophetic/BPO50. html). Developed by Woody Norris of American Technology, it is definitely the wave of the future in audio technology. HSS waves can be directed at a specific individual or group. They are encased in the HSS sound beam. *Only those in the sound beam can hear the beamed music or message.* The quality is so good, the listener feels like the sound is being generated from inside his head. The sound waves can travel 160 yards without distortion or loss of volume. Other uses of this technology include:

1. Listen to a movie or record at home while the children sleep.
2. Sports coaches could communicate with members of their team on the field without taking a time out.
3. Shops in a shopping mall could advertise their specials as people pass by.
4. Ambulances could warn cars to move without waking the neighbors.
5. Pointed messages could be sent from lifeguards to specific swimmers.
6. It could be used for crowd control during riots.

7. It could be used to increase the realism at movie theaters by causing voices to follow the actors.

HSS sound technology does have a potential military and law–enforcement use. A sonic gun, shaped somewhat like a large flashlight, can be pointed at the criminal or enemy and a release of 150 dB of sound can be pumped into his or her ears, causing excruciating pain without affecting anyone outside of the beam.

It has been likened to a flashlight beam that only illuminates the area within the beam. At 30,000 cycles, the sound quality is so real that the listener feels as if the sound is being generated *within his head.* This beam can travel up to 160 yards without any distortion or loss of volume. On the military side, if the volume is advanced to 145 dB, a burst of HSS sound could confuse and destroy an enemy by bouncing the sound off walls, buildings, etc., making the sound seem as if it is coming from many different directions (*Newsweek,* "Hearing Is Believing," August 5, 2002).

According to the same article in *Newsweek,* an experimental police whistle of 1.3 meters in diameter produced an infrasonic pitch of *37 cycles per second.* The sound produced violently shook the walls of the entire laboratory complex, even though its intensity was less than two watts.

Nicholas Tesla, a contemporary of Thomas Edison, was a brilliant eccentric who was ahead of his time in many ways. One of those ways was his research with sound. Tesla nearly destroyed his own laboratory on Houston Street with his experiments with infrasonic sound. He later tested infrasonic impulse weapons capable of wrecking buildings and whole cities on command. He artificially produced a small earthquake in Colorado Springs Colorado, with one of his experiments in the early 1940s. Tesla died almost penniless in New York City right after WWII. Before the FBI could get to his apartment, Russian KGB agents had already been there and confiscated his notes concerning his research over the years.

We are beginning to see now why music and sound is such an important means of communication. Its effects are cultural, psychological, and physical. No wonder the ancient Greek philosopher Plato claimed that if he controlled the music of a society, *he could control the society.*

Music elicits emotions. Music that produces sadness leads to slower pulse, raised blood pressure, a decrease in the skins conductivity, and a drop in body temperature. Fear produces increased pulse rate. Happiness causes faster breathing. Most of the time, music with a rapid tempo and written in a major key induces feelings of happiness. A slow tempo and a minor key induces sadness, and a fast tempo combined with dissonance (clashing intervals) induces fear ("The Biology of Music," *The Economist,* February 11, 2000).

Julius Portnoy, a leading scientific musicologist, has found that music can "change metabolism, affect muscular energy, raise or lower blood pressure, and influence digestion, but it may be able to do these things more successfully . . . than any other stimulants that produce these changes in our bodies" (ibid., p. 138).

I Think I'm Going Out of My Head

"To maintain a sense of well-being and integration, it is essential that man is not subject too much to rhythms not in accord with his natural bodily rhythms" (ibid., p. 199).

The sharp backbeat of the drummer in rock music is (soft–loud) the *antithesis* of the natural rhythm of the heart (loud–soft). The automatic nervous system will try to adapt to (homeostasis) to its most immediate aural, visual, and physical environment. The reverse pattern of the natural heart rhythm can cause heart arrhythmia and other cardiac problems if prolonged, or if the person has a heart problem to begin with. This might explain the rash of young people dying of "heart attacks" at ages way below the normal for that type of physical degeneration.

Do You Hear What I Hear?

Audiologist Kathleen Bulley tests and evaluates hearing at Scripps Hospital in LaJolla, California. She has noticed an increase in young adults coming forward with hearing loss. "Whether there really are more with hearing loss is hard to say. Actually, when President Clinton admitted he had a hearing problem (he also likes to listen to loud rock music—read the new book *Air Force One*) and not being an elderly president—it inspired a lot of people in their thirties and forties to come forward."

Bulley says there is a real danger to listening to loud music, especially in closed area like a car (or a church). "When people expose themselves to excessive noise levels, the ear is being bombarded with the pressure of the sound and, depending on how long they are exposed, the volume level of the sound; it can result in a temporary hearing loss. It usually starts out in the high-frequency range—like how your ears feel stuffed after a loud concert."

To show specifically how hearing loss can be incurred by listening to loud music, Bulley cites OSHA guidelines for noise exposure. "This is their criteria, but it is a governmental guideline. It can vary because people are individuals. For example, it says that 90 dB for eight hours can cause permanent hearing loss. It goes pretty fast after that: at 100 dB, it's two hours. At 105 dB, one hour. At 110, 30 minutes. At 115, 15 minutes."

What does this mean for the people McCullough mentioned who regularly listen to 160 dB or more? "The hearing may not go on one exposure. Did he really say 200 decibels? Because at 180, *people start feeling like they are coming apart!*"

No Neutral Ground

Like human nature itself, music cannot possibly be neutral in its spiritual direction.... Ultimately all uses of tone and lyrics in music can be classified according to their spiritual direction, upward or downward. To put it plainly, *music tends to be of either the darkness or of the light.*

—Ibid., p. 187

Fans of loud, syncopated, repetitious music, often with salacious or anarchistic lyrics, claim that all art, including music, is "amoral," without moral intent, innocent of any "feelings" except those projected on it by the listener. There is no logical or scientific support for such a statement, yet it is made to justify the evil and health-damaging music sold in this country to the tune of $15 billion dollars a year . . . more than the profits from cinema, live concerts, and professional sports combined (*San Diego Reader,* Calendar/Music Scene, p. 9, April 18, 2001).

Summary

As you can see from the brief sampling of recent research on sound and music and their effects on the human body and mind, we have entered the "twilight zone." We can no longer pretend that some types of music are harmless, nor can ignore the increasing evidence that music has a bright future in modern medicine. This information needs to be widely dispersed, discussed, and acted upon.

Chapter 11

Power of Music Updates

There have been so many new discoveries and research on the power of music since this book was originally conceived, it has been hard to keep up with it all. More and more research centers, educational institutions, and teachers have made important breakthroughs. We are discovering that music can heal, inspire, increase learning speed and capacity, and effect almost all areas of physical and mental health. As a society we are finding that music can bring us together or divide us even further. We are just beginning to understand the increasingly powerful role that music plays in our lives.

Solid scientific research has determined that certain styles of music can play havoc with our physical and mental health. Extremely loud, percussive, and aggressive music can stunt growth and maturity in different species of laboratory animals as well as kill plants of all types. Like tobacco, there are very powerful business interests in this country that do not want that story told. The record industry today is almost a $20 billion a year business, most of it in sales of dangerous music—music that can cause mental illness, as well as physical damage to our nervous systems, hearing, and immune systems.

This chapter includes recent interesting and important research in music. Please feel free to contact me with articles, lectures, and discoveries of your own regarding the power of music. I am constantly looking for new evidence of music's power.

We are discovering that taste in music is not the problem. The problem is in ignoring solid scientific research that tells us how dangerous music affects us—in all areas of our lives.

Dr. Jack Wheaton
P.O. Box 1331
Rancho Santa Fe, CA 92067
email: jcwprod@cox.net

Recent Research on Music

According to a CNN special report on May 20, 2009, "Soft music, like laughter, can open the blood vessels and produce protective chemicals within our body. Constricted blood vessels can lead to high blood pressure, which can increase heart attack risk. Hospitals across the country now use music therapy to help patients heal."

A scientist at the Montréal Neurological Institute for instance, have found dramatic evidence on brain scans that the "chills" or a visceral feeling of awe that people report listening to their favorite music are real. Music that a person likes—but not music that is disliked—activates both the higher thinking centers in the brain's cortex, and perhaps more important, also the "ancient circuitry, the motivation, and reward system" says experimental psychologist Robert Zatorre, a member of the team. It is this ancient part of the brain that, often through the neurotransmitter dopamine, also governs basic drives such as food, water, and sex, suggesting the tantalizing idea that the brain may consider music on a par with these crucial drives (Boston.com/yourlife/health/articles/2007/10/29/the powerofmusic).

According to the same article, listening to music can also reduce the intensity of pain and the need for narcotic drugs.

"Music therapy may also improve mental state and functioning in people with schizophrenia according to a 2007 Cochran review. Premature infants who listen to lullabies learn to suck better and gain more weight than those who don't get music therapy. There is evidence in improvement of the immune system in hospitalized children who played, sang, and created music.

"Information learned in song, rhyme, or rap is more easily recalled when in a state of high arousal (anxiety). This is due, of course, to the fact that this information is stored in a different fashion than traditional verbal cognitive information" (www.yellodyno.com/html).

"Music can increase endorphin levels. Endorphins, the brain's own 'opiates,' the healing chemicals created by the joy and emotional richness in movies (movie soundtracks, religious music, and marching band and drum ensembles) enable the body to create its own anesthetic and enhance the immune functions. The *Journal of the American Medical Association* reported in 1966, '. . . Music stimulation increases endorphin release and this decreases the need for medication. It also provides a distraction from pain and relieves anxiety'" (ibid., p. 71).

Ulman Lindenberger of the Max Planck Institute for Human Capital Development in Berlin, Germany, says: "To my mind, this study highlights one of the great joys of playing music, one voiced by many musicians: *a sense of self–transcendence.* Playing music together creates a rare chance to step outside of our small concern and ourselves and join our minds wholeheartedly with others in creating something no individual could make alone. Seen in this light, creating beautiful music is simply a wonderful by–product of a larger reward—connecting deeply with other human beings."

In the article "Music's Affects on the Human Body," we read, "Music does many things for the human body including, masking unpleasant sounds and feelings, slowing down and equalizing brain waves, affecting respiration, affecting the heartbeat, pulse rate, and blood pressure, reducing muscle tension and improving body movement and coordination, affecting the body temperature, regulating stress-related hormones, boosting the immune function, changing our perception of space and time, strengthening our memory and learning, boosting productivity, enhancing romance and sexuality, stimulating digestion, fostering endurance, enhancing unconscious receptivity to symbolism, and generating a sense of safety and well-being" (hs.riverdale.k12.or.us/~dthompso/exhib_03/jasonc/Music's_Affects_on_the_Human_Body.html).

In *Music and the Brain*, Laurence O'Donnell relates that the way Einstein figured out his problems and equations was by improvising on the violin.

"Classical music from the Baroque period causes the heart beat and pulse rate to relax to the beat of the music. As the body becomes relaxed, the mind is able to concentrate more easily. Furthermore, *Baroque music decreases blood pressure and enhances the ability to learn.* Music affects the amplitude and frequency of brain waves, which can be measured by an electroencephalogram. Music also affects breathing rate and the electrical resistance of the skin. It has been observed to cause the pupils of the eyes to dilate, increases blood pressure, and increases the heart rate." Mozart's music and Baroque music, with 60 beats per minute beat pattern, activate the left and right brain. The simultaneous left- and right-brained action maximizes learning and retention of information. The information being studied activates the left brain, while the music activates the right brain. Activities which engage both sides of the brain at the same time, such as playing an instrument or singing, causes the brain to be more capable of processing information (ibid.)

King George I of England had problems with memory loss and stress management. He called on his court composer, George Frederick Handel, to write and play certain styles of music to soothe his moods and restore his sanity, as King David and the Bible was called upon as a youth to play and sing to soothe the troubled spirit of King Saul. Frederick Chopin, while a young, brilliant pianist/composer and still living in Poland, was likewise called upon to write and play soothing music for his king.

An Australian physician and psychiatrist, Dr. John Diamond, found a direct link between muscle strength/weakness and music. He discovered that all the muscles in the entire body go weak when subjected to the "stopped anapestic beat" (soft/loud/soft/loud etc.) of music performed by hard rock musicians. He called it a "switching" of the brain. Dr. Diamond said the switching occurs when the actual symmetry between both of the cerebral hemispheres is destroyed causing alarm in the body along with lessened work performance, learning and behavior problems in children, and a "general malaise in adults" (*Music and the Brain,* p. 6)

Tests on the effects of music on living organisms besides humans have shown that special pieces of music (including "The Blue

Danube") aid hens in laying more eggs. Music can also help cows to yield more milk. Researchers from Canada and the former Soviet Union found that wheat would grow faster when exposed to special ultrasonic and musical sounds. Rats were tested by psychologists to see how they would react to Bach's music and rock music. The rats were placed into two different boxes. Rock music was played in one of the boxes, while Bach's music was played in the other box. The rats could choose to switch boxes through a tunnel that connected both. Almost all of the rats chose to go into the box with the Bach music even after the type of music was switched from one box to the other (ibid.).

Music and Learning

1. Music relaxes the mind and lower stress levels that inhibit learning.
2. Music acts directly on the body's metabolism and heartbeat, as well as being able to trigger the brain to release endorphins, reducing a tranquil state that leads to faster learning.
3. Music stimulates and awakens, reviving bored or sleepy students and increasing blood and oxygen flow to the brain.
4. Certain musical structures stimulate brain circuitry that help to decode complex ideas.
5. Music inspires emotion, creating a clear path to long–term memory.
6. Music modifies the environment, helping to get students into an effective learning state.
7. Music is a universal language. Students can better understand a foreign culture through listening to their music.
8. Music is a powerful anchor that moors learning in memory
   —Dr. Jeanette Vos, "An Introduction to the Music Revolution,"
   www.thelearningweb.net/music

In 2005, the Israeli Defense Forces stopped a Palestinian riot with a sonic weapon that broadcast a musical frequency that when played loudly and projected with a small but intense beam causes intense acoustic discomfort and renders potential militants incapacitated (*Jerusalem Post,* June 3, 2005).

In November of 2008 pirates who tried to hijack a liner off the coast of Somalia were exposed to a new sonic weapon, a long-range acoustic device, or LRAD, which is a high-tech loudhailer capable of causing permanent damage to hearing from a distance of more than 300 meters (984 feet) (BBC News, Tuesday, November 9, 2008.

> Music is the most powerful stimulus known among the perceptive process. Music is made up of many ingredients and according to the proportions of these components, it can be soothing or invigorating, ennobling, or vulgarizing. It has powers for evil as well as good.
>
> —Dr. Max Schoen, *The Psychology of Music*

> You can hypnotize people with music and when you get people at the weakest point you can preach into their subconscious whatever you want to say.
>
> —Jimi Hendrix, well-known early rock guitarist,
> *Rolling Stone* magazine, January 1970

Music and Society

Chapter 12

I Am Music

I am music, most ancient of arts. I am more than ancient; *I am eternal.* Even before life commenced upon this earth, *I was here*—in the sounds of the winds and the waves. When the first trees and flowers and grasses appeared, I was among them. I heard the first birds sing and the song of the giant whales.

And when men came, I at once became the most delicate, most subtle, *and most powerful medium for the expression of man's emotions.* When men were little better than beasts, I influenced them for their good.

In all ages I have inspired men with hope, kindled their love, given a voice to their joys, cheered them on valourous deeds, and soothed them in times of despair.

I have played a great part in the drama of life, who's end and purpose is the complete perfection of man's nature. Through my influence human nature has been uplifted, sweetened, and refined. I am the bridge between the temporal and eternal.

With the aid of men, I have become a fine art. From the harp of David and the lute of Orpheus, from Stradivarius to Mozart and Beethoven, a long line of the most inspired minds have devoted themselves to the perfection of the art—the means through which men may utilize my powers and enjoy my charms.

I have a myriad of voices and instruments. I am in the hearts of all men and on their tongues, in all lands and among all peoples; the ignorant and unlettered know me, not less than the rich and learned. For I speak to all men, in a language that all understand. I bridge age, gender, race, religious, and cultural gaps of all kinds.

Even the deaf hear me, if they but listen to the voices of their own souls. I am the food of love. I have taught men gentleness and peace; and I have led them onward to heroic deeds. I have let them hear the songs of the angels, the heavenly choir.

I comfort the lonely, I entertain the bored, I educate those thirsty for knowledge, I preserve the history of mankind in song, and I harmonize the discord of crowds. I inspire and help lead man toward his destiny. I am a necessary luxury to *all men*. I AM MUSIC!

—Anonymous

Chapter 13

Seven Basic Human Emotions

Introduction

There are seven separate elements that are part of music: (1) rhythm, (2) form, (3) melody, (4) countermelody, (5) harmony, (6) texture (tone quality and register), and (7) style (dynamics, tempo, and articulation). There are also seven basic human emotions: (1) mad, (2) glad, (3) sad, (4) scared, (5) sensual/erotic, (6) humorous and (7) inspirational (religious, patriotic, humanistic, and ecological).

Music is a language of emotion. Every part of a musical performance or composition expresses one or more emotions. The more clearly the conductor, performer(s), or singer(s) understand the emotion the composer intended, the more impact the musical performance will have on the audience. The performing musicians must *understand and feel* the emotions of the music themselves if they are to impact an audience

This is not always easy to do, since some musical compositions express very subtle emotions, rapidly changing emotions, or a combination of two or more emotions. It is important for the audience to feel the original emotional intent of the composer as powerfully as possible for maximum aesthetic effect

Audiences go to concerts to "feel" the emotions behind the music. Failure to "feel" the emotional intent of the music results in the audience not being able to connect with the music or the artists performing it. When this happens boredom, frustration, and even irritation can set in. Lyrics and music under drama (opera, film, television, or radio drama) help the viewer/listener to more easily relate to the music, *if the musical style fits the drama or kinesthetic action on stage or screen.*

Kinesthiology is the science of bodily movement. The Max Plank Institute in Germany is one of the most advanced research centers for studying movement, particularly as it is related to competitive athletics. Music behind drama, particularly cinema or television, *must* also understand how to amplify the physical movements and expressions of the actors/singers with appropriate music. *Each of the seven basic human emotions expresses itself in specific physical movements directly related to that emotion.*

For instance anger is physically expressed by grim visual expressions, tightening of the jaw, squinting or bulging eyes, a general tightening of all the muscles of the body, and the drawing in of the body mass to the center. Pointing, shoving, pushing, grabbing, and hitting are all variations or extensions of the basic emotion of anger. *The accompanying music must amplify these physical manifestations of emotions to be effective.*

In each of the seven categories of human emotion there are degrees of expression, from a very subtle, mild expression to a complete giving–over of the individual or individuals to the emotion(s) being expressed. *The accompanying music must adjust to the subtle changes in the emotion or emotions being expressed.* Listed below are the seven basic emotions and some of the suggested characteristics for appropriate accompanying music:

Mad
» *Rhythm:* fast, syncopated (offbeat accents), loud
» *Form:* random, wandering—follows the emotion on stage or screen
» *Melody:* use of dissonant intervals (minor second, augmented fourth, major seventh, minor ninth), large leaps, melody is short, dissonant and disconnected
» *Countermelody:* same as melody—with occasional clashes between the two
» *Harmony:* dissonant chords, disjointed chord progressions, unresolved dissonances

» *Texture:* range—extreme high or low tone, very bright or raspy
» *Style:* tempos—fast; dynamics—loud; phrasing—staccato (short notes)

Sad

» *Rhythm:* slow, repetitive, non-syncopated (few if any offbeat accents), simple rhythm patterns
» *Form:* Simple—AB or ABC or ABBA or ABCD, etc.
» *Melody:* dissonant intervals emphasized (same as above)
» *Countermelody:* simple, non-obtrusive, repetitive (repeated bass pattern)
» *Harmony:* minor, diminished, and augmented chords emphasized
» *Texture:* middle or low register, occasionally "sobbing" high register patterns; tone quality—dark
» *Style:* tempos—very slow; dynamics—soft to medium loud; phrasing—legato, smooth and connected

Glad

» *Rhythm:* cheerful, slightly syncopated, often repeated rhythms (children at play), 6/8 triplet feelings: yaa—da ya—da, etc.
» *Form:* simple and repetitive: AD, ABA, ABC
» *Melody:* emphasis on consonant (thirds and sixths) intervals, an occasional perfect interval for contrast (P4, P5, and P8)
» *Countermelody:* simple and repetitive
» *Texture:* middle or high register; tone quality—bright or clear
» *Style:* tempos—medium to fast; dynamics—medium to loud; phrasing—legato with some staccato for contrast

Scared

» *Rhythm:* highly syncopated and repetitive
» *Form:* Wandering—follows the action on screen or stage
» *Melody:* Very dissonant intervals, emphasizing augmented fourths, major sevenths, minor ninths.
» *Countermelody:* Very repetitive, often clashing with melody
» *Harmony:* dissonant chords with unresolved dissonance random chord progressions, extreme open or closed chord voicing

» *Texture:* extreme low or high register; tone quality—dark, raspy
» *Style:* tempos—extremely slow then gradually speeding up; dynamics—extremes, very soft and then suddenly very loud; phrasing—smooth to staccato

The other three emotions—sensual, humorous, and inspirational—can be analyzed and musically "framed" in a like manner.

Some composers intuitively know how to select the right ingredients in their musical compositions to express the emotions they wish to convey. Others must be trained to be able to do this. A careful observance and listening (with the musical score, if possible) of some of the great examples of emotional expression in music would help both the student and the listener to have a deeper understanding regarding emotion and music.

Some suggested musical examples to listen to for music analysis regarding emotion might include:

» **Mad:** "Overture" from *Romeo and Juliet* (ballet) by Tchaikovsky. This single short example expresses beautifully in music anger (mad), love (inspiration), and death (sadness).
» **Sad:** "Funeral March" by Chopin. This piano piece is often played at state funerals. Rachmaninoff's "Isle of the Dead" is another appropriate example.
» **Glad:** "Overture" to Rodger's and Hammersteins' *Oklahoma* or *The Sound of Music.*
» **Scared:** "A Night on Bald Mountain" by Moussorgsky, or "The Witches Sabbath" from Hector Berlioz' *Symphony Fantastique.*
» **Sensual:** "Bacchanal" from Saint Saen's opera *Samson and Delilah,* as well as Maurice Ravel's "Bolero" (used so effectively in the film 10).
» **Humorous:** "The Sorcerer's Apprentice" by Dukas or the "Overture" to Shakespeare's *Midsummer Night's Dream* by Mendelssohn, or Leonard Bernstein's "Officer Krumpke" from *West Side Story.*
» **Inspirational:** Religious—"Hallelujah Chorus" from Handel's *Messiah;* Patriotic—"Stars and Stripes Forever" (March) by John

Phillip Sousa; Humanistic—"We Are the World" by Stevie Wonder; and Ecological—"Afternoon of a Faun" by Debussy, "The Pines of Rome" by Rhespighi, and "Rocky Mountain High" by John Denver.

Summary

The more you realize that music is a language of emotion, the more it will change your listening habits. You will begin to search for music that expresses the emotions and feelings *you* want to hear, rather than being a *victim* of mass media by being bombarded by random musical selections via radio, recording, film, or television.

One of the important signs of a mature art form is its ability to express itself in *all seven* of the human emotions. Some musical styles, though widely popular, are limited in their range of emotional expression. From a historical standpoint, it lacks the ability to permanently affect the direction of music or to be accepted into the hallowed halls of more mature forms of musical expression. A musical style that concentrates on sex, anger and fear cannot be considered a mature musical form.

Chapter 14

Advertising

We take it for granted we see and listen to hundreds of ads a day, via print media, radio, television, even waiting for the local movie to start. You can't go to a professional ball game today in the United States without being bombarded with loud music and advertising. In the new, romantic world of the Internet, we have unsolicited advertising called "spam." Fortunately, so far, it is not accompanied by loud, blaring rock music.

Advertising, for the most part, gave up a long time ago on the basic announcement of a product, why it's the best buy, its cost, and availability. Today we are lured to buy things we don't need and haven't thought about with prices beyond our ability to afford. After all, what are credit cards for? Credit card debt is at an all-time high, and one of the reasons is the success of modern advertising. Intensive research over the years by the world's biggest advertising agencies has revealed that the greatest seduction force in modern advertising is *music*. Why? Because *music triggers a subconscious reaction on the part of the listener that is permanently associated with the product and stored in the long-term memory side of the brain* (left hemisphere).

Recent research has already shown that music has tremendous power to overpower our conscious will. Music is used to seduce the potential customer into a receptive state of consciousness; creating an aura of warmth and familiarity with products many of us have never seen and will never buy nor care to. The proper use of music in advertising, along with color, drama, exaggeration, repetition, and fantasy (sometimes humor) all work to draw us closer to the product being sold.

Mass advertising today is a *science* and an *art*. Marshall McLuhan, the well-known Canadian sociologist, said that the high art of the 21st century would be the best of our television ads. Today, the Cleo Awards is an annual event honoring the best television commercials internationally.

McDonald's Corporation, one of the heaviest advertisers in television ($300–500 million annually) tests all its new television commercials with carefully screen and selected audiences before the ads are released on television. These well-paid recruits are not only interviewed and probed afterward for their reactions, they are "wired" with special apparatuses that measure everything from their heart rate and respiratory rate to the rate of pupil (eye) dilation and blinking.

Product identity is sought after at an early age. Major foreign auto corporations like Toyota and Nissan provide logo uniforms to their schools, along with "play" production lines and tools that simulate working on or building a car. In the United States today, giant corporations woo school kids early on with free study tools, notebooks, etc., with their corporate logo attached. Even T-shirts today reflect the "hottest" advertising market among young adults.

Pavlovian Conditioning

One of the most powerful devices for developing product identity today is the music used behind familiar television commercials. As we have already pointed out, music subconsciously ties the listener in with the product and triggers long-term memory. We respond just as the great Russian behaviorist Dr. Pavlov's dogs, who salivated when they heard the bell that signaled food.

Today, most young children between the ages of 3 and 7 are able to recognize—and in many instances sing—the themes to their favorite television shows and commercials. Commercial music from radio and television advertising has, for the most part, taken the place of nursery rhymes and traditional folk songs. Classical music today is thought of in terms of popular motion-picture soundtracks, particularly to movies series like *Harry Potter*, *The Lord of the Rings*, and *Star Wars*.

Stop for a moment and consider how many product themes or television and movie themes you can remember, even if you can't hum or sing them. Write their names down. Now, ask yourself how many nursery rhymes or folk songs you can remember. Which can you most readily recall? Those of us who grew up in the United States in the 1930s and 1940s, the pre–television era, can *still* remember and hear in our heads the themes to our favorite radio shows, like "The Lone Ranger," "The Green Hornet," "The Shadow," "Captain Midnight," and "I Love a Mystery."

In most instances, unless you are trained in music at an early age or had parents who seriously screened what you listened to, you will mostly recall music from radio and television commercials of that period, as well as some movie themes. If you are over 35, you should be able to identify or hum themes to such popular early television shows as "Bonanza," "Peter Gunn," "I Love Lucy," "M*A*S*H," and "The Disney Hour." Now, can you hum or recollect popular themes for Chevrolet, Pepsodent, Alka–Seltzer, Doublemint gum, or Wheaties? How many more can you remember?

The survivors of the 1960s recollect mostly big hit songs of their favorite rock artists. Today, if you drive across the country and listen to radio, the four biggest music-format radio shows you will hear will be, (1) nostalgia rock, (2) soft rock, (3) pop–rock, and (4) country–western. In some more urban areas you might find R&B (including Motown) or jazz or classical music stations as well.

Two giants in innovating and developing commercial, piped–in background music for business are *Muzak* and *Seeburg*. When I was working on my doctorate degree at USC, my composition professor, Ingolf Dahl, presented his students with his greatest wish for his 70th birthday: that someone would sever the main communication lines that fed Muzak into thousands of businesses in the Los Angeles Basin. He could not stand this crass manipulation of the American consumer and their musical tastes through forced–listening to meaningless (to him) piped–in music. No one volunteered to do the deed.

Are We Being Programmed?

Muzak and Seeburg have spent millions studying how to manipulate our emotions via music. Their music is tailored for each type of business, and the style of music also changes for the time of day and the time of year, as well as the day of the week. If the customers are primarily male, the music is different than if the customers are mostly teenagers, women, or families. If there are heavy concentrations of minorities, the piped-in music is adjusted to fit the ethnic makeup of the neighborhood and the regular customers.

Geographical location and the education levels, as well as primary businesses in the area, are also considered when customizing a piped-in music program tailor-made for their customers recognizable patterns. The music used is also adjusted for the type of business. Supermarkets hear different piped-in music than banks, for instance. In other words, *they know who we are and how to program us via music.*

Hidden cameras have revealed that the average person goes into the first stages of hypnosis when shopping in a supermarket as a result of the music, the layout of the store, the colors used in selling the products, and the room temperature of the store itself. Maybe that's why I sometimes come home with the wrong thing or additional items when my wife sends me to the supermarket occasionally! *Music can be a very subtle form of subliminal advertising, particularly in trying to connect the music to the product or service.*

The primary purpose of piped-in music, according to these two biggest producers, is to adjust the mood of the potential customer. Some businesses required lively music to stimulate buying, like sports car dealerships, swimsuit stores, and motorcycle dealerships. Others require a lush, romantic style, like women's lingerie, cosmetics, wedding accessories, and romantic getaways.

Victoria's Secret, a lingerie store, is the largest distributor and seller of classical and semi-classical music in the United States. The combination of sensuality and elegant classical music has served them well. They discovered gold when they not only used the music to sell their products in the store, but then turned around and sold the music in a CD format to the customers as well!

Since music triggers long–term memory and long–term memory is stored in the right hemisphere of the brain, the same part of the brain that stimulates our emotions, manufacturers and businesses work hard to get us to associate their product (in a warm, fuzzy way) with the product theme and the overall emotion of the commercial (usually happy, humorous, or inspirational). The purpose of music in a commercial is to (1) adjust the potential customer's mood to be receptive to the product; (2) help the customer remember the product's brand name; (3) overpower left–brain logic or hesitancy to buy; (4) briefly entertain the listener/viewer in such a way that they would like to hear and see more; and (5) make a strong positive connection of personal pleasure with the product.

Music, Emotion, and Commercials

Again, music is a language of emotions. So, what emotion or emotions are the most important to bring out in a potential buyer? Obviously, that depends on the product. A quick review of the basic emotions would include mad, sad, glad, scared, sensual or sexy, inspirational, and humorous.

Okay, what are we selling? Let's see how products line up with certain emotional force fields:

Emotion	Product
Mad (angry, frustrated, etc.	service–oriented businesses, bookkeeping, income tax, political parties, escapes, vacations
Sad	funeral services, environmental warnings, insurance, growing old, weight control, budget control
Glad	family restaurants, theme parks, family vacations, new homes, Christmas, birthday, anniversaries
Scared	burglar alarms, self–defense classes, anti–drug anti–gang ads, AIDS, drunk driving, marital counseling, bail bonds, terrorism, assault

Emotion	Product
Sensual (sexy)	women's clothes, particularly swimsuits and lingerie, libido drugs (Viagra), cosmetic surgery, cosmetics, designer clothes (male and female), shampoo, jewelry, diet ads, perfume
Inspirational	military service—recruiting ads, environmental protection, patriotic ads, religious ads, historical places, historical books, movies, TV dramas
Humorous	toilet paper, antacids, kid's toys, movies, books, plays, TV comedies, cereals, insurance

Next Step

First, the product; second, the emotion; third, the creation of the right music. This demands on the part of the composer a detailed knowledge of musical clichés that amplify and trigger a specific emotion.

We are all victims of conditioning. We've been "conditioned" to associate certain rhythms, forms, types of melody, harmony, choice of instruments, and style, with certain emotions. In other words, the commercial composer/arranger must be able to *press the right buttons* musically with the correct emotion for the ad. This takes great skill, sensitivity, and a good memory for what turns people on in these seven emotional force fields.

The highest paid, regularly salaried composers today are those who wrote the music for radio and television advertising. Their cleverness can make or break the selling of a new product. Remember, they usually only have 30 or 60 seconds to work their magic, although some infomercials run longer. For many years I have recommended to students who are interested in trying to enter this lucrative field to begin audiotaping commercials for different products. I suggest to these students that they break the music down into its seven basic components (rhythm, form, melody, etc.) and identify the musical clichés they use to trigger an emotional response to the product and then store that information for later use. Should they actually get an opportunity to work in this field, they will already be miles ahead of those who are trying to earn while they learn. These students do not have to make exact copies of already existing commercials (what would be the point?), but they can work from the same template of emotional stimulus that already exists. Why reinvent the wheel?

Chapter 15

Music for Cinema and Television Drama

Until the 1920s motion pictures were silent. Usually there was a pianist, organist, or small orchestra to play appropriate music for each scene portrayed on the screen. *Silent movies without music were not believable.* Music was the necessary link in getting the audience to relate emotionally to the action on the screen. There was even a monthly magazine for those musicians engaged in this business. The necessary dialogue for silent films was printed underneath the action on the screen.

A friend of mine presented me with an excerpt from one of the issues of an old magazine published in the 1920s for silent–movie musicians. It was a typical musical insert (for piano or organ) entitled "Music for Storm or Battle." It was always fun to play occasionally and imagine oneself in the pit at a movie theater back in the 1920s.

The first motion picture with a dialogue and a prerecorded music soundtrack was Al Jolson in *The Jazz Singer* (1926). The immediate success of this new innovation quickly threw over 25,000 musicians out of work in movie theaters across the United States, at the same time opening up a lucrative studio orchestra recording business for skilled musicians in Los Angeles and New York City.

Over the years, the recording technology (driven by huge profits from films) continued to improve, until today, where the most sophisticated recording and playback systems available are used to provide super realism and drama in film soundtracks, including special speakers that produce extreme low and high frequencies, quadraphonic sound, stereo, digitally recorded (no loss of quality on replay, plus a more realistic tonal quality), and computer-cued to fit difficult action scenes. The most effective music/special effects and dialogue playback systems are found in our local theaters. A well-mixed, realistic soundtrack adds to an already overwhelmingly realistic screen presentation.

I've had the pleasure of writing music for several Hollywood commercial films (MGM, Universal, etc.). It is an exciting and challenging business. The producer and director usually wait until the very last to enlist the composer to write music for the film. The film composer is always under pressure to write appropriate, exciting, and new music—quickly!

It is necessary to "spot" the film with the director. This means going through the unedited film, scene by scene, discussing where music is appropriate and where it is not. Scenes requiring music have to be analyzed by the director and the film composer. The basic emotions and kinesthetic action for each scene requiring music have to be identified, discussed, and analyzed. Then the historical style of the music (you can't use ragtime piano in a science-fiction film), and the choice of instruments, length of music, visual and aural cues for music to begin, are chosen. It is a tedious process, since most films before the final edit are four or five hours long. *It usually takes two to ten days to thoroughly "spot" a film.*

There are actually three different soundtracks to a film: the dialogue track, the special effects track (doors slamming, people running, etc.), and the music track. Usually the dialogue and special effects tracks have been recorded and are in place *before* the music track is added. The final mix of all three soundtracks is of vital importance. The music and/or the special effects tracks should never bury or cover up the dialogue. The balance between these three soundtracks is constantly shifting. The mixer must listen very carefully and make adjustments accordingly. Poorly mixed soundtracks have seriously damaged many potentially successful films.

By the time the composer sees the film, the dialogue and special effects audio tracks are usually in place. I usually sit with a stopwatch in one hand, a portable digital recorder in the other to tape specific remarks and recommendations by the director for each scene, a clipboard, notepad, and pencil, as well as a few sheets of blank manuscript paper to sketch musical ideas. Each piece of the film that requires music is logged and timed accurately. Usually it reads something like this: *"Reel #1. Scene #3 (love scene). 2:30 sec (suggest strings, soft voices—dir.)."*

The primary purpose of the music is to enhance the drama on the screen. No matter how "musical" the score, if the musical ideas do not enhance the realism and emotional impact of each scene, then it is a waste of time. Poorly composed musical scores have irreparably damaged many potentially great movies. It's up to the director to ride herd on the film composer, to make sure the music fits.

Two blockbuster films of the past, *Lawrence of Arabia* and *The Right Stuff*, had film soundtracks tossed and new scores written at the last minute because the director was not happy with the early result. Maurice Jarre replaced Dimitri Tiomkin for *Lawrence of Arabia,* and Bill Conti replaced Jerry Goldsmith for *The Right Stuff.*

Talent is not enough in writing music for film. *Empathy* is of equal importance. The composer must deeply feel the intended emotional impact of each scene before he or she can write appropriate music. Some film composers can write well for action films, but cannot write effective music for love stories. Comedies are often the hardest to write for, because the essence of comedy is exaggeration, timing, and subtlety.

Film composers must also sense what types of instruments are the most appropriate. Sometimes one or two instruments are more effective for a scene than a full orchestra. Some composers can adapt to changing emotional character of each film project; others cannot.

Another factor is trends. When Jan Hammer chose to use an all–synthesizer–produced soundtrack for the wildly successful "Miami Vice" television series, suddenly all electronically scored music soundtracks for contemporary films and television projects became the trend. Usually the first question asked by film directors or agents when I was active as a film composer in Hollywood in the 1980s was, "Can you write like Jan Hammer?" Soon, the powerful impact of John Williams' music, beginning with *Jaws,* started the next trend.

Directors and agents were then asking, "Can you write like John Williams?" A standard joke floating around Hollywood for years was about the three stages of a film composer's career. Stage 1: "Have you heard the film music _____ by Jack Wheaton?" Stage 2: "Get me Jack Wheaton, no matter what the cost!" Stage 3: "Whatever happened to Jack Wheaton?" Some film composers have been fortunate and talented enough to adapt quickly to the changing musical tastes in Hollywood.

The film composer, once he has spotted the film with the director, must now choose the right ingredients from the seven elements of music. The choices have to be made based on what emotion or emotions are being portrayed on the screen at that moment (a chase scene, a fight scene, a love scené, etc.), along with complimenting the movement or kinesthetic action on the screen at the time.

Kinesthetics is the science of motion study. The music selected must match the physical activity on the screen: are the actors walking, sitting, lying down, dancing, standing still, etc. So, the composer must enhance the emotion and drama of the scene as well as the motion and movement. Both tasks are important. Consideration for dialogue and other special effects must also be part of the equation.

Once the emotions and the kinesthetic action have been analyzed and the appropriate music composed, it must then be orchestrated for whatever instruments and type of orchestra are most appropriate. I've composed musical scores for films for full symphony orchestras (*Guns and the Fury*, Rome Opera Orchestra) as well as a recording studio full of high–tech synthesizers and drum machines (for television commercials) played by one to three players, sometimes programmed to play themselves on cue.

Source music is music in a specific scene in a film that is not background music. The music is part of the scene itself, coming from a radio, television, live orchestra, etc. In writing source music, the director and the film composer must decide if they use authentic pre–recorded commercial examples for the scene, or does the composer write "new" source music, but in the historical style necessary to fit the scene. Woody Allen's funny and nostalgic film *Radio Days* used both. Woody borrowed examples of old radio shows, but when necessary the film composer filled in with appropriate new music.

I once had to write an original Italian–style disco tune typical of the 1970s for source music for a spy–murder film titled *Escape*. For that particular scene, the music was coming through a small radio in her apartment. The female actress begins to dance to the music, her lover enters the apartment and begins to dance, and then . . . sorry, I can't tell the rest. You'll have to rent the film from Netflix.

I had already agreed to do the film. The director could not find any commercial examples of Italian disco that he liked. I was stuck. I had to write authentic and appropriate music for the scene. I rushed to Tower Records on Sunset Boulevard in Hollywood and bought several CDs of typical Italian disco.

I ran back home, listened to the CDs, broke the basic style of Italian disco of the 1970s into its seven musical parts, analyzed the typical musical clichés used in each of the seven parts, and then preceded to write my own Italian disco tune. I carefully chose the right instruments—including a funky, old, cheap–sounding *Farfisa Organ* sound (which, for some reason, the Italians liked) and then recorded the music. I was able to duplicate the Farfisa Organ sound on my Yamaha DX–7 synthesizer, as well as the guitar, bass guitar, and special "sweetening" effects (an added string track).

Increasingly, film directors are looking for additional income for a film from the soundtrack CD. To promote a film, a producer looks for needed airplay. Commercial radio seldom, if ever, plays instrumental excerpts from a new film, but they will play the featured song or two from the score of the new film, particularly if it is recorded by a well–known pop artist or group. These added songs with lyrics, usually done in a contemporary "pop" manner—regardless of the historical period of the film—usually occur at the beginning of the film, *a la* James Bond, or the end of the film, as in *Titanic*. Celine Dion, the popular Canadian songstress, was selected to make the recording for the *Titanic* project, and it helped guarantee airplay and additional income for the project.

Sadly, most of these songs tacked onto the closing credits to boost airplay are inane and often at odds with the overall impact of the film. Usually they are "soft rock" in style to appeal to the teenage audience, the most loyal film fans, with inane lyrics that celebrate nothingness. In spite of the system, some great films, musical scores, and even featured songs sneak through occasionally, and brighten the lives of those of us who are above the dumbing–down barrier.

Then we come to the editing process. The role of the music editor is an important one. This is the person that makes the final decision on what music goes where in a film. Usually the composer and the music editor work together with the director in making these final decisions. Sometimes the music editor steps out on his own, usually with disastrous results.

A few years ago I attended the premiere of a film I had scored. The music editor made critical decisions after I had left for another assignment without my input. As a result, several of my musical cues were in the wrong place! My wife and I slowly slid down in our seats and left the theater hurriedly afterward. Ironically, this particular film, *Penitentiary II,* has gone on to become a "cult" film and is often shown on late–night television. Watch for it. See if you can tell where the music cues do not seem to fit the action on the screen!

Without writing out specific musical examples, which would be useless without the reader's ability to see the scene they were written for, you by now should have a general idea as to how a film or television drama composer goes about their work.

The most important lesson to be learned when scoring for film or television drama is the basic fact that *music must enhance the drama onscreen without distracting from it.* Many talented composers cannot write good film music. They cannot keep the music underneath the drama. The result is that the music distracts rather than enhances the scene.

A Tribute

Some of the greatest music composed in the United States over the past 70 or 80 years has been written for motion pictures. As a tribute to some of these great but seldom recognized composers, I would like to list some names, not all–inclusive, of my favorites by decade:

1930s   Ernest Korngold, Alfred Newman, Max Steiner, Franz Waxman

1940s	Victor Young, Miklos Rozsa, Alex North, David Raskin
1950s	Bernard Hermann, Johnny Greene, Jerry Goldsmith
1960s	Elmer Bernstein, Jerry Goldsmith, Dmitri Tiomkin, Michelle LeGrand
1970s	Henry Mancini, John Williams, Leonard Bernstein, Maurice Jarre
1980s	John Barry, Bruce Broughton, Johnny Mandell, Nino Rota, Lalo Schifrin
1990s	James Horner, Danny Elfman, Bill Conti, Allyn Ferguson, David Grusin
2000s	David Shire, Alan Silvestri, Ennio Moricone, Patrick Williams, Randy Newman, and many other new, emerging stars

Summary

Motion pictures have had the greatest impact on world culture than any other medium. The United States is still the leader in producing great films. Music from the beginning has played an important, even essential, role in enhancing the dramatic effects of cinema. In many instances, films have been forgotten, but the melodies from those films linger on. I believe that someday future scholars will go back to the rich legacy of film music and discover that many of the world's greatest composers have been hiding before our very eyes—buried in the musical scores to thousands of films. Hooray for Hollywood!

Chapter 16
A Brief History of Rock 'n Roll

In the 1950s, the United States saw the birth of the most influential style of music of the latter part of the 20th century—*Rock 'n Roll.* This new style, a combination of Afro–American rhythm and blues with country–western, with occasional gospel overtones thrown in, created the most important style of music in modern history.

In the early 1950s, Allen Freed, on his popular radio show from Cleveland, Ohio (now the home of the Rock 'n Roll Hall of Fame) asked Bo Didley, a popular R&B songwriter/guitarist/singer, to explain what this new term "rock 'n roll" meant. Bo Didley explained that it was the casual black term for sex in the back seat of a parked car. At a critical moment, the car would often "rock 'n roll," even though parked with the ignition off.

Freed was somewhat of a visionary, because he tried to secure control of the term as registered trademark. Alas, the cat was out of the bag, so to speak. This mostly "black" music, now leaking to the mainstream of American popular music (and soon to take over) was already being referred to as *rock 'n roll.* In the black ghettos of the United States, the music, prior to this point, had been called *rhythm and blues.* Alan Freed was unable to secure a trademark of the term, and had to settle for a brief moment of fame as one of the first disc jockeys to call this new and exciting music *rock 'n roll.*

In one of my earlier books, *The Technological and Sociological Influences on Jazz as an Art Form in America* (University of Michigan Press, 1976), I pointed out the close interaction on the development of jazz with the major technical innovations (particularly in the area of transportation and communication) and the shifting social scene in our country. For instance, rock 'n roll would never have made the successful leap from the black ghettos to mainstream USA without the development of a wide network of independent FM radio stations, independent recording labels, innovative television shows like Dick Clark's "American Bandstand," and new magazines focusing on this revolution like *Rolling Stone*.

The improvement in air transportation and the development of our intercontinental highway system allowed musicians to travel long distances swiftly and at reasonable fares. The growing financial affluence of the middle class, the emerging huge bulge in our population charts called the "baby boomers," and the large discretionary income of the American teenager all contributed to the success of this new music.

The baby boomers began growing up. The racial barriers between black and white were slowly being broken down. White teenagers no longer had to seek out black music in the "other" part of town. They could tune it in on FM radio, buy the record at local record stores, attend mixed racial concerts, and watch and hear some of the major artists on "American Bandstand."

Dave Bartholomew, producer/director of the Dominos, once said: "Rhythm and blues and rock 'n roll are the same thing, but they [the whites] stole it from us [the blacks]." The major black artists who managed to successfully "cross over" to this more lucrative market—now open to white as well as black listeners and fans—included Bo Didley, Chuck Berry, Little Richard, James Brown, BB King, Fats Domino, Louis Jordan, Dinah Washington, Ray Charles, Aretha Franklin, and many others. Major record companies, fearing the possible rejection of a huge wave of mostly black artists, began developing white "cover" groups and singers, like Bill Haley and the Comets, the Everly Brothers, Pat Boone, Jerry Lee Lewis, and eventually the King himself, Elvis Presley.

Many black R&B artists, for one reason or another, failed to make the leap to the larger, more lucrative market. The best of these groups continued to sing, write, and record good music until the second wave of black musical styles began to cross over—*Motown*. Barry Gordy and his huge stable of Motown (Detroit, Michigan) artists like the Supremes, the Temptations, the Jackson Five, and Stevie Wonder eventually captured the mainstream American pop record market, with few if any successful "cover" groups. At last the United States was ready for honest black music, written and performed by black artists, and recorded, produced, and marketed by black businessmen.

An often-overlooked influence on the birth of rock 'n roll was country music. Afro-Americans contributed R&B, and early white rock 'n roll artists contributed country. An interim style was called "rockabilly," made famous primarily by one recording of one tune: Carl Perkins' "Blue Suede Shoes" (later recorded by Elvis Presley).

Rock 'n roll was loud, lascivious, anarchistic, rebellious, and introduced a new ingredient, at least to white audiences: music as a drug. The volume, sharp backbeats of the drummer, syncopated rhythms of the melody, and the repetitive lyrics all contributed to a physiological state of extreme alertness coupled with a loss of individual consciousness to group consciousness . . . a cathartic experience that can be traced back to the jungles of Africa, India, and Asia.

Just as the post-WWI culture experimented with jazz, bootleg gin, and the "Charleston," the WWII culture began experimenting with R&B (soon to be called rock 'n roll), abandoned dance styles (everyone doing their own thing!), recreational drugs like marijuana, LSD, and cocaine, and sexual promiscuity.

The open expression of sexual desire separate from "romantic" love was a sociological phenomenon as well. Here, the discovery of the birth control pill, freeing responsible women from unwanted pregnancies and freeing male lovers from long-term commitments combined to produce major changes in our nation's sex habits—changes led by the music and made possible by the slogan of the Dupont Corporation: "Better things through chemistry."

What Was That?

Around 1968, I was on my way to a meeting at Capitol Records in Hollywood, California. Screaming teenagers, mostly girls, surrounded the building. An armored Brinks truck was backed up to the back door. Soon four young men dashed out, jumped in the armored van, and the van tore out of the parking lot with some teenage girls trying to jump on. It was truly a mad, mad scene! At first I thought it was from a movie one of the studios was shooting.

When I entered the building I asked the person I was meeting with, "What was that?" His answer was that it was a new rock group from England called the Beatles. Capitol Records was their United States distributor, and they were there for an important meeting. I said, "Oh, oh, here comes the British!" I was right. The Beatles and later the Rolling Stones went on to become two of the most popular pop music groups of all time.

Roots

Rock music was a derivative of the earlier style of the '50s rock 'n roll. Rock music was actually born in Europe and imported back into the United States, even though its roots were American. Rock music was group oriented, whereas rock 'n roll elevated soloists as well as groups. Rock music was louder, angrier, more rebellious, and less "black" in its content and presentation. Rock music was born in the 1960s, and was the first of what could truly be called an "international" style of pop youth music.

The major innovators and pioneers came mostly from Great Britain, with the Beatles and the Rolling Stones being the two strongest European forces in early rock music. The Stones are still performing, even though several are grandfathers today.

The battle cry of the culture–rebellious hippies of the 1960s was "Sex, Drugs, and Rock 'n Roll!" Today, the musical style of rock and its billions of fans are just as closely tied to this motto as ever: "'In rock, you're supposed to be outrageous,' says Lou Cox, a New York–based psychologist who specializes in addictions. 'Being bad is good. The culture is not only supportive of addiction,' he continues. 'It's as if there is a demand for it—like its part of the *credibility package*,'" (Michael Paeoletta, *San Diego Union Tribune,* May 2004).

Is There Something In the Music?

The average life expectancy of a full–fledged rock 'n roller is very short. So many of the greats have checked out early, from the Doors'

Jim Morrison, the Who's Keith Moon, the Sex Pistols' Sid Vicious, then there's Jimi Hendrix, Janis Joplin, and the Rolling Stones' Brian Jones, to contemporary artists such as Sublime's Bradley Nowell, Blind Melon's Shannon Hoon, and Nirvana's Kurt Cobain.

A growing awareness of the fact that death is nature's way of telling you to "slow down," as well as the economic reality that dead artists can't sell records . . . and reap any benefit from their fame, has caused many rock superstars like Whitney Houston, Courtney Love, Natalie Cole, Ozzy Osbourne, Mary J. Blige, the Red Hot Chili Pepper's Anthony Kiedis, , Billy Joel, and Dr. John, to admit addiction and submit to professional treatment. "In the mid–1980s Aerosmith broke down the door that made it OK for big–name artists to go public with their sobriety, according to industry observers. In the years since, Eric Clapton, Boy George, Bonnie Raitt, James Taylor, Elton John, and others have made their sobriety known" (ibid.). Michael Jackson, who had admitted to having a prescription drug problem, died of heart failure brought on by a suspected drug overdose on June 25, 2009. Today being a former addict to pills, pot, booze, or harder drugs is more a badge of honor than shame.

That fact that so many of the leading artists of rock music are addicted to drugs or alcohol or have died from overdoses, along with a very high percentage of their fans can't help make one wonder if there is something in the music itself that contributes to this plague. The jazz musicians of the 1930s through the 1960s had their bouts with booze and drugs—but on a much smaller scale.

The environment of the rock world suggests moral decadence, aggressive music, outrageous lyrics, and even more outrageous behavior on stage and off. Months and years of this can't help but take its toll on any attempt to survive and live a somewhat normal life. Paul McCartney, of the Beatles, and Mick Jagger are two superstars who seem to have run the gauntlet and survived. Not only have they survived, but the Queen of England has knighted them. Today they are "Sir" McCartney and "Sir" Jagger. Can you believe it?

Moral Anarchy

I believe there is something intrinsic in rock music that contributes heavily to drug and alcohol addiction. First, the volume itself, along with the sharp after-beat of the drummer, triggers the "fight-or-flight" response, which causes the body to self-medicate via the brain from the adrenal glands. The artists themselves after a concert are so pumped full of adrenaline, it is no wonder they go back to the hotel and destroy their rooms.

Second, I believe the anarchistic lyrics of the songs themselves promote and even glorify drug use, sexual promiscuity, and social rebellion. The costumes alone tell us that these are not normal human beings on stage. Even life-after-death gets the rock treatment with songs that argue for Hell rather than Heaven because of the big "party" that will be going on there. Apparently some rock artists are on a first-name basis with some of the most evil Satanists on this planet, and they seem fascinated with the concept of demons, possession, and evil. There is even a rock style called "gothic" that focuses on these issues.

The third issue is accessibility. These groups are constantly surrounded by sexual, drug, and alcohol temptations. A Trappist monk wouldn't survive a week on the road with the Rolling Stones without eventually coming around and joining the 24-hour party. What's amazing is the fact that many of these artists have lived as long as they have, considering their lifestyle.

Troubled Teenagers

The second greatest cause of death among teenagers today is suicide (auto accidents are first). Studies reveal that many of these tragic suicides were at least partially a result of listening to too much rock music and then the eventual use of drugs. According to most psychologists, aggression is either turned outward or turned inward. Suicides are often a result of uncontrollable anger and aggression that is turned inward. Suicide is often a form of "payback" to those that ignored or were not aware of their problems.

There is a consistency with heavy metal rock music being a major part of the suicide environment here that is disturbing. The lyrics to many rock songs taunt the listener regarding death and challenge the individual regarding suicide. Death is looked upon as no big thing, and the promise of an eternal party in Hell sounds attractive to an emotionally depressed or disturbed teenager.

Sooner or later, just as society had to crank up the courage and collate the overwhelming facts to challenge the tobacco industry, concerned parents and citizens in our society will have to challenge the powerful multibillion–dollar per year recording industry. This will be no easy task, but to stand by and turn a blind eye to the power of rock to destroy individual lives and health can no longer be ignored. Something has to be done. Someone has to step up to the plate.

This will be no easy task. Many of these artists have reached levels of popularity that virtually make them untouchable, unless they commit mass murder at high noon on the steps of the Capitol, and even then a clever lawyer can probably get them off. Rock lawyers may argue that their artists did not throw the bomb, but the victims and their parents can realistically argue that rock music was the match that lit the fuse.

Summary

Two of the most critical decades in American history took place in the 20th century: the 1930s, and later the 1960s. Both produced fantastic technological innovations that completely changed our lifestyles, as well as major social changes that completed the United States from a stiff–necked "Puritan" culture to a more "sensate" culture—one bent on pursuing that promise offered in our nation's Bill of Rights, the right to the *pursuit* of happiness.

Music was along every step of the way: the innovative classical musical styles and jazz music of the 1930s; and the emerging third-world ethnic blend of new and tribal in the rock 'n roll music and later rock music, as well as the emerging Latin music styles of the 1960s. Music led the way in both revolutions.

Is all rock music bad? No! But most of it is . . . particularly when performed at such high decibel levels. Is rock responsible for most of society's ills today? Again, no, but if you have a troubled teenager, he or she is like a bomb waiting to go off, and rock is often the match that lights the fuse. We must do, as we did with cigarette advertising, (1) deglamourize the habit, (2) examine the damaging fallout systematically and logically, (3) report the results, and then (4) move to correct the abuses. Failure to do so is failure of our government to protect its citizens, one of the primary reasons for government in the first place.

The great breakthrough in music was the discovery in rock music that the music itself can activate automatic nervous systems in the body and act as a drug. As a society we have spent billions fighting the drug war, while rock music slipped in the back door and turned on the youth of America . . . with few the wiser.

In general rock music is the most dangerous and potentially destructive musical style ever created. The health damage and social fallout from its obsessive use will be great and sobering. The longer we wait, the more damage we face in the younger generations coming up.

Any civilization that sees a threat to its citizens and turns and looks the other way is neglecting one of the primary reasons for government in the first place: protection. Failure to act will encourage the other dangerous serpent let loose with rock music; social anarchy. Historically, social anarchy is always followed by a dictatorship.

Now is the time to act!

Music and Religion

Chapter 17

New Age Music

Music in ancient Egypt was used to alter the emotions, it was used to create mass hypnosis, and to incite immorality."
—Ernest A. Budge, *Osiris,* University Books, 1961, p. 245

Another new and popular music style is called "New Age music." Born out of the rapidly developing field of music therapy and the rediscovery of ancient third–world musical practices, New Age music is primarily used to create and/or enhance emotional moods. It is not designed to entertain intellectually. It is often deliberately repetitive and even boring. *New Age music's primary task is to bring you into its emotional force field and keep you there until you surrender your individual identity to group consciousness.*

Although quieter and less obviously sensual, and less rhythmic than rock music, it can help a person relax, but its repetitive and deliberately monotonous sameness can also be addictive and hypnotic. If "rock" represents the stimulants of the drug world musically, New Age music certainly represents the depressants, the opiates, and the hallucinogenics. Improperly or unscrupulously used, New Age music—in a different way than rock—can be dangerous to your health.

The constant repetition of a simple musical phrase, with or without a lyric, can induce the first stage of hypnosis. Modern advertising would like to use it more, but most radio and television ads are too short to maximize its potential narcotic effect. However, in controlled environments, like stores, offices, theaters, concert halls, and automobile and home sound systems, the use of musical repetition can be "hypnotizing."

New Age music sets out to (1) get your attention, (2) hold your attention, (3) adjust your mood to the music, and (4) hold you there long enough to lose your normal strong sense of self-identity. At first glance it seems boring and repetitious. It is deliberately so. The object is to blend you into the sea of group consciousness. This little escape from self can be uplifting and pleasant. It is therapeutic, but in a different and potentially more dangerous way than regular music therapy. *New Age music is a rediscovery of an ancient way to use music. It goes way beyond entertainment.*

In the early years, beginning for the most part in the 1960s during the great cultural revolution in the United States, New age music was used primarily to create an emotional force field around one particular emotion (sensuality, fantasy, escape, repose, etc.), in which the listener could step into and flee the hostility and violence of today's modern society. This was the "Yellow Submarine" the Beatles wrote about, or "Lucy in the Sky with Diamonds," a song title that was code for the newly popular hallucinogenic drug LSD.

So much of the contemporary commercial music from the 1960s forward promoted drug and alcohol use, illicit sex, and social anarchy. Eventually, many devoted listeners to these new sounds were burned out. They needed to detox from the frantic intensity of contemporary rock and take a "mind bath" in the soothing sounds of New Age music. Just as the drug world has uppers and downers, so does the world of music. The trigger with New Age music is not a loud, pulsing beat, but rather a constantly repetitive, simple phrase which lulls one into a hypnotic state.

Rapidly developing technological changes in the field of electronic instruments soon led to the invention of the sampling synthesizer, an electronic keyboard instrument that could "sample" and then reduce to a digital computer code *any* sound, musical or non-musical, into organized musical notes that could be played and recorded from a regulation keyboard.

The invention of the sampling synthesizer led to an entirely new development in music, where a composer's choice of musical sounds used to reproduce his or her musical ideas was now *limitless.* Everything from the sounds of mating whales to the sound of a jet engine could now be manipulated into musical tones.

This new field of sound was dubbed *environmental music.* Today there are a growing number of talented young composers grinding out CDs using sounds never used in music before. These specialized hybrids are usually sold at stores with strong environmental biases, as well as at art galleries supporting nature art and photography. The voice of the sperm whale meets the jazz giant John Coltrane, or something like that.

Mood Control Through Music

Early canned–music distributors like Muzak and Seeburg, two post–WWII music services that specialized in piping in music to businesses, soon discovered that certain types of music promoted or enhanced certain emotions. These two companies, and others, began writing and recording music that did not necessarily challenge the intellectual side of the brain, but rather, created this audio force field that could whisk the listener out of a stressful environment, musically relax them, and put them in a more positive shopping mood.

The background music you hear on the elevator, in stores, in businesses, and in offices you enter, is usually very carefully chosen to match the time of day, average age of the customer, time of year, product or service being offered, and even racial and cultural biases of the customer. The music may seem to be random and even mindless in some instances, but it is not. The sounds you hear have been tested and successfully applied to enhance the appeal of the product or business you are patronizing. Elevator music was the beginning of New Age mind manipulation through repetition.

Most New age music is deliberately monotonous. Its growing popularity has even spilled over into the classical world of music, creating a new, contemporary compositional style called "minimalism," with recognized composers like Philip Glass, Vangelis, and others writing, recording, and performing successfully this one–dimensional style of music. *With New Age music and minimalism, you no longer "listen" to music in the traditional sense; instead, you "feel" it.*

Minimalism is taking simple melodies with as few notes as possible, smooth rhythm patterns, nonthreatening chords, etc., and making the combinations you can create from this limited menu last as long as possible. In other words, doing as much as you can as a composer with as little as possible in raw material. We have seen the same minimalism in visual arts as well (think of a monochromatic painting of basic geometric shapes). *Non-evolutionary* could be another name for this style of music, which shows up in movie scores, concert halls, and even for contrast occasionally in the pop/rock world.

The left hemisphere of the cerebral cortex part of our brain, according to recent research, is the dominant brain in our modern technological culture. Non-emotional, logical, linear, and goal-oriented, this brain gets "tired," burned out. New Age music appeals to the right brain—the seat of our emotions, fantasies, pleasures. This side of the brain is non-linear. Right-brain art and music do not have to "go" somewhere or have deep hidden intellectual meaning. They are a refuge for the uptight.

New Age music is therapeutic for those intense left-brain careers in medicine, law, engineering, science research, and politics. They can "escape" into fantasyland and, like a child, listen in awe and wonder until they are bored. *Your boredom threshold is related to your intellectual bias.* The more "left-brain" you are, the sooner you will be bored with New Age music.

All right-brain music has to do is distract, entertain, and relax. Businesses that are particularly left-brain in nature (doctors, lawyers, brokers, teachers) all tend to suffer from *left-brain burnout.* A relaxing romp with minimalist New Age music is often just the ticket. Check your critical nature (also left-brain) at the door. Comparing this style of music to classical, jazz, or Broadway melodies is a waste of time. It's like comparing apples with oranges. The two don't relate.

The Greek-Judaic-Christian culture that we inherited is very "logos," or logic-driven. This is a left-brain skill. *Until recently, most art of our Western civilization had to be logical.* This means that it had to have a beginning, a development section, and a logical conclusion—the climax of the story, piece of music, ballet, novel, what have you.

Right-brain cultures (mostly tribal) do not demand logic from their art. All they demand is something pleasing, exciting, and repetitious. Like a child at play, their art will keep doing the same thing until the "child" is bored and then turns to something else. This drives left-brainers mad, causing them to stomp out of performances, smash CDs, and break up with friends or girlfriends who are not left-brain biased, because in their world *everything has to mean something.*

One of the characteristics of this music that clearly identifies it as "right-brain" bias is that it does not develop the major musical themes introduced to a climactic, logical conclusion. The music is non-evolutionary. It just keeps repeating a pleasant sound until the composer becomes bored with it, and then he or she moves on to another pleasant sound.

Cultural Differences

The differences are dramatic between a left-brain biased culture and a right-brain biased culture. India, not the modernized, Anglicized India, but ancient India, for the most part is right-brain dominant. Their music does not build . . . it is charming and goes loping along on the sitar and tabla drums until the composer yells "Change," and then it takes off in another direction. *It ends when the creator is tired, bored, or out of new ideas.* Even the religions of right-brain biased cultures are different. Hinduism and Buddhism, India's two native religions, see life as cyclic, not evolutionary, hence the emphasis on reincarnation and karma.

Islamic cultures have weak musical systems. Music, for the most part, is forbidden. Tribal dance music, celebrations for weddings, funerals, etc., are allowed, but the listening of music for pleasure is forbidden in the Koran. *Islam, for the most part, sees all artistic expression as an attempt to distract mankind from the deity.*

Those of us who treasure the arts had better hope and pray that Islam does not someday conquer the world, as the Koran demands. If they do, that's the end of opera, ballet, concert music, jazz, pop, and all the rest. Only the lonely sound of the muezzin chanting his call from the minaret five times a day would break the monotony of an Islamic culture without music.

In New Age music, endings are no big deal. The favorite ending for this kind of music, as well as for Motown and pop/rock ballads, is to keep repeating the last phrase and gradually fade the music out, like a band marching down the street in a parade. These types of endings are called "board fades," meaning the recording of the piece creates the illusion that technically the music never ends. Contrast this with the end of a Mozart or Beethoven symphony. Now that's an ending!

The birth of rock music in the 1950s contributed to the development of New Age music. Both presupposed that their audience was more interested in "feeling" the music than in being intellectually challenged by it. Today "rap" music and most of "hip-hop" fall into this same category. How can you really "listen" to a rap artist?

Hip-hop and rap are the antithesis of New Age music, except for the use of constant repetition. Besides the street dialect that dumbfounds and is even untranslatable by major black entertainers like Bill Cosby, the words go by so fast and are so drowned out by volume, dialect, and special effects (record-scratching) that you can only hear one or two distinct words occasionally . . . and that is usually a derogatory term for women, police, or society, three favorite targets of urban rage. And don't you find it a little hypocritical to watch angry rap artists on MTV with huge diamond rings, gold crosses, and multimillion dollar a year record contracts complaining about social injustice? How many of these studs share their wealth with the "hood"? Not many.

The appeal of this music is that the fatigued left brain escapes into the intellectual simplicity of the right brain and gets to relax for a bit. There is no harm in that, as long as you understand that the simplistic world it describes is fantasy and can never cross over to the real world.

Those who try to live a right-brain lifestyle in a left-brain world are doomed, unless they are fabulously wealthy and can insulate themselves from the wolves around them. Alas, that is a left-brain skill, so you have classic burnout by former stars who, like children, do not understand how the left-brain culture works and usually end up penniless. There is a long list of wildly successful right-brain musical artists that are prematurely dead, broke, or severely damaged physically or mentally by their stubborn efforts to live a right–brain life. That should be warning enough.

As in rock, this new music can be hypnotic and can also lead to a form of psychological addiction, hence the constant presence of a CD or MP3 player and attached headset for today's teenagers and young adults. The magic wand of New Age music can help erase the anger–producing reality of an ugly urban environment, or a disappointing life, or a left brain worked too hard for too long.

It's like visiting Disney Land. It's a fun place to visit, but you wouldn't want to live there. Tragedy occurs when some individuals decide that they can live comfortably and happily in a left–brain culture, yet almost totally hiding out in their right–brain. When movies and television shows portray computer nerds or geeks, they almost always portray them as constantly listening to rock or New Age music. Here we go again: the human being trying to seek balance through homeostasis.

When an individual today is ping–ponging back and forth between left–brain work and right–brain entertainment, they can lose their balance and fall into the black hole. They can literally forget who they really are and what values are real. This childhood naïveté has produced many urban tragedies, suicides, drug overdoses, and mental illnesses. We must learn to live in the real world with a balance between left– and right–brain parts of our society.

The ancient Greeks often claimed invisible spirits were the source of most artistic creativity, sharing their ideas within willing practitioners of the art. Inspiration to them was "waiting on the muse." Today in New Age music, this idea has been reborn.

Some of the people who produce New Age music are not aware that their "muse," an imaginary artistic partner that lives within but identifies him or herself as a separate personality, can mentally unhinge them or lead them down self–destructive paths. Many rock artists openly boast of their muse, as does Joni Mitchell and many other rock artists/composers.

Then there are the "mythical masters." Some medical experts and religious leaders suggest that these mythical masters could be from the dark, occult side of the universe and could be dangerous to those allowing them into their consciousness. One particular demon (called "friendly spirits," "spirit guides," or "totem animals" by the New Agers) named *Koothoomi* has appeared to a number of New Age artists and given them musical ideas. In David Tame's *The Secret Power of Music* we read, "From far away I heard the strains of an organ with which was mingled the sound of voices so pure and ethereal as to suggest the changing of a celestial choir. . . . It was my brother's [spiritual guide] Koothoomi playing on the pipes. Suddenly a voice spoke out, 'Listen well, and remember, for one day you will give such music to the world.'"

Purpose

Today New Age music is designed to bring the listener into a peaceful but unrealized hypnotic state—always mentally and physically dangerous, for if they are truly disembodied spirits, demons, they are always looking for a mind they can easily enter and eventually control. If they are not from the dark side, they are still dangerous, for the individual has created a false universe that will some day collide with reality. New Age music is often called "electronic meditation."

A wide range of self-appointed musical therapists, in so-called "healing" sessions, is using this potentially harmful music. I believe that a great deal more research needs to be done before this style of music is used in a therapeutic manner. As Christ pointed out many times in His teachings, what good is it if we gain physical health, wealth, prosperity—a false "peace"—and lose our soul in the process?

"Brother" Charles, a New Age musical adept, recently told *Meditation* magazine, "I can open the doors of your [brain's] databanks. . . . As you're listening, the rescripting process is happening automatically via subliminally recorded messages." All this may be as harmless as Casper the Friendly Ghost. However, the mind is a dangerous place to experiment with using dangerous and untested ideas and concepts. Remember, Sigmund Freud once championed cocaine as a "miracle drug," especially for schizophrenics, before studies revealed its terribly addictive and harmful side effects.

Many today believe marijuana and New Age music are both harmless. Wrong on both counts. In-depth studies of chronic marijuana use show a consistent damage to long-term memory, motivation, and the autoimmune system. Recent studies are turning up some disturbing facts regarding the dangers of certain types of hypnotic New Age sounds, as well.

Although outwardly soothing, this new type of music can be in some ways more dangerous than rock, because it taps into very subtle occult conditioning techniques that have been around for eons. The subliminal messages hidden in this type of music are often "secret" and generally "unknown" to the listener, and in many cases overwhelm the senses, just as the chanting of a mantra in the name of a Hindu demon (as they do in transcendental meditation) can somehow soothe the 21st century mind. Soothe, yes, but at what cost?

Summary

New Age music is not new; it is ancient. Its basic concepts have been around this planet for eons. Our culture is literally rediscovering this ancient form of music. It appears innocent and harmless, but it can be terribly addictive and destructive. It must be used with great appreciation regarding the power of music. Unsupervised and uncontrolled use of new musical sounds has caused great damage to some over the past 100 years or more.

We need to cautiously enter these new, different, and unexplored worlds with a rope that securely ties us to reality.

Chapter 18

Quotes

In doing the research for this book I have come across many interesting quotes regarding the power of music. Below are just a few of what I believe are most important.

Order Out of Chaos

Music creates order out of chaos -- for the rhythm imposes unanimity upon the divergent, melody imposes continuity on the disjointed, and harmony imposes compatibility on the incongruence.

--Yehudi Mentuhin, 1972, world-famous violinist/conductor

Monkeys and Worship

Research with primates [monkeys] reveals that when tensions between individual monkeys exists, they are sometimes resolved by synchronizing and coordinating vocal expressions. *That's what humans do when they worship together;* they synchronize their emotions by singing a hymn, a praise song, or chant -- to unify the worshiper with fellow worshipers to.

—Jane Brewer, *Contemporary Therapies in Nursing and Midwifery* (1998, Harcourt And Brace)

If I Had My Life to Live Over

If I had my life to live over again, I would have made a rule read some poetry and listen to some music at least once a week; or perhaps the parts of my brain now atrophied would have thus been kept alive through use. The loss of these tastes is a loss of happiness, and may possibly be injurious to the intellect, and more probably to the moral character, by enfeebling the emotional part of our nature.

—Charles Darwin, *The Forbes Scrapbook of Thoughts on the Business of Life* (Forbes, Inc., New York City, 1976)

Sing!

Give us, O give us the man who sings at his work! Be his occupation what it may, he is equal to any of those who follow the same pursuit in silent sullenness. He will do more in the same time ... he will do a better ... he will persevere longer. One is scarcely sensible to fatigue while he marches to music. The very stars are said to make harmony as they revolve in their spheres.

—Carlyle, ibid.

Life and Music

Life is like music, it must be composed by ear, feeling and instinct, not by painting by the numbers. Nevertheless one had better know the rules, for they sometimes guide in doubtful cases.

—Samuel Butler, ibid.

Music Turns on Your Body

Psychologists have found that music does things to you whether you like it or not. Fast tempos invariably raise your pulse, respiration, and blood pressure; slow music lowers them.

—Doron K. Antrim, ibid.

Be Nice!

Music is the only language in which it is hard to say a mean or sarcastic thing.

—John Erskine, ibid.

Don't Kill Enthusiasm

There exists a passion for comprehension, just as there exists a passion for music. That passion is rather common in children, but gets lost in most people later on. Without this passion there would be no mathematics nor natural science.

—Albert Einstein, ibid.

Music, A Bridge to Heaven?

Music makes me forget my real situation. It transports me into a state which is *not my own.* Under the influence of music I really seem to *feel* what *I do not understand,* and to have powers which *I cannot have.*

—Leo Tolstoy

Profound

Life without music would be a mistake.

—Frederick Nietzsche

Escape

"Making music demands attention and focus to the point that it's impossible to do anything else," said Alicia Ann Clair, director of the music therapy program at the University of Kansas in Lawrence. "If you want a break from all the things that are bothering you and upsetting you, music gives you time out from the distress."

—*San Diego Union Tribune,* January 28, 2002

I Need a Music Teacher!

The fastest growing group of aspiring pianists in the U.S. is adults ages 25 to 55, according to the National Piano Foundation. For more information on where to find the keyboard teacher, visit the Private Music Instructor National Directory at www.overwer.com/pmind. For teachers of other instruments, contact www.teachlist.com.

—Ibid.

Music and Surgery

A little soft jazz or maybe the sound of ocean waves piped into the operating room along with whispers of encouragement from doctors and nurses might help post-surgery patients get back on their feet. Swedish researchers found that patients soothed by music and words of comfort during surgery have less pain and fatigue during recovery.

—Dr. Colwell, Scripps Hospital, LaJolla, California

Listening While Unconscious

A team led by Ulric Nillson, M.D., of Orebro Medical Center Hospital, confirmed that the brain is aware of sounds even when the patient is anesthetized. They reported their findings recently in *Acta Anaesthesiological Scandinavica*.

—*AARP Bulletin,* February 2002

Music and Diet

Listen to beautiful music and you could forgo a junk food binge. Researchers at Montréal Neurological Institute found that the emotional responses generated by pleasing music activates the same feel-good center of the brain that eating your favorite foods and sex do.

—*First for Women,* "Help for Emotional Eaters, March 25, 2002

From the Bible

And it came to pass as they came, when David was returned from the slaughter of the Philistine [Goliath], that the women came out of all cities of Israel, singing and dancing, to meet king Saul, with tabrets, with joy, and with instruments of musick.

—1 Samuel 18:6

Therefore I will give thanks unto thee, O LORD, among the heathen, and I will sing praises unto thy name.

—2 Samuel 22:50

And the priests waited on their offices: the Levites also with instruments of musick of the LORD, which David the king had made to praise the LORD, because his mercy endureth for ever, when David praised by their ministry; and the priests sounded trumpets before them, and all Israel stood.

—2 Chronicles 7:6

[They] chant to the sound of the viol, and invent to themselves instruments of musick, like David; That drink wine in bowls, and anoint themselves with the chief ointments: but they are not grieved for the affliction of Joseph. Therefore now shall they go captive with the first that go captive. . . .

—Amos 6:5–7

Now his elder son was in the field: and as he came and drew nigh to the house, he heard musick and dancing.

—Luke 15:25

And the voice of harpers, and musicians, and of pipers, and trumpeters, shall be heard no more at all in thee; and no craftsman, of whatsoever craft he be, shall be found any more in thee; and the sound of a millstone shall be heard no more at all in thee.

—Revelation 18:22

And the doors shall be shut in the streets, when the sound of the grinding is low, and he shall rise up at the voice of the bird, and all the daughters of musick shall be brought low; Also when they shall be afraid of that which is high, and fears shall be in the way, and the almond tree shall flourish, and the grasshopper shall be a burden, and desire shall fail: because man goeth to his long home, and the mourners go about the streets.

—Ecclesiastes 12:4–5

And they [angels and those in Heaven] sung a new song, saying, Thou art worthy to take the book, and to open the seals thereof: for thou wast slain, and hast redeemed us to God by thy blood out of every kindred, and tongue, and people, and nation; And hast made us unto our God kings and priests: and we shall reign on the earth.

—Revelation 5:9–10

Chapter 19

Rock Music in the Church

The incredible power of rock music and its universal appeal to young people began to enter mainly Protestant non–denominational churches in the late 1960s and early 1970s. Was it the "devil's music," as some conservative Christian leaders claimed, or was it possible to use this universally popular music to attract more young people to church, as more liberal church leaders preached? Was it the "hook that would help stop the decline in church attendance, particularly among young adults?

An interesting development within the "hippie" movement of the 1960s through the 1980s was the birth of what came to be known as the *Jesus Movement.* Burned–out hippies, with lives shattered by illicit sex, drugs, alcohol, and a voluntary descent into hell through hallucinogenic drugs began turning to Christ for salvation and for help.

Many had tired everything else, and they had nothing to lose. Buddha couldn't do it. Mohammed couldn't do it. Krishna couldn't do it. Lao Tse couldn't do it. Marx and Lenin couldn't do it. None of these seemed to work in giving purpose to their lives, in making their lives happier and free them from their self–destructive ways. Maybe Jesus Christ and Bible–based Christianity was the answer! For millions Christ and biblically–based non–denominational Christianity was the way out of sin and into the way of salvation.

In Costa Mesa, California, a young pastor by the name of Chuck Smith, disenchanted with the tunnel vision and legalism of mainline denominations, began his own independent ministry. His area was a Mecca for surfers, hippies, and those desperately looking for some way out of the self-created hell of their lifestyle. Chuck Smith invited these burned-out hippies to come to his church "just as you are," with cut-offs, sandals, beads, long hair, and hollowed eyes. However, allowing them to bring into the sanctuary the most pagan musical style the world had ever seen—rock—seriously compromised this tremendous Christlike act of compassion. While this new music had lyrics that honored Christ, the Bible, salvation, etc., as the research in this book illustrates, *the musical style always overpowers the lyrics* when the two are in contrast with each other. Never in the history of music has there ever been such a wedding of opposites: carnal music and spiritual lyrics.

This new way of casual worship spread like wildfire, within and without the United States. Soon recording studios were crowded with young Christian musicians recording their new songs. Christian music record labels and publishing companies sprang up, along with independent FM stations to broadcast the music. *Many young singers, composers, and bands that could not make it in the more commercial world of rock turned to the still lucrative new field of contemporary Christian music.*

Another vein of gold was discovered in youth music in America, a vein that would have far-reaching effects on the record industry and on the definition of worship within the church and would eventually account for almost one-third of all contemporary music recorded and sold in the United States. Contemporary Christian rock music today is a $3-5 billion a year industry.

Early pioneers in Christian rock included *Al Greene,* a popular black R&B singer who decided to concentrate on contemporary Christian music; *Andre Crouch,* a powerful singer/songwriter with an excellent ensemble who could have gone on to make zillions of dollars in the wider commercial world of rock, but chose to stay with contemporary Christian music (CCM); *Ralph Carmichael,* a Hollywood studio composer/arranger who turned to this new field of music; and *Sandy Patti,* a young girl with a Metropolitan Opera-worthy voice that was thrilling to hear. Other pioneers included *Bill Gaither,* who combined the traditional Southern gospel style with the new music, *Amy Grant,* and many others. *Pat Boone,* already a widely-known pop singer, *Johnny Cash, Tennessee Ernie Ford,* and even *Elvis Presley,* the "king" of rock 'n roll, all recorded albums of Christian music. Elvis recorded two Christian albums before his untimely death for this rapidly growing market.

Rock Music in the Bible?

Art in its final degradation exists only to shock.

—George Orwell

First Rock Concert

The Bible is full of expositions on sacred rock music. Music was an integral part enkephalins all ancient cultures. We can go back to the Exodus and we are told in 1 Corinthians 10:11 that these things were written in Scriptures as examples or guidelines *for us today.*

The first powerful rock concert recorded in the Bible was the one that the children of Israel participated in while Moses was up on Mount Sinai receiving the Word of God in the form of the Ten Commandments along with the dimensions and decorations in the construction of the tabernacle. Bored, irritated, and frustrated, many of the children of Israel began to pressure Aaron, Moses' brother, to let them return to the worship of the Egyptian gods. They wanted to make a calf out of gold and to feast and celebrate.

We read in Exodus 32:6 "And they rose up early on the morrow, and offered burnt offerings, and brought peace offerings; and the people sat down to eat and to drink, and rose up to play."

When Moses came down from the mountain, he and Joshua could hear the music long before they saw the celebration. Lo and behold, Aaron, Moses impatient brother and appointed high priest, had allowed the children of Israel to melt down some of their gold jewelry and make an idol, a golden calf, and then begin to celebrate with a Jewish "Woodstock" in the middle of the desert. "And when Joshua heard the noise of the people as they shouted, he said unto Moses, There is a noise of war in the camp" (Exod. 32:17).

Then we read in Exodus 32:19–21: "And it came to pass, as soon as he came nigh unto the camp, that he saw the calf, and the dancing: and Moses' anger waxed hot, and he cast the tables out of his hands, and brake them beneath the mount. And he took the calf which they had made, and burnt it in the fire, and ground it to powder, and strawed it upon the water, and made the children of Israel drink of it. And Moses said unto Aaron, What did this people unto thee, that thou hast brought so great a sin upon them?"

The outcome was not pleasant. Moses was not amused. In fact, he was so mad he threw down the Ten Commandments, freshly chiseled into granite by God Himself, and waded into the party. He quickly divided his followers into those who were not part of the "Dick Clark Bandstand" and those who were. Those who were partying were swallowed quickly into the ground when suddenly opened up.

So ended the first attempt to "liven up" worship with secular music.

David Boogies with the Ark

The second attempt was when King David moved the Ark of the Covenant from Shiloh to Jerusalem. David was dancing naked in front of the procession to wild, secular music, and he got careless. He ignored the very specific commands on how to move the ark given by God in Leviticus. As a result, one of the unauthorized men carrying the ark, Uzza, died when the ark tipped and he tried to catch it. Uzza and David, along with all the rest, were guilty of *deliberate disobedience,* because only Levites were allowed to carry the ark. David later realized his mistake and repented.

Third Attempt

After the Jews were taken into captivity in ancient Babylon by the armies of Nebuchadnezzar, the Jewish advisors to the king, Meshach, Shadrach, and Abednego, were told to bow down and worship the golden statue of Nebuchadnezzar when *they heard the accompanying loud music.* These three young Jewish boys got it right and refused. They were thrown into the fiery furnace, but survived when a mysterious fourth man suddenly appeared in the furnace and delivered them from harm.

There are several other attempts in Scripture to use pagan music to attract or liven up a Christian worship service. It never happened. God is a holy God and does not need our cheap form of sleazy entertainment to attract true worshipers. In fact, who wants a person whose is only half clean?

Pagan religious services were almost always accompanied by *loud, syncopated, repetitious music.* Christ Himself in Matthew 7 warns His followers when they prayed, "not to babble [mindless repetition] as the heathens [pagans]." Even today, you will not find contemporary so-called "religious" rock music in a Jewish synagogue. They had to learn their lesson the hard way, and so far have resisted the inroads of this style of music into their worship services.

Compromise

The Christian church was successful in keeping pagan music out of the sanctuary and worship until the second half of the 20th century, when cultural pressure began to build to compromise in what music was appropriate for worship. The power of mass media—films, radio, television, the recording industry—all lent a subtle form of pressure to finally give in on this one-time inviolate principle. Dollar signs and increased attendance were the carrot; many fell into the trap.

Compromise is the basic rule in politics. In religion it can be fatal. When you begin to compromise basic beliefs that have been in place for centuries, you fracture the identity of the belief system and weaken it, eventually to the point where it almost totally changes its identity to keep up with the constant pressure.

Moral Corruption

Then the question becomes, if going to church is like watching "American Bandstand," only with different lyrics, why bother going to church? Because according to David Tame in *The Secret Power of Music,* "The technical different between 'serious' [modern classical] music, jazz, rock, or any other form of modern music were less important than the underlying factor that *they're philosophical basis was more or less one and the same: hedonism and anarchy."*

In a 1966 *Rolling Stone* interview, rock legend Bob Dylan said, "If people knew what this stuff was about, we'd probably all get arrested."

The music that Moses and Joshua heard coming down the mountain was sensual, occult, loud, repetitious, and trance inducing. Moses and Joshua heard the celebration from afar (Exod. 32:5). Joshua thought it sounded like "the noise of war in the camp." Were they rewarded for the musical celebration? Hardly. Swift and severe judgment followed (Exod. 32:18–ff).

Later in Scripture, in Leviticus 10:1–2, we find that the sons of Aaron (levitical priests serving in the tabernacle) were swiftly punished for mixing *the sacred and the profane.*

In the book of Numbers, Balak, king of the Edomites, hired Balaam, a local prophet/priest (of unscriptural practices), who tried to put a curse on the children of Israel as they migrated through the land of the Edomites on the way to the Promised Land. Failing each time to put a curse on Israel, Balaam finally confessed that the only way to weaken Israel morally and spiritually would be to send the most seductive young native women (along with their seductive native dances) to the young Israel men and soon they would intermarry and eventually embrace false gods. *Idolatry was a major problem for Israel from that moment on* (around 1200 B.C.) until the *end of the Babylonian captivity* (around 536 B.C.). Certainly pagan music was a pivotal part of these pagan, sensual practices.

Spiritual Deception

More than any other form of the misuse of sound, it is rock with which we must deal today. . . . It is a global phenomenon; a pounding destructive beat which is heard from America and Western Europe to Africa and Asia. Its effects upon the soul is to make nigh–impossible the true inner silence and peace necessary for the contemplation of eternal verities. . . . How *necessary* is it in this age *for some to have the courage to be the ones who are "different", and to separate themselves out of the pack* who long ago sold their lives and personalities to this sound? . . . I adamantly believe that *rock in all its forms* is a critical problem which our civilization *must* come to grips with . . . if it wishes to survive.

—David Tame, *The Secret Power of Music,* p. 204

In the dramatic and prophetic outline of end-time events just preceding His return, in what Bible scholars called the Olivet Discourse (Matt. 24–25; Mark 13; Luke 21), Christ warns that the single most predominant signs of the end times would be *spiritual deception.*

As we know from Ezekiel 28 and Isaiah 13, Satan was at one time in charge of worship and understood well the power of music. The Apostle Paul says in 2 Corinthians 11:13–15 that Satan and his fallen angels can transform themselves into "angels of light," meaning false teachers, singers, and musicians within the body of Christ. Second Thessalonians 2 echoes the tremendous and powerful deception that will take place *within* as well as without the body of Christ.

We read in Amos 5:23, "Take thou away from me the noise of thy songs; for I will not hear the melody of thy viols."

Music was an important part of ceremonies and worship in ancient Babylon under King Nebuchadnezzar (Dan. 3:5). End-times "Babylon" is full of "harpers, musicians, pipers, and trumpeters" (Rev. 18:22). We are told to *come out* of that kind of environment, not bring it into the church.

Throughout history, there has only been two choices: either take the church of Christ out into sinful society, or allow the regular practices of sinful society into the church. Compromise may be the heart of politics, but it is deadly dangerous in the spiritual realm. *There can be no compromise with God's Word or His practices without bringing judgment.*

One of the most frightening passages in the Bible is found in Matthew 7, toward the end of the Sermon on the Mount. Christ warns that there will be many who will someday stand before Him for judgment and will claim that they preached His name, healed in His name, and, I'm sure," sang and played music in His name. Christ's answer is chilling: *"Be gone; I never knew you."* How can contemporary pastors today play fast and loose with God's Word, God's guidelines for worship, and God's strict regulations concerning the church?

Marked for destruction, the great spiritual harlot found in Revelation 12–13 and destroyed in Revelation 17 is called a "harlot" because she openly mixes *the sacred with the profane.* Music can and has become part of this unholy mixture. For almost 2,000 years in the Christian church and another almost 2,000 years of Judaism preceding Christ, very specific guidelines were given for worship. Suddenly these guidelines are being ignored and the mixture of the sacred and the profane is openly practiced and boasted of. How can this be? Is there no fear of the living God?

Paul said in 2 Timothy 3:5 that we are living in a time when we will talk more and more about Jesus, but remain the same in our carnal nature. That's why our Lord Jesus Christ told us to look for the "fruits" of the ministry. Today the divorce rate, child- and spousal-abuse rate, and other moral corrupting behaviors, are almost as high within the church in the United States as without. Babylon has so closely counterfeited worship that it is unsafe to judge worship by *our feelings alone.* Everything must line up to Scripture—in context, not out of context—or *it does not belong.* This includes the guidelines for music.

Scripture Twisting

Larry Norman, frequently dubbed "the father of Christian rock," makes the statement that rock 'n roll music *originated in the church hundreds of years ago, and that the devil stole it.* His battle cry is to *take rock music back for Jesus' sake.* But on his website (www.bible-truths.org/living/RockMusic.html), Wayman Zeldon writes: "Rock music calls to all the baser instincts of man—riots, rebellion, sexual sensuality, sexual gratification, self-glorification. Rock music was designed to excite and stimulate the flesh."

Defenders of Christian rock point out that the Bible commands us to "sing a new song unto the Lord" (Ps. 40:3). Does this mean we stop singing the sanctified hymns and praise songs of the past? *I don't think so!* What does the Bible mean about singing a "new" song? In the prophetic book of Revelation 15:3 we see that this *new song* is *none other than the 3,500-year-old song from Exodus: the song of Moses and the Lamb.*

When one wishes to escape the hustle and bustle of the modern world, its aggressive, narcissistic self-centeredness, and its relentless pumping of loud music and obnoxious images into our consciousness, where do you go? There are only two places left: the quietness of nature, and the sanctuary of the church. Sadly, the church is quickly disappearing as a sanctuary, as a "holy" place where one can go and hear the "whisper" of God through prayer, Bible study, and meditation.

In the shadow of the great cathedrals of Europe, when you visit you are always cautioned to dress appropriately and to *be quiet!* These ancient cathedrals are living monuments to a time when the line between the sacred and the profane were based upon Scripture and were clear and inviolate.

Two Choices

It's a great blessing to leave a worship service feeling calm, loving, and spiritually uplifted. It is quite another to feel agitated, vexed, anxious, embarrassed, and resentful after being subjected to the loud, syncopated, repetitive noise of most "modern" churches in America today.

Throughout the history of the Christian church, believers have always had one of two choices to make: either take the church out into corrupt, sinful society, or invite the corrupt, sinful practices of society into the church in the hopes of winning converts. Scripture endorses only one: the church must go out *without compromise to fulfill the Word of God.*

For 300 years, from the time of the resurrection of Jesus Christ (A.D. 32), the church was small, persecuted, and centered on the Word of God and the guidance of the Holy Spirit. When the church became the state religion through the Roman Empire under the edict of Emperor Constantine (A.D. 312), the church *compromised* and allowed many ancient pagan customs, which could be traced back to ancient Babylon, into the church. The church grew in size *but diminished in spiritual power.*

Sensory Overload

The extreme volume, heavy backbeat, repetitive phrases, and syncopated rhythm patterns of rock music all combine to create a sensory overload that triggers the "fight–or–flight" response, causing an inner restlessness and hard–to–control energy release that is *antith-*

esis to true worship in the Judeo-Christian tradition. Apologists for this new style of pagan music in the church claim the energy release is a result of the "power of the Holy Spirit." Although one can search the Bible from beginning to end to find an example of the Holy Spirit working in this manner, in fact just the opposite occurs: *rock music releases physical and emotional forces* that are just the opposite of historic, biblically–based worship. For the first time in our culture, music is being used as a drug . . . and now the drug is available in "sanctified" form within the church.

The Christian church resisted the desire to bring this music into the church until the 1970s, when the success of new ministries that allowed this kind of music (with Christian lyrics) into the sanctuary during the worship service rubbed off on more traditional churches who were losing members. *Biblical Christianity has never operated on the principle that "size" matters. In fact, it teaches us to be suspicious of sudden growth, particularly if it is based upon worldly principles, not biblical ones.*

Soon there was a whole new category of commercial music in the United States, "Christian rock." The records sold by early pioneers like the Maranatha Publishing Co., Bill Gaither, the Imperials, Dallas Holmes, Randy Stonehill, Keith Greene, and others, became the hottest–selling albums in Christian bookstores across the country, eventually representing $2–3 billion annually of the $15 billion–a–year record industry.

Today, every type of pop/rock music that is available commercially is also available in a more "sanitized" version in Christian music—rock, rap, hip–hop, gothic, heavy metal, punk, etc. Parents breathe a sigh of relief, because they believe (erroneously) that the occasional addition of "Jesus" and "amen" somehow sanctifies a musical style built on the slogan of "sex, drugs, and rock 'n roll."

As we've already seen in this report, this music is not new. In fact, it represents some of the oldest music in the world—the occult, pagan, blatantly sexual music of ancient Babylon, Egypt, Greece, and Rome, and their sensual religious cults.

And keep in mind, the human ear is a delicate mechanism. It does not take much volume overload to begin the deterioration process. Anything over 80 decibels is potentially dangerous. The average rock festival volume is around 90–100 decibels, depending on where you sit. Yet "modern" pastors like Rick Warren boast that their "Christian" music is very loud and rock/pop based. Isn't it interesting that the church used to be known for peace and quiet, but today you could actually damage your hearing by attending some of these loud Christian–rock led services?

As we've already studied, the constant sharp pounding of the rock drummer on the backbeats (beats 2 and 4) triggers the survival mechanism we call the "fight–or–flight" response. The sudden rush of adrenaline into the bloodstream gives us a "rush" and increases aggression. Sadly, the modern church mistakes this as a symbol of the presence of the Holy Spirit. Nothing could be further from the truth.

> I'm a single officer alone with my car, and you can hear this guy for blocks. He still hasn't turned anything down yet. It's a real low, bassy thing and you could feel it. If he'd had a cup of water on his dashboard it would look like Jurassic Park. I finally got him to turn it off by making gestures. I'm in shock that this guy can even hear me, then he reaches up behind his ears and puts in his hearing aid. . . . *He is 22 years old and is almost totally deaf in his right ear.* He's really cooperative. I asked him when he lost his hearing, and he said, "Oh, about a year ago—the doctors said to music that's too loud." I asked him why he did it, and he just said, "Cause, man, *it's the thing to do!*"
>
> —*San Diego Union Tribune,* "Music Scene," October 18, 2001

There is a *very real danger* in listening to *loud music.* Symptoms start out in the high frequency range—like how your ears feel stuffed after a loud concert. According to OSHA (government) guidelines, 90 decibels for *eight hours* can cause *permanent hearing loss.* At 100 dB, two hours; 105 dB, one hour; 180 dB, people start to feel like *they're coming apart* (ibid.).

Noise pollution is a very dangerous problem in our society today, and unfortunately, the new "seeker–sensitive" churches that not only allow but promote this kind of music are apparently unknowingly endangering the hearing of their congregation—even though there is ample scientific evidence warning us about the dangers of volume in music.

The Wrong Music in the Wrong Place at the Wrong Time

I strongly urge every Christian who attends church regularly to resist the efforts to bring Christian "rock" music into the sanctuary during worship. Please point out the dangers as illuminated by the material in this book, as well as my previous two books, *All That Jazz: A History of Afro–American Music* (Scarecrow Press) and *Crisis in Christian Music* (Bible Belt Publishing)—both available online at www. amazon.com. In addition, check out the Internet yourself. Though a search engine like Google, type in "Rock Music in the Church." You will get a ton of material from a wide range of sources all sincerely pointing out the dangers of this music.

Big Business

Christian rock/pop music is one of the fastest growing parts of today's $12 billion annual payroll. It is estimated that Christian represents $1–3 billion of that total. Most Christian bookstores today will tell you their primary money–maker is Christian rock CDs and videos. So many parents are under the illusion that if it is packaged and sold through a Christian bookstore it must be okay.

In most instances, it is not. Even the lyrics have become increasingly corrupted and have moved farther and farther away from Scripture and the glorification of Jesus Christ, and more into the camp of self–indulgent spiritual narcissism . . . "Jesus is my buddy," etc.

What Has Rock Done?

According to *U.S. News and World Report* (October 28, 1985), "It is not just a 'phase' that teens go through, as some have erroneously thought. The philosophy that a person fills his or her mind with at [age] 15 will, *short of an absolute miracle by God,* continue to permeate their thinking at 35 and beyond. And when one considers that today's teens listen to an average of 10,500 hours or rock music between the 7th and 12th grades."

Today, Christian rock imitates or "mocks" commercial styles and artists, even to the "gangsta" clothes, dress, sullen looks, and rebellious and sensual poses for CD covers. *The only difference is an **occasional** reference to Jesus Christ and Christianity.* The market is obviously aimed at preteens (8–12) and teenagers (13–20), with girls being the primary target. Stylistically, there is (1) mainstream Christian pop, (2) teenybopper rock (the youngest kids), (3) heavy metal, (4) gothic, (5) ethnic, (6) hip–hop, (7) rhythm and blues, (8) country–rock, and (9) rap/gangsta rap. Each of these popular styles has its followers among today's teenagers.

We now have Christian "rap" music, a musical style completely devoid of melody, harmony, dynamics, etc. This is a style of "protest" music that goes back to ancient Africa and the tribal griots (poet–musicians).

Christian "Evangelism" Through Music

Many of today's popular Christian rock groups state that their primary purpose is *evangelism,* although seldom in their concerts is the plan of salvation given or any Scripture read. The Bible states that music's purpose is primarily for worship, not evangelism.

There is not one instance in Scripture where music is the primary platform for evangelism. The Holy Spirit through the Word of God, the Bible, is what brings sinners under conviction, not suggestively clad, overtly loud, brazen, and prideful performances of wealthy and powerful Christian rock stars and groups.

Why do these groups advertise primarily on Christian radio and television and through supportive local churches? Because an estimated 8 percent of their income from record sales comes through Bible bookstores and churches. *It's a big business, folks, with bookstores, publishers, record companies, and megachurches all lining up for their piece of the pie.*

The World According to Rock Music

The growing "secret" epidemic of the incurable and eventually fatal AIDS among black people today prompted Jacob Levinson to write his book, *The Secret Epidemic: The Story of AIDS and Black America*

(Pantheon Press). According to Levinson's book, today AIDS is the No. 1 killer of black American men and women between the ages of 22 and 25. Levinson blames a lot of this on the pop music industry, MTV, Hollywood, and the angry, aggressive musical styles of hip-hop and "gangsta" rap.

Many commercial rock concerts, and even some rock clubs, offer what is called a "mosh pit" for "dancers." A mosh pit is an area, usually in front of the stage, where individuals and couples can go and *do anything they like* short of public sex or exposure. Mosh pits are often violent, with individuals hurling their bodies at each other. At commercial concerts, well-trained bouncers surround the mosh pit and stop any activity or individual that gets too far out of line.

Here's the surprise: *mosh pits are common events at most major Christian rock concerts.* Most Christian parents are not aware of this, nor do they seem to be aware of the dangers involved. A cobra is a deadly snake. You can dress him up, paint him, try to teach him manners, but he is still a deadly snake and will bite when given the chance. The same is true with rock music. It will bite when given the chance.

And then there is MTV. The power of MTV is enormous. The last time I visited Israel, I had the opportunity to talk to a major executive of an international hotel chain in Jerusalem. He told me that families from all over the world who come to visit Israel and Jerusalem insist on two things: access to CNN, and access to MTV—CNN for the parents; MTV for the kids. MTV now controls a great deal of the pop music industry, dominates the television channels for teenagers (who have the most discretionary income of all age groups), and now they've moved into producing motion pictures.

The programming of MTV is primarily a visualization of popular rock hits. These visualizations are often borderline pornographic, sensual, violent, and degrading to women (and occasionally children and animals). The major themes, over and over again, are sex, the occult (demons, charms, Satan, etc.), violence, lust, anger, power, gender hatred, adult hatred, hatred for society, hatred for law and order, and drugs. Love songs are satirized as "corny."

The videos produced by the top Christian rock groups are not much better, just a bit more reserved, with only ambiguous lyrics and motions regarding the most common topics of their commercial big sister. I challenge all adults, and particularly parents, to spend a few minutes watching MTV, realizing that they have a bigger impact on today's youth than *any other media.*

Even NBC Television's Tom Brokaw now openly associates the cause of much of our teenage social unrest, crime, murders, and rape with today's music and entertainment (*The Brokaw Report,* June 5, 1992).

The powerful signals sent by this occult–based music is hard to overcome. The "high" teenagers get from the fight–or–flight rush they get when they listen to loud music with a sharp backbeat is like a drug. Today, teenagers and many adults *cannot live without it. That's one of the primary reasons the rockers of the 1960s and 1970s have insisted on bringing their music, their drug, into the church.*

Nyet

The Christian church (evangelical/Protestant) in Russia today is more aware of the dangers of Christian rock than we are. Recently Peter Peters and Vasilij Ryzhuk, head of a Russian church conglomerate called the *Unregistered Union of Churches,* wrote a letter to major Christian "rock" stars and their record companies *urging* them not to bring that kind of music to Russia. The letter read:

> Our young people do not attend these concerts or meetings [where contemporary American Christian rock music is performed] because *we have all committed not to participate in secular entertainment.* Many come with Bible in one hand and rock CDs in the other. We are *embarrassed by this image of Christianity.* We abhor all Christian rock music coming to our country.
>
> Rock music has nothing in common with true ministry or biblically–based service to God. We are very, very against Americans bringing to our country this false image of "ministry" to God. We need spiritual bread—give us true bread, *not false cakes.* It is true that rock music attracted people to the church, but not to godly living.

—www.behtlministries.com/Russian.htm

Play It and They Will Come

The single most common argument from pastors, worship directors, and musicians themselves are that *young people will not attend church without rock music.* There are no studies that I could find that support that claim in any way. In fact, there are numerous studies that claim just the opposite: teenagers *do not want to go to church and hear "bad" or "amateurish" rock music. They go to worship as we do . . . with appropriate music.* One of the strengths of Christian music is its timelessness.

Dr. Barbara Resch conducted a survey of nearly 500 teenagers from across the United States on the appropriateness of music for the church. The findings are surprising. The vast majority of teenagers in this survey agreed on the following. The preferred music and styles were:

» Choral music, not instrumental
» Sung by a group of singers rather than a soloist
» Characterized by a simple musical texture and understandable text
» Musical examples reminiscent of popular styles (jazz, rock, and country) were *overwhelmingly rejected as church music*

The study goes on to record that though most of these teenagers like rock music and thought it was the right music for some times and places in their lives, *they didn't believe that the church service was that time and place.* Another surprise in the survey was the discovery that the responses were not significantly different from the teens who attended church regularly and those who did not. In fact, while listening to examples of Christian rock/pop, many responded, "This sounds like my parent's music!"

When asked regarding their feelings on the role of music in worship, the most common responses were (in order):

1. Church music should be an expression of religious belief
2. Church music is part of the presentation of God's Word (the Bible)
3. Church music is a way for people to use their talents to serve God
4. Church music establishes or changes peoples' moods

The final results continue to surprise us. Those surveyed showed a healthy respect for the corporate nature of their worshiping congregations. In other words, they were sensitive to the effects of introducing rock music on the older members of the congregation! The summary of this study is stunning: "Attempts by adults to present an appealing contemporary popular sound were apparently unsuccessful in winning over unchurched students, who measure that sound against cutting-edge pop music and *found it lacking*" (http://worshipo.Icms.org/insert/churchmusic/91teens.html).

I have run my own survey in this area, and it supports this study and others in their findings. *So why do pastors keep telling us the kids won't come to church without this kind of music?* I don't think that is the primary reason for its unpopular introduction into contemporary Christian worship. I believe it is all part of a vast pattern to secularize the church in an effort to attract more members . . . casual dress, drama sketches, guest musical artists, special lighting, emotion-wrenching testimonies, and ear-splitting music. *We have turned worship into a circus, leaving Christ outside to knock on the door and ask to come back into His own church* (Revelation 3—the Laodicean church).

Who's Influencing Who?

There are two arguments today about music. The first is that the ancients and the traditionalists believe that music affects character and society, and therefore the artist has a duty to be *morally responsible and constructive, not immoral and destructive.* The other argument is the opinion of secular humanists, the radical avant-garde—that music is basically "amoral," that is, neutral in its ability to influence either positively or negatively.

This point of view is part of the greater foundation of our culture philosophically today. We live in an era of moral relativism, born out of existentialism and socialism along with Darwinism . . . basically, man is only responsible for himself, and all his moral points of view are personal, not communal. Under this philosophy, a president of the United States could lie under oath concerning his "immoral" behavior in the Oval Office of the White House and *mean it!* No one takes responsibility for their lives; we are all victims of circumstance.

No wonder the gospel message is such a hard-sell today, for the God of the Bible holds us individually and collectively responsible for our behavior, and only through the shed blood of an innocent lamb, the Lamb of God, Jesus Christ, can the permanent blot of sin be erased and judgment spared. How ironic to see people today supposedly within the body of Christ taking the second position regarding their music, their lives, their way of worship, and their watered-down, often insulting, presentation of the path of salvation.

Hallucinogenic Music

Rock music is a sad, exaggerated imitation of authentic black American rhythm and blues. This music, born in the juke joints and honky-tonks of rural black America, crossed the color line into the white community in the 1960s. Black Americans understood the roots of this music and forbade its performance in black churches. It was called "the devil's music," and still is to most Afro-American Christians. To this day, the Afro-American church, for the most part, has resisted the intrusions of so-called "Christian" rock into their churches. They see the crass commercialism, distortions, and prideful nature of the music for what it is.

Thomas A. Dorsey, the father of modern black gospel, and the author of such wonderful modern praise songs as "Precious Lord," was himself a former "blues" singer by the name of "Tampa Red" before he was saved and turned his musical talents toward serving the Lord.

Whenever a foreign culture adopts the characteristics of another culture, the foreign culture always exaggerates the artistic styles of the culture they are borrowing from. While Americans took the native R&B of black Americans and distorted its rhythms, increased the volume of the music, and turned the lyrics into songs of rage and rebellion.

We all know that the 1960s and 1970s were decades of rebellion. Lapel buttons that read "Question Authority" were popular, along with a communal lifestyle and anything that could be seen as a rejection of traditional American cultural values. Sex became a sport, drugs a religious communal experience (as it still is among the Jamaican Rastafarians and certain sects of Hinduism), and the music had to overwhelm the senses and attack all traditional social values.

People stopped "listening" to music in an intellectual and emotionally stimulating (but controlled) way and started "feeling" the music instead. The critical nature was set aside as long as the music overwhelmed the senses. For this to happen, the music had to overcome the logical, deductive, and comparative–experience part of our brain and open us up to non–logical sensory experiences, foreign (until then) to most Western cultures. Music was used to create feelings and not new understandings.

Using music to open up man's mind to hallucinatory experiences is not new. It was and is quite common even today in many cultures. Even in the day of our Lord, this kind of music was common, particularly in the religious cults. Remember that it was Jesus who cautioned His followers not to "babble" (use non–logical repetitions to overcome critical areas of the brain) as the heathen (Matthew 16).

Music can be used as a drug. Loud, sudden sharp sounds, such as the backbeat of the rock drum, tend to activate the "fight-or-flight" response. Early man had to face sudden danger and consequently, *loud, repetitive, sharp sounds* were and still are interpreted by our brain as "danger." When this fight–or–flight response is activated, the brain sends a signal to the adrenal glands. Adrenaline is then dumped into the bloodstream, giving us a sudden surge of energy and aggression.

All cults use some form of repetitive chanting to break down individual consciousness. This is necessary to remove the "logical" part of our normal thinking. Otherwise, we would see through the charade of occult practices and realize that they are false and dangerous. *All forms of overly repetitive chanting or singing of a simple line over and over are dangerous and are contrary to biblical teaching.*

While researching my book *All That Jazz,* I discovered that most of the tribal religions of Africa, Latin America, Asia, and Polynesia, were demonic in nature and relied on certain rhythms to call up the demons peculiar to that religion. This discovery was later confirmed by a scholarly book called *Drumming on the Edge of Magic,* by Mickey

Hart, drummer with the well-known rock group The Grateful Dead.

Historically, the Christian church has long suspected that the deadly combination of the three musical characteristics given above was not only not scriptural but also contrary to true worship. For centuries the church forbade certain rhythms, restricted the volume of the music, and avoided mindless repetition. Even plainsong, or early Gregorian chant, though melodically repetitious, avoided mindless repetition of the lyrics.

Most sects within Christianity resisted secular music coming into the sanctuary until the 1960s. One of the concerns was the loss of the sense of "holiness"; another was the danger of church music moving from being a tool to promote worship to becoming a form of entertainment. One feels as if he or she is at a rock concert or some sort of spiritual pep rally. Holiness has been replaced with commercial slickness, light shows, loud bands, and other commercial ways to "dazzle" the congregation.

The Role of the Church

Until the mid-20th century in America, the role of the church was to take Christ and the church into the world, not bring the world into the church. Most pastors understood that the world and its sensual nature was incompatible with a life of holiness. Churches and pastors were more concerned with following the dictates of God in running a church as outlined in Scripture than in attracting hundreds, even thousands, to their services. Pastors, elders, deacons, and church congregations relied upon the Holy Spirit to attract new believers, not worldly mass-marketing techniques.

Today a staff at a megachurch looks, feels, and acts more like a corporate boardroom or a Hollywood studio than a spiritual gathering. The Bible, prayer, and reliance on the Holy Spirit for guidance in running the church has been cast aside for corporate pep talks, and a search for new and more exciting forms of entertainment, flashy special effects, etc.

Doctrine of the Nicolaitanes

The doctrine of the Nicolaitanes, which Christ said in Revelation

2 that he "hated," has leapt from the Catholic to the non–Catholic denominations. What is this doctrine? It is the doctrine that places church leaders *above* the laity, or congregation, meaning they are if not infallible, at least *not* subject to normal protests and questions of their authority. This feeling is so subtle that many churches and parishioners are not aware of it.

Seldom are pastors in churches *ever* approached with anything but accolades, unless he has blatantly broken the basic rules of morality, and even then it is more to avoid embarrassing the church than rebuking the pastor. Strong personalities who are not afraid to challenge authority in business and civic environments are often strangely silent in a religious context. Most believe that God is closer to the pastor and the church leadership than they are. As a result, rather than resisting change when it should be resisted, the people in the congregation remain strangely silent, or stop coming to church, or search out another body of believers.

This is contrary to Scripture. Even a casual reading of Acts, both 1 and 2 Corinthians, Hebrews, Galatians, and 1–3 John reveal and expose the facts that not only are we to speak up when we sense the pastor or the church is headed in the wrong direction, *we are spiritually obligated to do so.*

A Moment of Truth

Another sad by–product of allowing a commercial, worldly, sensual musical art form into the church is the trashing of over 300 years of often–sanctified church music. It seems as if the generation that grew up in the age of rebellion in America not only wants to bring their secular music into the sanctuary, but they want to dispense with most traditional church music, regardless of its beauty, spiritual honestly, and historical tradition. It's almost as if there is a perverse resistance to anything beautiful, quiet, introspective, and holy.

Could it be that the generation to which we are referring were so rarely exposed to beautiful music of any kind that they resist keeping it in the church because they do not understand or feel it? It is hard to comprehend how screaming electric guitars, sexy–sounding saxophones, throbbing electric basses, and clanging, banging drums could ever be considered holy, worshipful, or reverent.

Sooner or later, pastors, music and worship leaders, and elders of churches where this kind of music is glorified must ask themselves, *Is this a worshipful atmosphere? Are we polluting the sanctuary? Are people coming for a sensory experience rather than worship? Have we mistaken "getting high" on rock music with a true outbreak of the Holy Spirit?* Christ warns us in the Olivet Discourse (Matt. 24, Mark 13, and Luke 21) that the primary sign that will occur in the years just preceding His return will be *spiritual deception*.

Cleansing the Temple

Contemporary Christian music is big business. It's the fastest growing part of the secular music industry, rapidly approaching $3 billion annually. Many so-called "Christian" artists arrive in limos, have gone in and out of marriages like any other celebrity, and celebrate Christ less and less in their music, instead celebrating their own personal feelings and sensual experiences.

It is bothersome to me to walk into a church sanctuary to worship and be blasted out by a traveling "Christian artist," who also has a table full of CDs, T-shirts, etc., on sale in the lobby.

Whenever I've challenged the appropriateness of contemporary rock music being played in a formal church service, I'm always told, "They [the congregation] like it!" I'm here to tell you, that is in most instances not true. I challenge any music and worship leader or pastor to study the body language and participation of their congregation whenever the music is loud, repetitive, and overly syncopated. Generally, over two-thirds of the congregation *does not participate, they endure.* Those who come to church to be entertained are the only ones who "like" it.

Prophetic Fulfillment

By attending Christian rock concerts, does not one identify oneself with their ecumenism and their false doctrines and become a partaker of their evil deeds? (The Bible clearly teaches a theology of guilt by association; see John 10–11.) And since we will all be accountable to the Lord at the Bema Seat for our stewardship with the resources he has entrusted to us while on this earth, how can anyone possibly justify allocating any resources to the support of rock music?

—Tim Fisher, *The Battle for Christian Music,* 1992

In a positive way, the phenomenon of rock music in the church is a fulfillment of prophecy. Those who search the Scriptures honestly and diligently know that it has been predicted that in the last days there would be two churches, one devoted to Scripture and holiness, the other polluted by the world, the occult, and sensual practices.

Summary

Over 2,000 years *before the birth of Christ* the musical systems of China was both highly developed and central to its society. It was to this that the philosophers directed much of their attention. *Understanding its intrinsic power,* they carefully checked their music to make sure that it conveyed *eternal truths* and could influence man's character for the better.

—David Tame, *The Secret Power of Music,* p. 34

I have tried to understand the power that worldly music has over people and over the contemporary church. I believe it is a combination of naïveté—not understanding the physiological, emotional, psychological, and spiritual fallout that comes from bringing the music of rebellion, rock, into the sanctuary—and a form of pride.

To this end, tradition states that one [Chinese] emperor, by the name of Shun, would monitor the health of each of the provinces of this vast kingdom by simply examining the music they produced. *Course and sensual sounds indicated a sick society, one in need of his intervention and assistance.*

—Ibid., pp. 13–14

Satan's biggest tool over us all is pride. Man fell because of pride, and has still today spiritually deceived more non–believers and believers through pride than any other way, particularly in the church. Those of us in the church are aware of the too obvious sins, but pride, and particularly spiritual pride, is subtle, easily rationalized, and hard to resist.

Those who grew up in the decades of rebellion in America, the 1960s and 1970s, are the most insistent that rock music replace traditional church music in the sanctuary. They want to toss out 2,000 years of tradition. What a hold this music has on them!

The Nuts and Bolts of Music

Chapter 20

The Seven Parts of Music

An automobile engine has seven basic parts: (1) the engine, (2) the electrical system, (3) the cooling system, (4) the fuel system, (5) the steering system, (6) the brakes, and (7) the chassis. In a similar way, music is made up of specific parts: (1) rhythm, (2) form, (3) melody, (4) countermelody, (5) harmony, (6) texture (range, tone), and (7) style (dynamics, tempo, and articulation). These are listed in order of importance and development. There are standard clichés or simple formulas in each of these parts that can suggest a specific human emotion. The idea in musical composition, regardless of historical style, is to line up all seven parts so they are expressing or amplifying the same emotion.

Each of its seven parts can convey a feeling or suggestion of a specific human emotion. Interestingly enough, there are seven basic types of human emotion: (1) mad, (2) sad, (3) glad, (4) scared, (5) sensual or erotic, (6) humorous, and (7) inspirational (religious, ecological, social). When the seven parts of music all line up to suggest a particular human emotion, the results are powerful and spectacular. It is the composer's job to know how to do this. The skill is sometimes a learned skill; in other instances it is intuitive.

However, there is another consideration for the composer or songwriter. He or she must also understand the standard clichés for different cultural styles. These cultural styles include (1) ethnic (a musical style peculiar to a particular race or tribe), (2) religious (Judeo–Christian), (3) Western European classical, (4) Latin American, (5) Asian American, (6) Middle Eastern, and (7) United States (which includes Afro–American influences in gospel, jazz, and blues).

Today's composer has a wide range of musical and cultural styles, as well as the many choices in choosing instruments to express ideas. Deciding what *not* to do often takes longer than deciding *what* to do. Regardless, the seven parts of music are activated when the choices have been made. The most primary element, rhythm, must be dealt with first.

Rhythm

Rhythm is the most powerful element in music. Rhythm organizes melodies, chords, etc., into recognizable patterns. The human body and brain are about ten times more sensitive to rhythm than to pitch (melody). That's because our bodies are so rhythmic; our circulatory system, respiratory system, and other systems of the body are constantly creating internal rhythm patterns. The human heartbeat at rest is approximately sixty to seventy-two beats per minute, unless you are a professional distance-event athlete; then your resting heartbeat could be much slower. The heartbeat is not even; the first beat is three times as long as the second: boom . . . boom–boom . . . boom . . . boom–boom.

Our bodies are constantly trying to adjust to the constant changes in our physical environment. Our heartbeat, for instance, will increase gradually if there is a beat similar to the heartbeat that is repetitive and gradually increases in tempo. Many of the more sophisticated computer games today have musical soundtracks with strong repetitive typical heartbeat rhythms that gradually increase in speed as the climax of the game approaches. The player's heartbeat will gradually increase in speed as well, adding realism to the game.

This protective mechanism—unconscious constant adaptation to environmental changes—is called "homeostasis." It is one of the reasons the human species is so adaptable and has survived so many catastrophic changes in the Earth's environment. Rhythm is primarily a "right brain" (intuitive) musical skill. Music is something we "feel" as much as we "hear." The more emotional and spontaneous a culture, the more important rhythm is to their music. As our environment changes, so do the rhythm patterns that show up in our music. The rhythm of music even subconsciously imitates the natural rhythmic flow of each culture's spoken language: German, French, Italian, English—all these musical styles, and many others, suggest rhythmically the flow of the native spoken language as well as the rhythm of the basic emotion being expressed—no easy task!

Form

The next most important musical ingredient is form. Form is the organization of music into phrases, which are like musical sentences. Generally speaking, listeners like to hear a new musical idea, then contrasting ideas, followed by a repetition of the initial musical statement. This human desire for contrast and repetition has resulted in the development of several classical music forms that have guided composers for centuries in writing sonatas, symphonies, and concertos.

Form is primarily a "left–brain" skill in music, appealing to the logic, mathematical, organizational part of our brains. The more scientifically advanced (left brain) a culture, the more important form is to music. For instance, the tribal music of Africa has very little form, which is primarily the statement of one rhythm, then contrasted with another, and an eventual return to the opening statement.

Melody

Melody cannot exist without rhythm and form. Consequently, it is third in musical importance. Many of the world's more primitive musical cultures are built entirely around rhythm, form, and melody. Melodies are made up of intervals. Intervals are the distances between the notes. Each interval projects a particular emotional feeling. In the chapter on melody we will identify each specific interval and the emotional force field it creates. Melody is balanced between left– and right–brain; both hemispheres are involved in melody making.

Countermelody

A countermelody is another melody that runs simultaneously above or below the original melody in such a way that each melody compliments the other. In jazz or rock music, the countermelody is often in the bass line. Sometimes there are three or more countermelodies all interacting with each other simultaneously. This type of music is called "polyphonic" and takes great skill to compose. A countermelody adds energy, excitement, anticipation, and contrast to the original melody. Often the original melody is stated first and then the countermelody is added later.

An improvised countermelody like a jazz bass line is primarily a right-brain skill. Written countermelodies (a musical skill called "counterpoint") are primarily left-brain because of the mathematical relationships and the careful planning that has to go into writing counterpoint. Probably the greatest composer of this style of music (called "polyphony") was Johann Sebastian Bach, followed by Handel and Teleman.

Harmony

Harmony is the vertical organization of three or more notes, played or sung simultaneously. The intervals within the chord create emotional force fields that are magnified by the striking or singing of three or more notes simultaneously. Chords, like certain intervals, can create musical tension because of the dissonance in some of the intervals of the chord. These dissonances demand resolution to consonances (release of tension), and this process of dissonance resolving into consonance becomes a basic format for musical composition.

Harmony is primarily a left-brain skill and was developed primarily in the highly left-brain dominant literature cultures, like Western Europe. As far as I know, there is no tribal or third world culture with a highly developed harmonic system. Intricate form and countermelody is more the product of our Western European culture, a predominately left-brain society.

Texture

Texture is the choice of register (high, medium, or low) and the choice of tone-color (bright, clear, dark, or raspy a la Louis Armstrong). These choices have a great effect on the music being performed. Choosing appropriate ranges and tone colors credibly enhances certain emotions. These choices are part of a broader skill called "orchestration." Since these skills require foreknowledge and contemplation of action, they become primarily left–brain skills.

So much of what a composer does is internal. Just as the painter or sculptor must "see" in his mind's eye the finished product, the composer must "hear" in his mind's ear what will eventually become the final product.

Style

The seventh ingredient in music is called style. Musical style is primarily determined by tempo (fast or slow), dynamics (loud or soft), and articulation (connected or separated notes). These three divisions can change often within a musical composition, adding great contrast to the musical performance. Both hemispheres of the brain are involved in this final part of a musical performance, particularly when part or all of the music is being improvised.

What's Next?

The following chapters will examine these important seven parts of a musical work in more detail. In the meantime, it will enhance your listening pleasure to listen to your favorite music and try to analyze the musical clichés being used in each of these important areas.

Sadly, one of the weaknesses as well as one of the dangers of certain types of American pop music today is its lack of contrast. So much pop–rock music is loud, loud, loud, as well as lacking in contrast in phrasing (connected or separated notes). This lack of contrast creates a certain type of hypnotic monotony that apparently is deliberate in intent.

The auditory nerve is connected to the mid–brain, the part of the brain that scientists tell us is the seat of our emotions, bypassing the upper brain (cerebral cortex) which scientists tell us is the seat of all our deductive reasoning and creative thinking. What this means is that *music triggers emotions before we can control or modify them.* Have you ever been somewhere where the music is triggering emotions feelings inside your head that you may be uncomfortable with? I imagine the answer is "yes" in most cases. The only solution to that problem is to (1) turn off the music, or (2) change your environment so you cannot hear it any longer. That is why music is the bedrock to all radio and television advertising and is as important as the actors and the script in television and movie dramas.

When we wish to change our mood or modify our environment, we turn to music. If we wish to be happy, we seek "happy" music, and so on. There are some cultural differences in musical styles and choices of instruments, but the standard clichés in each of the seven parts are fairly universal in application and use.

The classical music of northern India is considered to be one of the oldest musical systems in the world. I was fortunate enough to study many years ago with an outstanding teacher and musician from northern India. She taught me "ragas," musical scales and modes, and common rhythms used in their musical system; she also showed me other cultural differences as well (form, choice of instruments, range, etc.). Most of the music of northern India is performed with one or more sitars (a plucked string instrument) and one or more tabla players (hand–held drums, like bongos). Often new rhythms are introduced by having the music stop and then the head drummer sings a new rhythm. The other instruments then fall in line and pursue this new path of excitement.

This ancient musical system of India is so sensitive to the effects of music on the listener that certain scales and rhythms are played (or listened to) *only* at certain times of the day and/or certain times of the year. There are "ragas" and rhythms suitable only for morning, afternoon, or evening; others are suitable only for spring, summer, fall, or winter.

According to the musicians and teachers of this system, to play these specific special scales and rhythms at any other time than designated is to *upset the internal systems governing the body,* which includes the respiratory, circulatory, endocrine, and digestive systems, brain waves, and natural endorphins. Recently, modern science has been able to confirm this earlier intuitive evaluation of the power of music and its effects on the body, the mind, and the culture.

I believe, like a lot of scientific discoveries we have made over the last one hundred fifty years or more, that we are just beginning to "rediscover" some of the hard-earned knowledge of older civilizations just in time to apply it to our hectic modern lives. We are discovering more and more natural healing substances in nature, and rediscovering natural painkillers and non-chemical anesthetics like acupuncture from China.

American medicine has painted itself into a corner, concentrating primarily on surgery or chemical medication for treatment. We are rediscovering the fact that nature itself offers many remedies and alternatives that are a lot less harmful to our bodies and minds. One of these discoveries is the use of certain styles of music to heal the body and the mind.

The constant roar of today's audio environment and the loud, uncontrollable, mostly rage-driven pop music of the day (rock, rap, and hip-hop) has created major health problems for our society. It's time to suggest solutions. That's one of the purposes in writing this book.

Someday prescriptions will be written for patients to listen to certain styles of music for healing purposes, as well as warnings to stay away from other styles of music because they can have serious negative effects on their mental, physical, and cultural health. What we need today is a "Pure Music Act," creating a federal bureau much like our Pure Food and Drug Act brought about. The primary purpose of government is to protect its citizens.

We need protection from intrusion of out-of-control music into our lives. It has created havoc wherever it has occurred, and long with our drug culture, it must go. "Just say NO to loud pop music" will become a popular slogan.

The argument for safe music today must be rescued from the generation warfare that is going on at the present. Teenagers dislike the music of their parents, and vice versa. Arguments must be sound scientifically, psychologically, sociologically, and culturally. This issue cannot be settled by too much emotion from either side. Only by new knowledge can we decide what is best for our children and for the mental, moral, and physical health of our society at large.

Music often seems to be a language of conflicting emotions—

emotions that change suddenly from sad to glad, scared to sensual, etc. Today's writer must make these changes at the exact spot dictated by the words of the song, the drama on the screen, or the desire of the composer.

Assignment

Following the examples given below, please write in the song or film soundtrack theme that best expresses in your mind that particular emotion. Examples:

Mad	—	Soundtrack theme to *The Terminator*
Sad	—	Soundtrack theme to *Schindler's List*
Glad	—	Soundtrack theme to *Titanic*
Scared	—	Opening theme to *Jaws*
Sensual	—	Ravel's "Bolero" in the movie *Ten*
Humorous	—	"Pink Panther Theme" by Henry Mancini
Inspirational	—	"America the Beautiful" sung by Ray Charles

Now, write in your own choices. The process of doing so will help you begin to identify the standard clichés in the seven musical categories that "create" a specific emotional force field.

Mad _____

Glad _____

Scared _____

Sensual _____

Humorous _____

Inspirational _____

Confessions of a Hollywood Film Composer

I've scored the music soundtracks to five Hollywood feature films. I enjoyed the creative process involved. A film composer must understand that his responsibility is to *enhance* the reality of the emotions (and physical actions) being portrayed on the screen at any particular moment. To do this, the composer must correctly identify the primary emotion being expressed and them amplify its intensity with appropriate music *without drawing attention away from the drama to the music.* This is not always an easy task.

I learned quickly how to underscore each specific scene that required music. Usually this is a collaborative effort with the director. Sometimes the music requires exotic cultural formats to fit the film. In each instance, while examining the scene with the director, I wrote down (1) the length of the scene, (2) the basic emotion of the scene, (3) the kinesthetic action of the scene (walking, running, talking, dancing, fighting, etc.), (4) exotic instruments needed to amplify the time and place of the scene, (5) the choice of instruments for the scene, and (6) the amount of dialogue or other extraneous noise going on at the same time.

After "spotting" the film, I then began to search for musical clichés in each of the seven categories of music. *Background music that distracts rather than amplifies the action on the scene is not appropriate, no matter how wonderful the music itself happens to be.*

My experience with film music sharpened my knowledge of musical clichés and how to apply them to create a particular emotional force field. These same techniques are used daily, hourly, in the music behind radio and television commercials.

Chapter 21

Rhythm

Music is the effort we make to explain to ourselves how the mind works.

—Mickey Hart, *Drumming at the Edge of Magic,* p. 118

He who makes a mistake is still our friend; he who adds to, or shortens, a melody is still our friend; but he who violates a rhythm unawares can never be our friend."

—Arab proverb

Listeners are much more sensitive to rhythm than any other aspect of music. Our bodies are walking, breathing, speaking rhythm machines. All of our automatic nervous systems—respiratory, digestive, and circulatory—are in a continuous state of rhythmic activity. From a kinesthetic standpoint we move, speak, exercise, sneeze, eliminate, and even sleep rhythmically.

The human body is an amazing machine. One of the reasons our species has been able to survive major climate or environmental changes is our fantastic ability to adapt. We are in a constant state of homeostasis; in other words, subconsciously our body, mind, and emotions are constantly adapting to our environment.

Power of Rhythm

Military drums play music designed to make your feet take you where your head never would. Music is as dangerous as gunpowder.

—N'omi Orr

Throughout military history, drums have been used to first unify, then lend courage, and finally enrage soldiers before and even during battle, helping them overcome their fear of death by beginning the drumbeats slowly and repetitiously, and then gradually increasing their volume, intensity, and speed. The youngest casualty in the American Civil War was a 12-year-old drummer in the Union Army.

The power of rhythm is amazing. A military unit marching across a suspension bridge must not march in step. The power of the sympathetic vibrations of all the soldiers' feet coming down at the same time can and would bring the bridge down. Sports stadiums must be built with sound baffles or barriers that limit the power of sympathetic vibrations from the fans stomping their feet or shouting in rhythm to affect the structure. "Africans, particularly West Africans, believe that the spirits ride the drumbeat down into the body of the dancers, who then begin the erratic shaking movements of the possessed" (Drumming at the Edge of Magic, p. 201).

George Otis, Jr., a well-known businessman and Christian author, traveler, and speaker, in his book *The Twilight Labyrinth* (Chosen Books, 1997), exposes the fact that demonic religions and cults throughout the known world *all* use certain rhythm patterns and sounds. These repeated, syncopated rhythms are used to "call up" their local spirits or demons. Often these supposedly demonic forces then take possession of one or more of the dancers. Once that happens, those "possessed" are petitioned by others present to give "supernatural" personal prophecies (1:36).

"During a possession trance, the consciousness of the possessed is said to leave and go wandering while the visiting spirit is in residence—typically they have no memory of anything that has happened and couldn't begin to tell you what the possessing spirit says through them" (ibid., p. 202).

Surprisingly, former rock drummer Mickey Hart of the Grateful Dead, in his popular book *Drumming at the Edge of Magic,* supports the occult research of George Otis regarding the use of rhythm to "call up spirits": "Great care must be taken that only the correct spirit takes up residence. The way this is accomplished is *with the drum. Particular rhythms are supposed to attract particular spirits.* An *Orisha* (demon god) like *Shango* (popular West African, Caribbean, and

Latin American demon god) *only comes when he hears his rhythm"* (p. 204).

"Imagine the soundscape thousands of years ago. Noise meant danger, possibly death, an understanding rooted in the oldest parts of the brain, in the fight–or–flight programs that activate the adrenals, preparing the organism for immediate action. This is what the Hindus knew on a cosmic scale; *there is terror in noise and in that terror there is also power"* (2:12).

There seems to be a morbid fascination on the part of some rock groups with the occult and the use of rhythms to attract "familiar spirits." For instance, on the Rolling Stones "Goat Head Soup" CD (a goat head is a symbol of Satan), they incorporate actual recorded excerpts of drums and chanting from Haitian voodoo ceremonies.

John Lennon, co-leader of the Beatles, said in a Rolling Stone interview (2/12/76, p. 100), "Rock and Roll gets through to people because of its *voodoo* beat. That's no bull, really. The best stuff comes from the natives. *Go to the jungle—they have the rhythm* and now it goes throughout the world [via rock 'n roll] and it's as simple as that."

Musicologist John Chernoff studied drumming in Africa, participating in animal sacrifices and other tribal ceremonies performed by the natives to appease the drum spirits. After these demonic ceremonies that often went on for hours, he claimed his arms did not tire and he "seemed to never make a mistake." Chernoff noted the close connection between the voodoo–type of African cult drumming and rock and roll: "Great drummers, aficionados, and scholars alike can trace the rhythms of the Latin dance halls of New York to Cuban and Brazilian cults and then to West Africa" (Chernoff, *African Rhythm and African Sensibility,* p. 29).

The most ancient of the more advanced civilizations seemed to suddenly appear out of the dusty mist of the post–Antediluvian age (after the flood of Genesis). This was the startling advanced civilization of the Sumerians. Archaeologists and scientists are finding out more every day about this ancient society that emerged in the fertile triangle between the Tigris and Euphrates rivers (modern–day Iraq).

They had advanced mathematical systems and writing systems

that seemed to leapfrog slow-developing tribal societies in the same area. They seemed to appear out of nowhere some time between 3500 and 2500 B.C. Many archaeologists have suggested that these are the descendants of Noah and his three sons, the only survivors—according to biblical legend (Gen. 6-9) of a worldwide catastrophic flood.

The ancient Sumerians also had an advanced knowledge of music, which they used in religious ceremonies and for healing, entertainment, education, and motivation of their warriors before battle. Some believe the instruments mentioned in the Bible (Dan. 3:5) that were used by a later great Babylonian ruler, Nebuchadnezzar (600 B.C.), were originally developed by the more ancient Sumerians.

Rumors abound of this civilization and later the Egyptians using sounds to actually lift and move heavy objects, like the stones in the great pyramids in Egypt. So far there is no conclusive evidence, but ancient writings suggest the future possibility of using music and sound on a much broader basis in the future.

The ancient Greeks had two types of religious music. The first was serious, idealistic, and inspirational, predominantly vocal, accompanied by the soft sounds of the hand-held harp using simple, non-syncopated rhythms. The popular Greek god most celebrated in this manner was Apollo. The music was melodic, quiet, serene, and relatively non-rhythmic.

The second most popular god was the ribald, bawdy, rowdy, lustful, and sensual god of wine and celebrations, Bacchus. His celebrations often degenerated into drunken orgies. The music was percussive, loud, and repetitive. The main instrument, a wind instrument called the *aulos,* had an eerie, loud sound not unlike the wailing of today's electric guitar.

Both types were deemed necessary to balance man's human nature. Both were considered cathartic and purifying. One appealed to man's noble nature; the other, to man's baser instincts. *Music played an important part in both.* However, the music used was radically different for each.

In his excellent book *Music and Trance,* Gilbert Rouget points out that the trance-ecstatic cults (like Bacchus) annoyed the Greek rationalist philosophers like Plato because they were *possession cults,* similar to voodoo in Haiti and santeria in Cuba. The rationalists resisted the surrender of individual consciousness to group consciousness. They cherished man's ability to think and rationalize. "The Greeks had known four different kinds of trance: erotic trance, poetic trance, mantric trance, and something Socrates called telestic trance. The last trance comes from the Greek word *teletai* meaning 'ritual.' Amidst frenzied dancing, which Plato in *The Republic* banned as 'unfit for our citizens,' the spirits of the cult came down and took up residence in the bodies of the dancers" (p. 241).

Rouget goes on to say that these were all surviving fragments of the ancient *goddess religions,* all of them *trance–possession cultures in which drums were probably the driving mechanism.*

Music and Science Today

Rhythm is vibration. Scientists tell us that matter itself is in a state of vibration. Every object has a sympathetic vibration and rhythm. Recent scientific studies have shown that certain sounds can affect inert matter.

Several years ago an industrial smokestack began vibrating violently whenever the ventilation fan was turned on. It seems that the ventilation fan was operating at the same frequency, or vibration, as the inert matter in the smokestack. The dangerous vibration suddenly disappeared when the engineers changed the speed of the circulating fan within.

I believe we are on the edge of discovering that music, rhythm, and sound have far greater benefits and in some instances greater dangers than we ever thought possible.

Most of the historical occult and hypnotic (trance–inducing) types of rhythms are repetitive, even monotonous. This is deliberate, for after more than one repetition of a rhythm the controlling left–brain reaction tends toward anger and then impatience, boredom, and finally surrenders, because it appears the music is not going anywhere. It doesn't make sense in a logical, deductive left–brain way.

After a few more repetitions, the left brain surrenders control to the right hemisphere, whereupon individual consciousness is then transferred to a collective group consciousness. The right hemisphere takes control and this transfer is okay with the right hemisphere of the brain, which likes group consciousness, play, and spontaneity.

After four repetitions of a particular rhythm, the critical mind (left hemisphere) "shuts down," allowing the subconscious (right hemisphere) to blend with other minds and the environment. This surrender of control can be exhilarating and cathartic (because in our culture most of the time the left hemisphere is in control), but there are dangers involved. Persons with mental problems and violent or difficult-to-control mood swings need to be careful about this surrender. Keeping some control by the rational left-hemisphere mind is important, particularly when an individual is already struggling with emotional instability.

Harold Courlander, in his important book *A Treasury of Afro-American Folklore* (Crown, 1976), discovered that the basic rhythms used to call up the "spirits" in the Tamil tribes of India, the tribal religions of native Africa, and their American variations, "voodoo" (Haiti), "santeria" (Cuba), and "condomble" (Brazil) are *very similar, if not identical.* They are loud, syncopated, repetitive, and layered (many beats interacting with each other). Also, the drum ensemble is usually the same: three or more drummers, with the "master" drummer playing the largest drum and providing the key rhythms to invoke the spirits.

Most of us are unaware that some of these same occult rhythms have shown up in jazz, pop, and rock music over the past fifty years. These rhythms are potentially dangerous and should not be put in the hands (or the ears) of those uninformed of their strange, potentially dangerous occult powers.

In the hippie era of the 1960s, the combination of drugs that altered consciousness (LSD, peyote, marijuana, and certain mushrooms) and newly-discovered rhythms often took the listener into dangerous places, places that could totally destroy individuals or permanently damage them. The "flower children" were playing with forces beyond their rational control, forces that have been around for eons and were being rediscovered, forces often driven by syncopated rhythms and loud repetitive music.

The Esalen Institute in Big Sur, California was, and still is (for the older hippie), the "in" place to visit, for workshops, therapy, and/or a general spiritual New Age tune-up. Uptight corporate executives fly into Monterey, California, and take a limousine to Big Sur, where they change into sweatpants and tops and are given a drum. They then join a drum circle, where a trained master drummer plays a rhythm and the uptight execs join in by playing the same rhythm on their drum. After awhile the master drummer changes rhythms and the others follow suit. This may go on for hours. At first it is fun, then boring, then irritating, and finally the surrender eventually takes place—at which point the right hemisphere of the brain takes over, giving the left hemisphere a much-needed break. The overall feeling is euphoric and restful. After a period of time, each exec's individual sense of identity is dissolved and somehow he or she finds himself or herself part of some group consciousness via the drumming. This frees the execs from stress.

It all sounds wonderful and fulfilling, but there are some dangers. Dangers involve suddenly switching control from one hemisphere to the other too often and/or to too great a degree. Like drinking, one drink relaxes, two drinks release social inhibitions, and three drinks enters the twilight zone.

As one visitor described it, he could feel his identity slipping away, replaced by some sort of group consciousness. Although frightening at first, most found it very therapeutic. Psychologists tell us we all need to "get away" from ourselves—to detach ourselves from our critical left brain.

Music is one way to do this, and repetitive rhythms are probably the fastest and simplest way to accomplish it. However, a safer way is to sing in a choir or small vocal group, take a piano class, or join an amateur concert, jazz or rock band, or orchestra. Extremes are dangerous in most areas of life, and this is one of them.

Today, "drum circles" are showing up in grade schools, college campuses, and corporate retreats. Many are finding this a fun way to escape left-brain linear goals and enjoy the emphasis on the group and the spontaneity of the moment. Properly used it can be therapeutic. But drum circles, particularly if the drumming goes on for too long and is too syncopated and repetitive, can eventually cause psychological stress. Collective drumming tends to break down individual consciousness and transfer each drummer's identity to what is called a "group" consciousness. This escape from self can be refreshing, but for those with psychological problems it can also increase stress. Careful management of drum circles is needed to avoid negative results.

Music and the Occult

Was there, immediately preceding Western "history," a drum-driven possession trance culture that worshipped the Earth in the form of a Great Mother?

—*Drumming at the Edge of Magic,* p. 207

In my book *All That Jazz: A History of Afro-American Music* (Ardsley House—Scarecrow Press, 1992), I discovered in my research of the tribal music of Africa, Polynesia, India, and some other third world countries, including Tibet, that music was *the most essential part of these pagan ceremonies.* The primary purpose of the music was twofold: (1) certain syncopated and repetitive rhythms *called up the spirit of demonic entity,* and (2) the repetitive sounds placed some in a state of self-hypnosis, then allowing the "demon" god or spirit to take over that person's personality temporarily, using them as a "channeler" for supposedly "spiritual" messages.

"Working our way through the crowd and peering through the doorway, we saw two Buddhist monks. One was *banging a brass plate,* while the other sat cross-legged in front of a small mound of red coals. The latter was a thirty-year-old medium that had been brought in to ascertain the source of the boy's physical problems. *We recognized him immediately as a weak-willed monk whose life was a revolving door for demonic spirits"* (3:26).

"Was the near extinction of the drum from Western European culture due to the fact that the drum had been part of a possession trance culture that had been surprised by its conquerors (the Indo-Europeans)?" (ibid., p. 209).

Slaves often brought demon-driven religions—their sacred rhythms—to the New World from Africa. In most instances, these rhythms combined with Western theology (adoration of saints, etc.) became an important part of native *religions* in Cuba (santeria), Haiti (Vodoun), and Brazil (condomble and macumba).

These hybrid demonic religions are here today, not only in the Caribbean and Latin America, but are now part of the United States' greater religious community, particularly among expatriates from Cuba, Haiti, and Brazil. Many of these demon-driven ancient African rhythms have drifted into the jazz, blues, Latin, and rock music worlds. Now they are showing up on the recordings of some of the more paganized so-called "Christian" rock groups.

"West African drum-driven religions preserved elements of the old goddess religion of the Neolithic. If this is true, then these rhythms are some of the most resilient on the planet. Five, ten, twenty thousand years—who knows how long they have been pulsing?" (ibid., p. 223).

African Christians and pastors immediately recognize these rhythms as spiritually *dangerous* and have issued warnings to their American brothers and sisters in the faith. Note the words from native Christian pastor Stephan Maphosa from Zimbabwe, Africa: "I am very sensitive to rhythms in music for I was a drummer in my village before I became a Christian who participated in demon-calling ceremonies using rhythms. I have recently noticed in many of the so-called 'Christian' music CDs given me by American missionaries and/or their children *the same beat or rhythm we used to call up our native gods*" (4:4).

In another instance, American pastor Joe Myers was visiting and fellowshipping with a group of native pastors in the Ivory Coast nation of Africa. He decided at one of their meetings to play some selections from his daughter's contemporary Christian CDs. "There was an instant verbal and violent reaction. Angrily, these pastors took us to task by asking why we were allowing believers in the USA to 'call up' evil spirits through *the native rhythms of tribal Africa?*" (5:4).

"When the slave ships began playing the waters between the New World and West Africa (1612–1860), everyone thought they carried just strong, expendable bodies. *But they also carried the new counter-culture—maybe even the [ancient] roots of the mother goddess-culture—preserved in the form of drum rhythms that could call down the Orisha (tribal gods) from their time to ours"* (Mickey Hart, *Drumming on the Edge of Magic,* pp. 209–212).

The story of the combining of African and Western European religious traditions on the island of Haiti in the nineteenth century is an interesting one.

The driving drumbeats, bloody sacrifices, and hidden societies are rooted in the fertile religious soil of West Africa. At the time of Napoleon, France owned Haiti. Around 1810 there was a successful Negro slave uprising on the island. Distracted by major wars in Europe, France did not send enough troops to reverse the takeover.

The African native who led the revolt openly boasted that he would turn the island over to the African "gods" if he was successful. Today Haiti, in spite of a potentially strong economy in sugar cane and other crops, is one of the "darkest" spots in the Caribbean, and representative Western democracy seems to have a difficult time finding roots on the island. Many superstitious people even today believe the island is "cursed" because of its dedication to dark spiritual forces.

Some scientists claim that they have traced the beginning of the outbreak of the deadly AIDS virus and its spread to the Western world to one or more of the young male prostitutes imported from Africa to Haiti for the pleasure of American and European male homosexuals on "vacation."

In the first major book on the AIDS epidemic, *And the Band Played On,* the author mentions that Haiti was one of the most popular spots for male homosexuals to vacation because of the easy availability of nubile young African and Haitian boys. According to the book, a very sexually active male airline steward visited the island and contracted AIDS, spreading it widely in various cities in and outside of the United States because of his constant travelling and sexual proclivities. The book also suggests that the young boy who infected the airline steward was brought over from Africa, where the disease supposedly originated.

There is still a lot of research going on regarding the roots of this deadly disease. We do know that the island of Haiti with its occult roots has contributed to the spreading of one of the most deadly viruses known to man.

"Vodoun" is the French name for Haitian voodoo, which thrives on repetitive, loud, syncopated drumbeats, bloody sacrifices, and hidden societies—all practices that originated in West Africa. The guiding spirits of vodoun are called *loas* or *guedes*. Originating in Africa, some of the names of the gods were changed to Catholic saints, but the practice of using repetitive syncopated drumbeats to call up foul evil spirits is as ancient as Sodom and Gomorrah.

Catholic folk culture and ancient African demonic rituals joined forces on the island of Cuba in the form of a native religion called *santeria*. In ethnic clubs known as *cabildos* or *reglas*, tribal drumbeats (on the male and female conga drums) announce the great festivals of Christian Epiphany—Carnival, Holy Week, and Corpus Christi (the week before the beginning of Lent). Members pour onto the streets of Havana (and now New Orleans, Miami, and Los Angeles) wearing masks of Yoruba (West Africa) tribal gods, while hosting icons of Catholic patron saints. Santeria or "the way of the saints" is a highly ritualized occult religion combining the two major influences. Devotees in training must wear pure white clothing. When you are in a Cuban community and you see someone dressed all in white, you can know that they are "in training" or one of the spiritual leaders of the local santeria cult.

There are many Native American religious rituals that involve drumming to a specific beat, dancing, and sometimes spirit possession. They too seek to call up "guiding" spirits. Tourists can visit the reservations of the Hopi and Navajo Indians in Arizona and, at certain times of the year, witness these dances. "Zuni Indians, for example, hold an annual *council of the Fetishes* [a fetish is an everyday object that is given supernatural power through a demonically–driven religion] in which gathered tribal fetishes are worshipped and energized by special night chants and offerings of prayer–meal" (7:10).

According to Joseph Campbell, a leading cultural anthropologist, the "shamans" or "medicine men" were probably the first spiritual leaders. Shamans were and still are master drummers. They are trance masters who have learned to use rhythm to create *altered states of consciousness* (8:163).

There are two types of drum–induced trance. The first is a possession trance. The spirits (called "loa" in voodoo) descend and invade the bodies of the dancers. The second type is a communion trance, where the spirit or soul of the drummer rides his drumbeat like a horse up to the spirit world where he (usually a male) transacts his business in an active rather than a passive (prayer) way (9:163).

There is a consistence to all the demon–driven religions of the world. Their ceremonies all involve ritual drumming, usually highly syncopated patterns, often very loud. Dancing is often part of the ceremony. At some point, someone or several people's personalities "are taken over" (possessed) by dark forces.

Often bloody rituals are included, like the sacrifice of a chicken or small animal, as well as occasional sexual abandonment on the part of the participants. *These same characteristics are often found today in our rock festivals and concerts.* When combined with the use of drugs or alcohol, these powerful forces suddenly unleashed in a naïve modern society can be morally devastating and deadly dangerous as well.

Rhythm and the Church

The early Christian church was well aware of the dangers of pagan, highly rhythmic, syncopated, sensual, loud, and repetitive drum–driven "religious" music. Even Christ warns His followers when praying not to "babble" like the heathen (Matt. 6). As a result, church leaders for almost two thousand years have watched carefully to prevent these kinds of musical practices from sneaking into church music. As late as the 1950s our culture realized and generally accepted that there were two basic musical styles: sacred and secular.

"With the adoption of Christianity by the Romans in A.D. 320, percussive music was banned as 'mischievous' and 'licentious,' the drum and cymbals were particularly singled out as evidence of the 'devil's pomposity'" (9:77).

Modern science recently affirmed the correctness on the part of the church to highly syncopated music. The teachings of ancient India predate recent scientific discoveries. In the Hindu (India) discipline of hatha yoga it is taught that there are seven chakras or energy centers, starting with the base of the spine and moving upward to the pineal gland, located between our eyes. Science confirmed these centers, only naming them as part of the endocrine system. Each of these glands seems to be particularly sensitive to certain types of rhythms and musical vibrations. Highly syncopated rhythms and low-frequency vibrations tent to activate the lower chakras, which then stimulate our sexual glands. A musical form of Viagra® is the result.

In Mickey Hart's book, *Drumming at the Edge of Magic,* he asks the question, "Why is noise that is produced by striking or shaking so widely used in order to communicate with the other [spirit] world?" (10:114).

Mickey later discovered the answer in an acoustic article by psychologist Andrew Neher, "A Physiological Explanation of Unusual Behavior in Ceremonies Involving Drums." Studying drumming in a laboratory setting, Neher found that he was able to "drive" or "entrain" the brainwaves of his experimental subjects down into what is called the *alpha/beta* border, which means that a majority of the electrical activity in their brains was pulsing at a rate of between six and eight cycles per second. The normal alpha/beta pulsation during activity is twelve to thirty cycles per second. This lower pulsation is similar to the deceleration that takes place just before falling asleep.

Neher goes on to conjecture that percussion, particularly drumming, fulfilled the role of "driver" because drums *produced a sound that was so dense, so inharmonic, so fast-decaying and scattered across the frequency band that it overloaded the hearing mechanism. And it was this overloading that helped induce trance* (11:114).

Besides activating the fight-or-flight response, loud, repetitious, syncopated rhythms can also stimulate the lower chakras, the energy centers of our endocrine glands, particularly the gonads or ovaries—the sexual glands.

Repetitive, syncopated, and loud rhythms can also lull the higher part of the brain into a state of hypnosis, allowing easier access to the mid-brain, the seat of our emotions. Actually, Madison Avenue, the center of American advertising in New York City, realized a long time ago that music was the most potent force in a radio or television ad *and rhythm was the most important part of the music in the ad.*

Unfortunately for advertisers, often the ads are too short to put the listener into a deeper state of hypnosis than the merchant would like us to be. Advertising agencies are always looking for ways to override the conservative and controlling left hemisphere of our brains so that the child-like, playful, but impractical right hemisphere can take over. When it does, we usually end up buying something we don't really want or need.

Radio and television ad music is highly definitive of the types of music that trigger certain emotions, depending on the product: lush, sensual rhythms for glamour products like clothes, shampoo, and perfume; Aggressive, loud rhythms when selling a pickup truck; inspirational sounds when dealing with family values, buying houses, family cars, etc. *No one has spent more time and money on how to motivate the buying public through the use of music than today's advertising agencies.*

Paganization of Christian Worship

Even in the black churches raised on spirituals, gospel songs, and other Afro-American music, they still understood the difference between the "devil's" music and the music of the church. Beginning in the late 1950s that barrier began to break down. Secular music has not only joined forces with traditional sacred music in many megachurches today, secularized music has replaced two thousand years of sacred musical traditions.

If these were just social adjustments and changes, the problem would be minimal. However, the belief that you can write religious lyrics to a demonically-driven rhythm and have the song be spiritually sanctified is naïve at best. As Mickey Hart explains, "These instruments [drums, percussion] are capable of releasing certain energies that you contact only when you play" (8:22).

In a recent article, pastor and author David Wilkerson (*The Cross and the Switchblade*) has closely monitored the penetration of liberal churches with contemporary so-called Christian rock music, and he claims that there has been a steady decline in moral sensitivity on the part of the young people and parishioners attending those churches since this trend. He sees Christian rock for the most part as a return to primitive occult worship repackaged with watered-down Christian dogma and words (6:3).

Types of Emotion

In the popular 1970s psychology book *I'm Okay, You're Okay*, Dr. Brendt identified what he called the four basic human emotions:

1. Mad
2. Sad
3. Glad
4. Scared

In my own research I would have to add:

5. Inspirational (religious, patriotic, brotherhood of man, etc.)
6. Humorous
7. Sensual

So there you have it—seven basic human emotions balancing the seven parts of music. When you line up the correct musical formula in each of its categories to reinforce the emotions you wish to portray, you have the "magic" of music, and its foundation is rhythm.

So, what types of rhythm reinforce these emotions? Let's look at the following examples:

» **Mad**—short, very jerky, exaggerated and syncopated rhythms, loud and unpredictable. Musical example: the famous shoot out at the OK Corral in the Wild West is beautifully captured in rhythm and sound by American composer Aaron Copland in his popular western ballet, "Billy the Kid.

» **Sad**—slow, mostly even rhythms with little or no syncopation, long note values. Musical example: "Somewhere" from Leonard Berstein's popular Broadway musical *West Side Story.*

» **Glad**—Fast, running rhythms, slightly syncopated, much repetition building to a big climax. Musical example: music by John Williams from the bicycle chase sequence of the Steven Spielberg film *ET: The Extraterrestrial,* or the scene from *Titanic* where Jack and Rose are both on deck on the highest, most frontal position, letting the wind blow through their hair.

» **Scared**—Slow, winding rhythms with occasional sharp, unpredictable percussion sounds, often with an increasing pulse–beat representing stress and fright. Musical example: opening theme music to Stephen Spielberg's *Jaws.*

» **Inspirational**—Kate Smith singing Irving Berlin's "God Bless America"; Woody Guthrie singing "Blowin' in the Wind"; civil rights protesters of the 1960s singing "We Shall Overcome"; "Battle Hymn of the Republic" on the Fourth of July.

» **Humorous**—Henry Mancini's clever opening theme to *The Pink Panther* with Peter Sellers as Inspector Clouseau.

» **Sensual**—"Dance of the Seven Veils" from the opera *Salome* by Richard Strauss, or the theme to the movie *Mambo Kings.*

The bottom line is that rhythm can enhance or even strongly suggest a particular emotion that the mind can and often does buy into. In other words, music can manipulate our moods (thank God), even without conscious approval. Like all powerful things in life, there's a good and bad side to all of this. On the downside, we are putty in the hands of Madison Avenue, who bombards us twenty–four hours a day with mass advertising on radio, television, and the movies. *Rhythm and music are manipulating us whether we want them to or not.* The good side is that powerful rhythms can enhance drama, cinema, dance, and even sporting events.

Eurhythmics

A relatively new science has been created sometime within the past fifty years: the science and study of rhythm, hence *eurhythmics.* A scientific approach to the mysterious power of music and in particular rhythm has resulted in a whole host of breakthroughs in sports, work, public speaking, singing, and acting as well as musical performance.

An enhanced rhythmic sense can improve our basic skills in one or more of the categories listed above. How do you "enhance" or strengthen your sense of rhythm?

Rhythmic skills are mainly enhanced through *moving to rhythm.* That's right; dance your way right into a more sensitive rhythmic sense! The contraction and relaxation of the large muscle groups of the body to rhythm strengthens our rhythmic sense. When I discovered this, I flashed back on an undergraduate college friend who was a good pianist but had a lousy sense of rhythm. After studying tap-dancing for less than a year his rhythmic sense in his performance improved *dramatically.*

Percussive sound or noise played loudly over time eventually overwhelms the hearing apparatus and this plays a large part in inducing trance—in a sense, it is a "sensory overload" (15:176).

Many believe Afro–Americans have a "natural" rhythm gene that is superior to that of other races. "Blacks have more rhythm!" has always been a common misconception. There is no gene for rhythm. Why then are they in most instances more sophisticated and superior in their rhythmic sensitivity? Primarily because in their subculture people *walked, ran, and dance to music more than the rest of society.* Other subcultures where rhythm is a strong element: Jews, Hispanics, and some Middle Eastern cultures also seem to have a more highly developed rhythmic sense.

Finally, in discussing rhythm in association with the research on the human brain hemispheres at leading medical centers like UCLA Medical Center in Los Angeles, California, research tends to support the fact that the rhythmic skills involved in playing music tend to reside in the right hemisphere of the brain, the gestalt, spontaneous, emotion, and non–linear side. Hence, those with a strong sense of rhythm tend to be in most instances *right–brain* dominant.

Summary

Rhythm is the most powerful part of music, and the most mysterious. We know so little about it. Still, for centuries certain rhythms have been used to trigger emotional responses that can be predicted and manipulated by the unscrupulous. We need to have a healthy respect for rhythm.

Rhythm is not emotionally or spiritually neutral. Music is the language of emotions, and rhythm is the most powerful element. For almost two thousand years the Christian church has had a healthy respect for strong, loud, repetitive, syncopated rhythms and for the most part kept them out of the church—hence the division between sacred and secular music, a division that no longer exists.

Today's champions of loud Christian rock music in the sanctuary are on shaky ground. There is no *biblical, cultural, scientific, or logical reason* to introduce this sensuous, non-sacred music into the sanctuary. Proponents show an amazing arrogance, pride, and lack of sensitivity to members of the congregation when they champion such dangerous changes in worship.

There is a type of music that ministers to and amplifies the carnal side of man. There is another which nurtures and amplifies the spiritual side of man.

"I know that it's possible to ride the rhythms of a drum until you fall into a state of receptivity that can be construed as the beginnings of trance" (Mickey Hart, drummer with the Grateful Dead, 13:176). Underestimating the power of certain rhythms to override your conscious control is just as naïve as believing you can drink a lot of liquor without feeling its effects. Properly and carefully used rhythm can inspire, elevate, relax, activate, and unify the listener. On the other hand, rhythm can be the catalyst that breaks down our cultural and religious barriers and takes us back to primitive, dangerous experiences.

Loud, repetitive, and syncopated rhythms can be a legal substitute for dangerous, mind altering drugs. More care needs to be taken to protect our society from the moral degeneration often found in contemporary music. Yes, there is a Pied Piper that can lead our children out of the village and into darkness, but he doesn't play a flute; *he plays the drums.*

> There have been many times when I've felt as if the drum has carried me to an open door into another world.
>
> —Ibid.

Chapter 22

Form

The second most important element in the seven parts of music is form. We can have "music" with just rhythm, but the minute we stop beating or tapping one rhythm and switch to another, we introduce the next musical element, *form.* Aesthetically, all truly great art offers a balance between unity and variety. Too much unity, boredom; too much variety, chaos. As a result, form, which monitors balance and contrast, is of vital importance.

The simplest musical form is A–B–A: a beginning musical phrase contrasted with a different melody and rhythm, then returning to the original theme. This is the underlying structure of most of the longer, more complex musical forms.

However, as we've already learned, new musical styles began to emerge in the 1960s that ignored these heretofore aesthetic facts. Beginning in the 1960s and much earlier in some musical circles, the new music began to be used as an emotional force field. Music became the cheapest and easiest way to modify an unpleasant environment. It's no accident that the large, portable CD/cassette players were called "ghetto blasters." You might say the uglier and/or more stressful the environment, the more the constant use of music to modify it.

When music is used in this manner, it becomes monothematic and has no more contrast than the patterns you see on wallpaper. *This type of music is totally right–brain driven since there are no intellectual attractions to monotonous repetition.* Today, our modern society has accepted this new type of alternative music—music with no other purpose than emotionally modifying the visual (and aural) environment.

Even classical composers, such as Phillip Glass, descend into the simplistic musical style called "minimalism." When writing this kind of music, the challenge is to see how creative you can be with as little raw material as possible. Obviously form suffers a blow—often almost disappearing—except for the almost inviolate necessity of contrast . . . at some point "A" has to give way to "B," which then must return to "A," although there are examples of modern works where that intellectual principle is ignored. When that happens, the phrases flow from one to another without repetition or, often, serious contrast. This use of musical form is called "through–composed," meaning no return to an earlier musical idea. Musical ideas wander from one to another with no attempt to connect, contrast, or develop to a climactic point, somewhat like looking out the window of a car while zooming along a highway noticing the billboards without any attempt to link them together.

However, even in the most bland and repetitive styles of "new age" or contemporary classical, rock, pop, hip–hop, and rap, you will find some use of musical form, even in the most extreme through-composed piece of music. Form is the organizing force in music, and without it you would have random noise and chaos. Even when music is reduced to its lowest common denominator (that of environment modification), form becomes a necessary ingredient. Below are listed some of the most common traditional forms used in writing songs.

The simple song forms still dominate the structure of vocal music. Folk, religious, ethnic, work and later pop songs traditionally favor one or more of the following simple forms, usually in eight-measure phrases:

» A–B — Two-part song form ("Yankee Doodle")
» A–B–A or A–B–B or A–B–C or A–A–B–A — Three- part song form ("God Bless America" — ABC)
» A–B–C–D or A–A–B–C or A–B–C–D–A — Four-part song form ("Star Spangled Banner" — AABC)

The period in Western Europe history known as the Renaissance (A.D. 1400–1700) was dominated by music written for the dance. Early instrumental music was primarily based on popular dance forms: *the minuet, gigue, sarabande, pavanne,* and many others. These early dances were often combined into collections of contrasting forms. These collections were called instrument suites and usually used the unifying factor of being in the same key.

The forms of this period in secular music were from the popular dances, usually simple two- or three–part song-form. The longest lasting form to come out of the Renaissance period and continue into the Baroque and even the Classical period was the *minuet,* an often-used form for second or third movements of sonatas, concertos, and symphonies. Minuets were usually in three–quarter time, divided into two parts, the second part modulating to another key and called the *trio.*

From the twelfth through the fourteenth centuries church music dominated the musical landscape with the music of the mass and other religious works becoming increasingly complex. Musical form became more and more intricate in the "classical" music of Western Europe from the seventeenth century on, almost as if the music was trying to imitate the complex architecture of the mighty cathedrals of Europe.

Although the Protestant Reformation, led by the former German monk Martin Luther, did return to simple song–forms for their hymns, the larger works (cantatas, oratorios, and masses) by Protestant composers like J. S. Bach and G. F. Handel remained complex in their use of musical form. One might say that the mighty fugues and canons of this period reached the ultimate in musical complexity in the use of form.

The four–voice fugal form became the most complex of the musical styles of the period, likened to the late–*Rococo* styles in church architecture and design. The fugue gradually introduced and layered—one on tope of another—four different *melodies.*

1. Like the manufactured gears of a fine watch, these melodies interacted with one another in the first part of the fugue, called the

exposition or primary statement. Each melody entered on a different note, often in a different key, but would combine smoothly with the original melody.

2. A developmental section where the composer would take portions of the melodic elements introduced in the first part of the fugue and combine them into new musical phrases and melodies would follow the exposition.

3. The final section was called the recapitulation, where the original melodies would return and combine once again with each other, this time all in the same key—followed by an extended ending called a coda.

Below is a diagram of the typical form of the exposition of a four-voice fugue.

1st Theme	Contrasting 2nd Theme	Contrasting 3rd Theme	Contrasting 4th Theme
	1st Theme	Contrasting 2nd Theme	Contrasting 3rd Theme
		1st Theme	Contrasting 2nd Theme
			1st Theme

The intricate musical forms of the Baroque in Western European music explored the extremes of complex musical form, never to be duplicated in later historical styles. Much like the complex architecture of the ancient cathedrals of Europe, the musical forms used in the Baroque were never surpassed in their intellectual and artistic beauty.

The famous Johann Sebastian Bach's composition for organ, "Prelude and Fugue in D minor" is a wonderful example of this most complex form of the Baroque period. Another famous example is the fugal form used in the overture to George Frederick Handel's beautiful and much-loved oratorio, "The Messiah."

The music of the Classical period (late 1700s to early 1800s) in the history of Western European music rebelled against the forms of the Baroque and gravitated to less complex forms. Out of the classical period came the standard form for the first movement of most later sonatas, concertos, and symphonies, a form that would be called the sonata–allegro form. Another form became popular for the last movements of sonatas, concertos, and symphonies—the Rondo form.

Just as the fugue was the ultimate form of the Baroque, the sonata–allegro form was the sine con non of the Classical period. The sonata–allegro form was much like the form of the fugue, in that it contained three large sections:

1. The primary statement of themes (usually two or more), often in contrasting keys. Note: these themes were not combined as in the fugue, but sequential, often with a short musical bridge between the two. Also, the second theme was often in a contrasting key or mode (major become minor, etc.). Like the fugue, this beginning statement of two or more (sometimes three) contrasting themes became known as the *exposition.*
2. The next section, as in the fugue, was called the developmental section. Again, as in the fugue, composers would take material from the earlier themes and explore their potential in combining, inverting, and modifying the earlier themes. This section usually included a great number of modulations to other keys, often staying in the new key very briefly before moving on. These fast–moving changes were called *transitory modulations.*
3. The final section of the first movement sonata–allegro form was called the *recapitulation.* In this section, the earlier themes stated in the exposition return, only this time in the same key and often shortened, followed by an extended ending, the *coda.*

Rondos were mostly used as the overall form for last movements of sonatas, concertos, and symphonies. They were usually brightly, lively, and full of energy and excitement. Basically the rondo form is based on a simple formula:

1. *Primary theme:* A simple, catchy melody is introduced, often after a brief introduction.

2. *Secondary themes:* A contrasting theme is then introduced after the original statement, followed by a return to the original theme. Again, a third theme is introduced, followed once again by a return to the original theme.

3. *Finale:* After several departures and returns to the original theme, there is a final, dramatic statement of the original theme, often decorated with parts of the secondary themes, all building to a grand climax and an extended ending called a *coda.*

The *rondo* and *sonata-allegro* forms became the most important forms to come out of the Classical period (1750-1825). The two greatest composers of that period were Mozart and Haydn. The Mozart "Jupiter" symphony and any of the Haydn "London" symphonies would be excellent examples in illustrating the rondo and sonata-allegro forms.

The rondo form, which originated in dance-forms of the pre-Baroque era, became very popular for the last movements of symphonies, concertos, and sonatas. Usually playful, done in a fast or bright tempo, it provided the necessary sparkle to end an extended work of music. The rondo form, usually after a brief introduction, introduces a simple theme, often a familiar folk song, as in the Schubert "Trout Quintet," or a sparkling theme like the one used by Beethoven in the final movement of his great "Pathetique" piano sonata. This simple theme is then contrasted by a series of variations or departures, each one followed by a return to the rondo theme: A-B-A-C-A-D-A-E-A-F-coda and ending.

The Romantic period of Western European-based classical music extends from the early 1800s through the 1920s in the United States. Few new forms developed. Most were adaptations or modifications to the forms already being used. As composers approached the twentieth century, they began to search for new forms but found very few that lasted. It seems that *form is the most difficult part of music to modify or change.* There are certain intellectual necessities to hold an extended piece of music together in our mind. Those necessities include a logical and meaningful form.

The twentieth century was one of the greatest centuries in mankind's history. More scientific discoveries were made in that single century than in all the other previous centuries combined. Our lives today are dramatically different as a result of the fantastic inventions and discoveries made. Probably the three most important and life affecting were in the areas of communication, transportation, and energy.

Great discoveries and experimentation were also going on the arts in the twentieth century. In music, probably the area of least change was form. It is very hard to come up with a new form that is pleasing and lasting to the listener.

Three twentieth century innovations are of some interest, however.

1. The first is what composers call *through-composition:* a form that does not recycle previously-heard material. A through-composed musical composition would have identifiable phrases, A-B-C, etc., but there would be no repetition of previously played material. This constant move forward using new material is often typical of the driving, relentless energy of the twentieth century in other fields.

2. Most musical phrases are in four or eight measure lengths. Twentieth century composers began experimenting with non-symmetrical phrases, where one phrase may be five measures, the next, seven measures, and so on. This produces an effect of "randomness" that can be quite effective, and when combined with melodic dissonance, somewhat unsettling and disturbing.

3. Minimalism was an artistic reaction to the extreme melodic and harmonic complexities of previous eras. Minimalism can and does affect all parts of music, including form. Basically minimalism is making music with as little material as possible. In form, it means simple, short phrases, often repeated. Minimalism concentrates more on creating an emotional force field with music that produces a particular mood than entertaining the logical left-brain through intellectual development of themes.

Form is a logical necessity to intellectually-based music. It is not important to dance music, or some types of religious or mood-altering music. Form is definitely the most "left-brain" of all the parts of music. By ignoring it, we ignore the desperate desire on the part of the intellectual part of the brain to keep track of all the themes and their development. Somehow this process is aesthetically rewarding.

The taller the building, the greater knowledge of architecture is required to build it. The longer the piece of music, the greater knowledge of form is required. Many so-called "popular" musicians have bravely ventured into the world of extended pieces of music (ten minutes or longer) and have fallen flat on their face. George Gershwin was smart enough to run to the New York Public Library and check out books on composition and form when Paul Whiteman commissioned him in 1924 to write "Rhapsody in Blue" and later the "Gershwin Piano Concerto" for the New York Philharmonic Orchestra.

Right-brain music is spontaneous and seldom preconceived. Consequently, the form is also immediate. In most instances, right-brain music relies on several basic forms: (1) theme and variations, (2) rondo, or (3) through-composed phrases.

When we begin to leave the world of form, we begin to shift music more and more to the right hemisphere of the brain, where music becomes a pleasant modification of our moods or our environment, but offers little or no intellectual stimulation. The rock group the Rolling Stones' popular hit "I Can't Get No Satisfaction" cannot be compared in any way, shape, or form, to a Puccini opera aria and certainly not to a Beethoven symphony. However, it is obviously rewarding to the right-brain dominant Rolling Stones' fan.

The twentieth century witnessed an extreme shift in our culture from being a left-brain dominant culture to being a right-brain dominant society. In music nowhere was that more evident than in the use of form. The intellectual demands of the left brain gave way to the playful spontaneity of the right brain, allowing for extreme repetition, simplicity, and contrasts in form.

Summary

We no longer build church buildings like the great cathedrals of Europe, and we no longer write music that challenges our left-brain.

Slick, sleek, modern, streamlined, fast, and repetitious—music reluctantly in some instances joins the shift from left to right, always still seeking balance when it can. By its very nature form is left–brain dominant because it involves organization, planning, and contemplation, as well as balance and logic.

Right–brain culture demands none of the above, hence, musical performances that are totally spontaneous and unplanned, much like a Jackson Pollack painting, where the frantic splashes of paint on a giant canvas during red–hot periods of inspiration sometimes (not often) result in a permanent thing of beauty that we can hang on our wall.

Chapter 23

Melody

Surprisingly, melody is third in the list of importance and necessity in the structure of music. A great deal of the music of the world today is primarily rhythmic in nature, including today's popular rap music. However, after rhythm and form, melody is the next ingredient in importance. Melody held top billing in the music of Western civilization until the increasing input from third world nations in the twentieth century. Today, rhythm holds the top spot, with melody coming in a close second in today's pop culture.

Cultures north of the equator (or extreme south) tend to favor melody over rhythm. There are some cultural, climatological, and geographic differences that caused music to go in different directions in Western Europe, away from the rhythmic emphasis and toward melody.

Melodic favoritism seems to be characteristic of left–brain dominant cultures. Most melody–dominant societies reside north of the equator. Sociologists tell us that, possibly, survival skills in this highly seasonal environment (particularly during the ice age) demanded a more linear, logical planned approach to survival. Severe climate change forced man to plan ahead—if he wanted to survive. Food, clothing, shelter, and wood for a fire had to be planned for and stored. These environmental survival necessities caused societies north of the equator to develop a left–brain bias. In music, this translated into an emphasis on melody, harmony, and form.

One could even say that one of the great cultural heritages in the world today is the vast repertoire of beautiful melodies that flowed out of Western and Eastern Europe and Russia. Later, North America would add to this cultural heritage of beautiful melodies.

Except for the brilliant bossa novas of Antonio Carlos Jobim (Brazil), the classical music of Villa Lobos (Brazil), Chavez (Mexico), and Ernesto Lecuana of Cuba ("Malagueña"), there have been few great melodies or classical works that became part of the music repertoire from Latin America. The music of the Middle East and Far East sounds exotic to our ears, but most of us find the melodic ideas simplistic, overly repetitive, and based on strange and unusual scales and intervals difficult for listeners from the Americas (Canada, United States, Latin America) to relate to. Some of the folk music to come out of Brazil, Mexico, Peru, and the Caribbean has been new and exciting, but for the most part North America continued the European tradition of exalting melody over rhythm in our music.

Melody is a combination of rhythm and intervals. An interval is the distance between two notes. The smallest interval in traditional music (some cultures have smaller intervals) is a half step. There are twelve half steps to an octave. An octave is a doubling of the vibration of the original note. For instance, if I play "A" (above middle C) on the piano, its vibration is 440 vibrations per second. An octave higher, the vibrations would be 880 vibrations per second. An octave lower would be 220 vibrations per second, and so on.

The human ear can detect low–frequency vibrations down into the low double digits, 18vb, etc., and on up at the higher end into the stratosphere, actually higher than any written note, somewhere around 12,000 vibrations per second. Women tend to have a greater sensitivity to high frequencies than men do. As we age, most of us begin to lose some of our natural ability to hear extreme high and low frequencies in music.

A woman's hearing loss in this area is generally less than a man. Could this be why classical music audiences today tend to be older, with women outnumbering men almost two to one? This faster degeneration on the part of men in hearing extreme low and high frequencies has nothing to do with the selective hearing husbands have used as an excuse when their wives interrupt their ball games on television to ask them to do a simple chore.

Those who have been exposed to loud rock music or industrial noise of 80db and above on a regular basis lose not only the ability to hear the extreme frequencies, *they also tend to lose their ability to hear mid-range frequencies as well.* Chronic use of some recreational drugs such as cocaine can flatten out the mid-range, making it difficult to perceive small adjustments in volume, tone, and pitch in recorded of live music.

Within the octave, as stated earlier, there are twelve half steps. By combining one note with another higher or lower note, we can produce a wide range of intervals. These intervals are classified as:

1. Perfect (P4, C–F; P5, C–G)
2. Consonant (Major 3rd, C–E; Minor 3rd, C–E♭; Major 6th, C–A; Minor 6th, C–A♭)
3. Mildly Dissonant (Major 2nd, C–D; Minor 7th, C–B♭)
4. Sharply Dissonant (Minor 2nd, C–D♭; Augmented 4th, C–F♯)

Any interval larger than an octave is called a "compound" interval and basically duplicates the sound of the original interval within the octave, only with greater distances in-between. Commonly used compound intervals include (remember, the second note is always beyond the octave):

1. 9th—Minor (C–D♭), Major (C–D)
2. 11th (C–F), Augmented 11th (C–F♯)
3. 13th (C–A)

Enharmonic intervals are intervals that sound the same but can be written two different ways. The reason for this is to allow the reader to see the interval within the context of the key, or tonal center of the piece. Common enharmonic intervals include:

1. Augmented tonic (C–C♯), Minor 2nd (C–D♭)
2. Augmented 2nd (C–D♯), Minor 3rd (C–E♭)
3. Augmented 4th (C–F♯), Diminished 5th (C–G♯)
4. Augmented 6th (C–A♯), Minor 6th (C–A♭)

Music is a language of emotion. Every interval in music conveys some type of emotional meaning or feeling. It is hard to define feelings with specific words, but basically each interval could be described as projecting the following emotional feelings, no matter how fleeting:

1. Perfect Intervals: Octave, Perfect 4th and Perfect 5th—Suggests space, power, the outdoors, grandiose ideas, panoramic scenes, and emotional stability.
2. Melodic Intervals: Major and Minor 3rds and 6ths—Express love, beauty, pleasant memories, places, people, and general happiness and contentment; Minor 3rds and 6ths have a touch of sadness, suggesting transitory happiness (not lasting).
3. Mildly Dissonant Intervals: Major 2nd, Minor 7th, Major 9th—These intervals suggest excitement, energy, forward movement, exhilaration, anticipation, a distant danger or subtle threat, a challenge, conflicting emotions.
4. Dissonant Intervals: Minor 2nd, Augmented 4th, Major 7th, Minor 9th—These harsh, clashing intervals suggest extreme danger, anger, pain, horror, bad memories, rage, tension, tragedy, sudden loss, and overwhelming fear.

The composer uses intervals within their melodies to set up an emotional force field for the listener. The more you wish to emphasize a particular emotion, the more you use those intervals in your melody. Want happy melodies? Write mostly 3rds and 6ths. Want melodies suggesting power and space? Emphasize the perfect intervals. Want elation, challenge, and positive anticipation? Emphasize the mild dissonant intervals. Want fear, terror, and negative anticipation (defeat, sorrow)? Emphasize the sharp dissonances in your melodies.

How a composer uses intervals is the primary determiner of the overall emotional impact of a specific melody. Let's say I was contracted to write the background music for a Hollywood film. This is not a new experience, for I have scored the soundtracks for five films, many documentaries, radio and television jingles, and have writing the "incidental" background music for a modern production of Shakespeare's Hamlet at the University of Southern California. Let's say I had to make decisions on musical intervals on the following scenes. The intervals listed below would be the dominant intervals, but others would be used as well to give coherence to the music:

1. **Love scene:** Intervals, Major and Minor 3rds, with some mild dissonant intervals like Minor 7ths and Major 9ths to express love's longing.
2. **Horror or Terror** (or coming disaster): Major dissonances—2nds and 9ths, Augmented 4th, Major 7th. These dissonant intervals are disturbing and threatening in sound; unpleasant because of the tension they produce.
3. **Power** (like the triumphant entrance into Rome of a returning army): Perfect 4ths, 5ths, octaves, and some mild dissonance. The most powerful sounding interval is the Perfect 4th. The hollow sound of the Perfect 5th suggests strength and triumph. Minor 7ths and Major 9ths suggest excitement and victory.

Obviously, rhythm, form, melody, countermelody, harmony (chords), texture (high or low register, tonal quality), and style (tempo, dynamics, and articulation) would fill out their important part of the emotional impact (as well as the choice of musical instruments or voices). *Each of the decisions made in choosing what and how to combine these musical elements either adds to or detracts from the drama being portrayed on the screen.*

Obviously some composers are better at this than others. Successful film composers like Maurice Jarre, John Barry, Elmer Bernstein, John Williams, James Horner, Jerry Goldsmith, Danny Elfman, and Bill Conti, and many more, have intuitively or intellectually understood the role of the film composer and how to mold their music to the screen, to specifically enhance and raise the intent of the film director's efforts to a new level. Not everyone can do this well. Even composers in other media who try their hand at film scores often fail to recognize the subtleties involved in using music to enhance drama.

Probably the most powerful musical form to come out of Western Europe was opera. In the early stages of opera's development (seventeenth and eighteenth centuries) the music was usually stronger and more emphasized than the libretto (story line). By the time of Richard Wagner and Puccini (1800s and 1900s), the libretto began to take center stage, dominating the music. All this anticipated the even more realistic and powerful development of modern cinema, where the visual effects, the drama, and music can combine to be almost overwhelming in power and scope.

One of the most important musical ideas to develop out of late operatic music–drama was the use of the lied–motif, the musical cue that follows specific characters in the opera through the entire work. Whenever that individual appears, or that particular coming-together of lovers or enemies, the same musical cue is used. This recurring theme attached to specific actors or combination of actors enhances the drama. The lied–motif has also been used successfully in film scores like Elmer Bernstein's *The Magnificent Seven*, Maurice Jarre's *Dr. Zhivago, Lawrence of Arabia*, and many others.

Melody and the Human Brain

According to recent discoveries in how the human brain operates, the right hemisphere seems to be the seat of long-term memory. It is also the storage space for melody. Our ancient forefathers must have intuitively known this because in more primitive societies *all important information is sung to an easily recognizable melody.* This guarantees long-term memory and makes it easier for a non–literate culture to store and preserve information to hand down to the next generation.

Nursery rhymes, lullabies, work songs, war songs, and historical legends, courting songs, songs related to marriage, birth, death, and humorous songs—all are stored in long-term memory by setting them to music. Not long ago well-known film and jazz composer Quincy Jones recorded an audio history of Afro-Americans, for truly their culture was until recently an aural culture, their history largely preserved in music.

There has never been a major cultural, political, religious, or artistic movement that was not led by a song or songs. Major traumas to a culture like the Great Depression of 1929-1939 in the United States, WWI, and WWII were preserved in melodies and folk songs like Woody Guthrie's "Blowin' in the Wind," the memorable "Fanfare for the Common Man" of Aaron Copeland, and Irving Berlin's "God Bless America."

The folk music of a culture can often reveal more about the culture than articles and books, particularly since music is a language of *emotion* and most of us are motivated more by emotion than logic, although we may deny it.

Summary

Melody is a most powerful ingredient in music. How we all cherish certain favorite melodies that we associate with important events in our lives, celebrations of life at its various stages. Writing a great melody is a great accomplishment, a difficult task for even the most gifted composer. Finding the right rhythm, the right form, the right intervals in the melody and in the case of song, the right lyrics and getting them to all line up and enhance one another, is one of the reasons great melodies, whatever the musical style, are rare and precious.

Chapter 24

Countermelody

It's hard for us to imagine in today's world that the concept of organizing notes vertically into what we call "chords" was foreign to classical composers in Europe until the eighteenth century. Simultaneous sounds that combined pleasingly were until then a pleasant surprise, a coincidental coming together of notes only as a result of a very careful combining of one horizontal melodic idea with another.

Most of the native music of third world countries today does not have a system of what we would call "harmony," the concept of organizing three or more notes simultaneously into what we call chords. The emphasis on chords and harmony became a primary characteristic of the music of Western and Eastern Europe, as well as the United States.

Counterpoint is the combining of two or more melodies in such a way that they complement one another. The art of counterpoint is called "polyphony," which means "many voices." This complex composing technique reached its zenith in the music of Johann Sebastian Bach at the beginning of the eighteenth century. Still today—even in jazz or rock groups, one often hears the primary melody played by the lead guitar or sung by the lead singer. The bass line becomes the countermelody, while the rhythm guitar and/or the keyboard player plunks down the chords, while the drum keeps time and add appropriate accents.

Counterpoint is a standard feature of the tribal music of Africa, India, Polynesia, and parts of the Middle East and Asia. In many instances there may be as many as six or seven independent rhythmic lines combining simultaneously. Each rhythm is generally added one at a time, often with the "master drummer" improvising the final rhythm on top of all the others. This exciting, churning, driving sound is preserved today in the Brazilian *samba,* the Cuban *mambo,* and the Dominican *meringue.* Today, this exciting, rich, rhythmically polyphonic style is also characteristic of the Caribbean *calypso* and the popular music of South Africa called *high life.*

Johann Sebastian Bach, the leader and most definitive Western European composer of polyphony in the late seventeenth and eighteenth centuries, was consumed with preserving the essence of this complex form of musical composition and expression called *counterpoint* or *polyphony.* Toward the end of his life, in an attempt to record and preserve all that he had learned about this complex way of writing music, he, himself, paid to have the printing plates engraved with the essence of his technique in a book called *The Art of the Fugue.*

The musical examples in Bach's *The Art of the Fugue* are performable. Although no specific instrumentation is given, most of the examples can be played on keyboard or by a woodwind, brass, or string quartet. *The Art of the Fugue* is a thesaurus, a reservoir of all the important techniques in this style of writing, that became old-fashioned even before Bach's death.

Johann Sebastian Bach and George Frederick Handel were the last of the great polyphonists, until two hundred years later when some twentieth century composers rediscovered this challenging art.

How Do You Recognize It?

When you hear a melody or rhythm and then perceive another melody or rhythm sounding against the original *at the same time,* you have *counterpoint.* In jazz, rhythm and blues, and rock often the bass line working against the original melody is the counterpoint. In Latin American music, when you hear two or more rhythms being played against each other simultaneously, you have rhythmic counterpoint.

Sometimes counterpoint expresses itself in simple "rounds," melodies that repeat with entrances at different points, producing overlapping melodies, like "Row, Row, Row Your Boat" and "Frere Jacques."

The overlapping counterpoint melodies can become incredibly complex, like the "Sextet" from the opera *Lucia DeLammor* by Donizetti, where the composer introduces melodically one person at a time, each singing his or her own song, which is added to *the others*. Donizetti adds to this complex polyphonic aria until there are eventually six melodies, all independent of each other, yet sounding musically okay when sung simultaneously.

More recently, Frank Loesser, the great Broadway and Hollywood film composer, reintroduced this quaint and complex way of writing in the opening of his wildly successful Broadway musical *Guys and Dolls.* The opening vocal number after the overture was called "Fugue for Tinhorns."

Summary

Counterpoint in the music of Western Europe reached its zenith in musical forms like the fugue, written by master craftsmen like Bach and Handel. In the eighteenth century the vertical organization of notes into "chords" began to take precedent as a compositional device—aided by the increasing popularity of opera.

The music of many of the third world nations is often polyphonic, but the counterpoint is primarily rhythmic rather than melodic. Today we hear it often in the music of the Native American Indians, the Middle East, parts of Asia, Africa, Polynesia, and Latin America, particularly the widely popular *samba* and *bossa nova* from Brazil.

The brain enjoys the challenge of trying to keep track of the multiple sensory inputs it is receiving from polyphony. The right brain is challenged and excited by the complexity of the music; the left hemisphere is challenged intellectually in being able to distinguish and identify the various melodies and/or rhythms being sounded simultaneously. Although polyphony in the classical sense died out as the dominant musical style by the middle of the eighteenth century in Europe, today most of our ethnic and pop music is polyphonic—primarily rhythmic in character.

Chapter 25

Harmony

As we stated earlier, all seven parts of music help to create emotional force fields that are conveyed to the listener through the auditory nerves which are connected directly to the midbrain, the primary source of our emotions.

Again, as recorded earlier in this study, the wide range of human emotions can be reduced to seven basic ingredients: (1) mad, (2) sad, (3) glad, (4) scared, (5) sensual, (6) humorous, and (7) inspirational. Music's job is to trigger one or more of these emotions through musical ideas expressed via the seven parts of the musical performance.

A composer's failure to understand this process results in a hit-or-miss attempt at trying to communicate emotion through music. *If the composer does not know what emotion or emotions he or she wishes to express through music, the audience will fail to understand the purpose of the performance or the reason for writing that particular piece of music.*

After the politically extreme horrors of World War II, there was a group of Western European composers who tried to write "emotionless" music. Terrified by the emotional excesses of fascism and communism, these composers, including such names as Schoenberg, Berg, Boulez, Stockhausen, and Schillinger, tried to divorce themselves from emotion of any kind when composing. They used mathematical principles developed by Schoenberg and Schillinger. They called their new style "patterns of sound," and attacked any critic who attached an emotion to any part of their work. Needless to say their music today is seldom programmed, played, or enjoyed.

Our consumer–led radio and television advertisers have precon-ditioned us to respond to certain styles and types of music behind familiar ads for commercial products, television show themes, or motion picture soundtracks. Madison Avenue and Hollywood have done a good job preconditioning us to react to basic musical styles that are carefully researched and designed to trigger specific emo-tions. Young children of today can sing many of the television show themes or the music used behind popular commercials, but few can sing nursery rhymes, native folk songs, or patriotic favorites. "See the USA in your Chevrolet" (song) has replaced "Polly Wolly Doodle" (folk song).

Lining Up Together

When all seven parts of a musical work line up expressing the same emotion, the results are very powerful. When the various parts of a musical composition send conflicting emotions, the result is often confusion and disappointment. *When all seven parts set in motion the same emotion the results are powerful.*

One could go so far as to say that one of the fundamental and most objective criteria for determining whether a particular musical work is "good" or "bad" is determined by how well these seven parts support each other by expressing the same feelings. We forget that audiences crave to "feel" through music. They pay to hear music that triggers emotions, memories, and precious moments in life. Sadly, too few composers today realize this, being too caught up in their own ego, demanding audiences react to music that is not emotion-ally expressive or is full of conflicting ideas.

In harmony, every chord, every chord progression, every chord voicing, sets in motion some type of emotion. Harmony is the com-bining of three or more musical sounds vertically (all sounded at the same time) into what are called "chords." Generally it takes three notes to have a "chord," although chords can be suggested with even two notes.

Philip Rameau, eighteenth century French court composer, wrote an article in an early musicological journal around 1725 argu-ing for a new and exciting concept in musical composition that he had just discovered—the organization of three or more notes sounded together and conceived vertically, to be called "chords." The invention of chords naturally led to a wide range of chord types, chord progressions, and chord voicing.

The great German composer Johann Sebastian Bach wrote a rebuttal to Rameau's article, claiming that the approach to composition would "destroy" and/or replace polyphony—the favorite musical style of the Baroque, which it eventually did. The new style ushered in the "Classical" period, most ably expressed by Franz Joseph Haydn, Muzio Clementi, Wolfgang Amadeus Mozart, and other lesser-known composers. Chords underneath melody, not counterpoint, became the prevalent style. Opera had a great deal to do with this, with its increasing popularity and emphasis on arias (songs). Another name for this new style is *homophony.*

Three-note chords are called "triads." Four-note chords are called "seventh chords." There are basically four things you can do to a chord: (a) you can alter it (raise or lower one of the notes one-half step), (b) extend it (add additional intervals; sevenths, ninths, elevenths, thirteenths, etc., (c) substitute another chord for the original chord, and (d) voice the chord—open, closed, or partially open.

Chords in these early stages of harmonic development were built on the interval of the third: major and minor thirds. When the system, called *tertular harmony,* reached its maximum potential in the early twentieth century in Western European classical music, composers began searching for other intervals upon which they could build chords besides major and minor thirds. Eventually they settled on the new sounds of chords built on fourths. This new harmonic system was called *quartal harmony.*

This new system gradually emerged from esoteric classical pieces into jazz and pop music by the end of the century. Quartal harmony creates an entirely different emotional force field than tertular—projecting a feeling of power, openness, and ambiguity that is not only new and refreshing, but more accurately reflects the culture of our time.

The most common chord progression in early music, both in major keys and minor keys, is the progression based on the chord built on the first degree of the scale, moving to the chord built on the fourth degree of the scale, moving to the chord built on the fifth note of the scale. This chord often extended through the seventh (four-note chord).

The late Romantic-era classical composers like Brahms, Wagner, and Richard Strauss, and later jazz composers and arrangers like Stan Kenton and Duke Ellington, explored the extremes of chord extensions (9ths, 11ths, 13ths) until composers began searching for new ways of using chords, which led eventually to moving away from tertular harmony to quartal harmony.

Art tends to mimic its environment. The sounds commonly heard by classical composers—mostly rural in nature—have been replaced today by the harder, more ambiguous mechanical and electronic sounds of our urban environment. The fast-paced, high-stress environment of today suggests different rhythms, form, melody, countermelody, harmony, texture, and style. In harmony this was reflected in a move away from tertular harmony (chords built on thirds) to quartal harmony (chords built on fourths).

The only other possible harmonic structural system besides tertular and quartal is cluster harmony. In this system, chords are built on seconds, sevenths, and ninths. Chords built in this manner are usually highly dissonant and independent of smooth chordal progressions. Again, this system is refreshing, but it moves to the edge of the possible disappearance of any type of harmonic system at all.

Chords can be voiced or played in three different ways: (1) closed, (2) partially open, or (3) wide open. Closed voicing of a chord occurs when all the notes of the chord are as close together as they can be written. Partially open means one or two notes of a chord are dropped or raised an octave. Wide open means that there is as much space as possible between chord tones.

1. Closed voicing of chords suggests high energy, fast-paced action, powerful forward movement, brilliance, and enthusiasm or busy kinesthetic (movement) activity.
2. Partially-open voicing makes the chord sound more mellow, richer, thicker, and slightly more powerful (more weight).

3. Wide-open voicing makes the chord sound big, heavy, and very powerful. This voicing also suggests open space—sparse landscape, outer space.

4. In dance or cinema, fast-moving scenes demand closed voicing. Occasional accents require partial-openness, while dramatic climaxes, strong accents, awesome power, or inspiration demand wide-open chord voicing.

Western European music for the most part was built on the major scale (do-re-mi-fa-sol-la-ti-do) and the minor scale (la-ti-do-re-mi-fa-sol-la). Later, other scales, sometimes called "modes," were introduced. Initially these new scales were built on other beginning and ending notes of the major scale. For instance, the *Dorian* mode begins and ends on the second note of the major scale (re-me-fa-sol-la-ti-do-re). Surprisingly, this sleight-of-hand (building new scales on other notes of the major scale) opened up a whole Pandora's box of new feelings and expressions.

Later, more exotic scales were introduced: the chromatic scale (every note within an octave—twelve notes); the whole-tone scale (all whole steps); the pentatonic scale (five notes), so peculiar to Chinese and Japanese music (do-re-fa-sol-la); and the exotic Middle Eastern scale (do-rah-mi-fa-sol-leh-ti-do), or its Jewish cousin (do-rah-mi-fa-sol-leh-the-do).

Later, in the Afro-American music developing in the United States (spirituals, gospel, blues, jazz, rhythm and blues, etc.), one of the most common scales of our time developed, the "blues" scale (do-re-meh-fa-fi-sol-lah-the-do). A "blues" scale is a major scale with the third, fifth, and seventh notes lowered one-half step *without altering these notes in the harmony or the accompanying chords.*

The dissonance or clash between the lowered notes in the melody and the regular notes in the chords produce the "blues" effect, a musical sound that has made the blues scale the most popular scale in the world beginning in the second half of the twentieth century.

When two or more notes of a chord clash, they create tension, which is called "dissonance" in music. Dissonant chords suggest negative emotions—mention, fear, anger, rage, envy, anxiety, discomfort. Dissonance demands resolution, just as we look for ways to solve problems in our life that create tension. It is aesthetically very satisfying to the listener to hear the tension–producing clash of a dissonant interval or chord "resolving" to a less dissonant interval or chord.

This tension–release principle is found in all the arts. Circumstances in the plot line of a play, TV show, or movie create tension (example: car chase scenes). These tensions usually build to a climax through a series of ever–increasing tension–release scenes until the final tension is released, once and for all. This same aesthetic effect is common in most music. Dissonance melodically or harmonically demands resolution to consonance. Dissonant chords demand resolution to consonant chords, satisfying the listener's desire for release of tension.

Just as Western civilization pioneered architecture in the building of taller and taller buildings—something not possible before the understanding of stress and balance via advanced mathematics like trigonometry and calculus—our civilization built larger and larger chords, even developing new systems for building chords until the potential emotional effect in these new areas had been exhausted. While tribal Africa music emphasizes multi–layered rhythms and cyclic forms, Western European art-music emphasizes melody, harmony, and form as its greatest means of musical expression.

Today, many serious composers in our culture have totally discarded the traditional harmonic systems and have begun to explore new ways to express themselves through modern music, *independent of the guiding rules and practices of the past.* One of the most innovative and popular new systems to develop out of this experimental phase of modern music has been the development of what is called *dodecaphonic, serial composition,* or *twelve–tone composition* (one and the same).

This system uses complex mathematical formulas in place of traditional melodic and harmonic practices. Serial composition takes the twelve half–steps within the octave and randomly selects notes to make up a melody. *No note can be repeated until all twelve notes have been introduced.* Generally speaking, the composer is careful not to outline a familiar tertular chord with his or her selection of melodic notes. Emphasis is also in dissonant and mild dissonant intervals, followed by perfect intervals. Composers avoid the warm, fuzzy sounds of the major and minor thirds and sixths as much as possible.

Once the twelve notes have been selected, the new melody can be played forward or backward, inverted, or transposed up or down through the eleven other half–steps available within the octave. A grouping of twelve different notes within the octave in this manner is called a *tone row*. As you can see, this system can generate a large number of melodic ideas from one tone row.

Accompaniment chords can be created in the same manner. Group the first four tones into one chord (1–2–3–4), then the next four notes into the second chord in the progression (5–6–7–8), and finally the third chord in the progression by grouping the final four melodic notes into a chord as well (9–10–11–12). Another way to create new chords is to skip a melodic note (i.e., the first chord could be 1–3–5–7 notes of the tone row).

The mathematical possibilities are endless. This return to early Greek concepts of marrying music and mathematics has produced some revolutionary new ways of writing music. Many of these techniques are extremely helpful to commercial composers, particularly those who write for film, since divine inspiration is no longer the driving force behind creation.

Composers no longer have to wait for a musical idea, but can instead, by using some of these techniques begin composing new music *immediately.* This is a great help when it is two a.m. and you—the film composer—have a recording session for a new film soundtrack scheduled for nine a.m. Pioneers in this field were mostly German composers active in the early twentieth century—Arnold Schoenberg, Alben Berg, Stockhausen, and the French composer Pierre Boulez. The system works something like this:

1. Write out the chromatic scale (C–C♯–D–D♯–E–F–F♯–G–G♯–A–A♯–B–C.)
2. Select notes randomly to include in a melody . . . never repeating

a note until all others have been heard. (C–F♯–F–B–C♯–G–G♯–D–D♯–A–A♯–E).

3. Play this melody forward, then backward, then invert it (turn it upside down), and then transpose it up or down by a half-step until you have built this same melody on every note of the chromatic scale. You will discover that this one tone row can generate thirty-six new melodic and harmonic possibilities!

4. Make up accompanying chords in a like manner, building for instance a four-note chord on the first, fourth, lowered fifty, and seventh notes of the scale, and so on.

This style of music is so intensely dissonant and disconnected, it is often uncomfortable to listen to for long periods of time. However, it has proven to be extremely valuable in commercial writing, where modern times require modern sounds to reflect the alienation, open exploration of space, and other anxieties that attack us today.

George Gershwin used some of these techniques in writing his folk opera *Porgy and Bess,* and Glenn Miller used some of these techniques in writing arrangements for his popular swing orchestra. Most Hollywood film and television background music composers use the above techniques regularly. When there is a balance between true artistic creativity and new mathematical techniques applied to writing music, the results can be exciting and even spectacular.

The Future

Today it seems that composers have exhausted all the potential of harmonic systems; taking the building of chords and chord progressions to their maximum potential As the world and our society moves slowly toward a more right-brain bias, we find the popular music of the day moving away from using any harmonic system at all. A good example is rap and a lot of hip-hop music of today. Melody and harmony are losing their supremacy in twenty-first century music, while rhythmic counterpoint and electronic special effects are beginning to take their place.

The only new avenue to explore is the use of intervals slightly smaller than the half–step, the smallest interval used in our music up until now. Interestingly enough, third world cultures from Africa, India, Polynesia, and the Middle East are already using intervals smaller than our half–step, and have been using them for centuries.

One of the reasons we settled on our half–step was because of the technical demands of the keyboard. Playing a keyboard instrument would become incredibly more complex if there were more than twelve half–steps to an octave. Today tonal–sensitive synthesizer keyboards can play micro–intervals by changing pressure by bending the finger to the left or right on each key. As a result, there is a great rush in both classical composition and pop/rock to explore micro–intervals in writing, playing, or singing new music. Afro-Americans have been using micro–intervals already in their sliding vocal and guitar styles in blues, rhythm and blues, jazz, and hip–hop.

Harmony reflects the complexities of the Industrial Revolution, which reached its zenith in the early twentieth century, and is today being challenged by the new developments in electronics, nuclear, solar, and thermal energy, and biotechnologies.

Summary

I'm sure composers will eventually discover new and wonderful ways of expressing the times in which they live, using this modern technology to do so. Stan Kenton, the great jazz composer/band leader once said that all true art must express itself through the environment of its time. I believe that is a correct assessment. In the meantime, it is still a pleasure to hear a beautiful chord resolve to another beautiful chord underneath a lovely melody.

Chapter 26

Texture

The sixth characteristic, or part of music, out of seven is *texture*. Texture can be divided into two parts: (a) tone quality, and (b) register (high, medium, low). Then there are four distinct types of musical tone quality: (a) bright, (b) clear, (c) dark, and (d) raspy (a la Louis Armstrong).

A "bright" tone has a metallic ring or zing to it. It is an edgy, penetrating sound. The trumpet has been traditionally the "brightest" sounding instrument in the orchestra. Today, the electric guitar, when the player turns up the treble controls and turns down the midrange and bass control, can produce a very bright sound. In orchestral music, the piccolo, the trumpet, bells and the xylophone probably have the "brightest" sounds. Singers vary with the tone quality they favor.

Ethel Merman, a great star of Broadway shows in the 1920s–1940s, had a very "bright" tone could cut through the orchestra and could easily be heard in the back of the theater. A bright tone is edgy, metallic, and cuts through other tone qualities in an ensemble. "Bell-like" is another way of describing a bright musical sound or tone. A bright tone suggests enthusiasm, happiness, and excitement, building toward a climax and sometimes danger

A "clear" tone is the most common tone quality in music. Violins, flutes, saxophones, jazz guitars, muted trumpets, and most sopranos and tenors have a "clear" tone. Violas and cellos can have a "clear" tone in their higher register, as do trombones, clarinets, and French horns. A clear tone suggests stability, positivity, being comfortable, and usually is connected with positive emotions and positive kinesthetic action by dancers and/or cinema scenes.

Dark tones are characteristic of clarinets in their lower register, along with trombones, flugelhorns, French horns in the middle and low register, English horns, and bass clarinets. Many Afro–American singers and speakers have a "dark" tone (no pun intended), as well as jazz singers like Sarah Vaughan, Billy Eckstein, and Nina Simone. A "dark" tone suggests intimacy, sexiness, hidden danger, male virility, and female sexuality, and can suggest strength and power as well. It is used in dance and cinema to amplify those emotions, plus the openness of physical space (the rolling prairie) or outer space.

The popularity of the "raspy" tone grew out of tribal African instruments like the gourd–shakers and scrapers (the Latin guerro and the Brazilian afouce). This type of tone has a "buzz" to it. The great Afro–American trumpeter and jazz singer Louis Armstrong helped to make this tone widely popular. Many lead rock singers have incorporated this tone into their musical style, like Joe Cocker and Rod Stewart. There is no orchestral instrument that normally produces this type of tone. Trumpet, trombone, and saxophone players can produce this sound, as can electric guitarists. Today this tone quality is so common in blues and rock music that it has become the preferred sound, particularly for male singers. Again, this tone suggests male virility, female intimacy, warmth, extreme emotions, power, and sometimes anger. Dance or cinema scenes use this tone as well to suggest potential danger or attack.

The choice of tone in composing or orchestrating is important. The composer/-arranger's choices again amplify or detract from the emotional impact of the music. Intent on the part of the composer is amplified by the tone quality of the instruments he or she chooses to present their musical ideas.

Register

The highest pitched instruments in the orchestra include the piccolo, violin, bells, and xylophone. In jazz, popular, and rock music, the synthesizer or piano guitar, clarinet, and trumpet produce the highest pitches. Most of us hear higher frequencies and registers more clearly than lower registers, particularly women. For some reason women tend to be more sensitive to volume and register than men. Extremely high register suggests excitement, building to a climax, sudden danger, rapid movement (dancers or cinema kinesthetic action).

Most music, except for the bass lines and drums, is performed in the middle register. This is a stable, positive sound that can suggest beauty, inspiration, positive action, or movement. It is within the boundaries of pitch for the most common male or female spoken voice register. Common musical instruments in this range include violin, viola, cello (high register), trumpet (low register), trombone (high register), flute (low register), saxophone (alto/tenor), clarinet, and French horn. The middle register is the most commonly used register and is usually associated with positive emotions and lyric delivery by singers. In dance and cinema, this register is only avoided when it conflicts with dialogue or more extreme emotions or movements.

The low register, when used in music, usually expresses power, size, looming danger, conflict, large obstacles to overcome, and/or deep, dark, foreboding of coming dangers or disaster. In dance and cinema, it is raw power, approaching danger, overwhelming energy or excitement, foreboding, or an attempt to describe musically something very large and/or very powerful.

Summary

As we have already seen in earlier examples, each and every part of music aids in dramatically enhancing one or more human emotions. When these seven parts are put together carefully and with awareness of how the pieces should fit together, the power of music is overwhelming. Texture plays its role as well in enhancing drama, emotion, and movement in music, cinema, and dance.

Chapter 27

Style

Style, the seventh and final part of the mechanics of music ("seven" is considered the number of completion in the Bible) is made up of three separate parts: (a) tempo, (b) dynamics, and (c) articulation.

Tempo is how slow or how fast the primary beats or counts of a piece of music are. Music varies from an extreme slow of 40 beats per minute (bpm) to a hyper–velocity of 240 beats per minute.

Extremely slow tempos suggest sadness, grief, great loss, and major inspirational thought, the grandeur of nature, and relaxation and repose. Slow tempos can also suggest fatigue, defeat, age, and depression. Slow tempos run from the very slow 40 bpm to 80 bpm.

Medium tempos run from 72 bpm (there is some overlap here) to approximately 132 bpm. Moderate tempos suggest happiness, stability, and sometimes marching, or dancing, or walking as well as strong feelings about specific emotions.

Fast tempos pick up at 132 bpm and run all the way up to 240 bpm. Fast and extremely fast tempos suggest excitement, danger, thrill–seeking, great anticipation, tension, anger, speed, running, confrontation, fighting, building to a climax, events out of control, etc.

Interestingly enough, certain events, like describing a battle scene, a love scene, or a chase scene via music, all suggest beginning with a slower tempo and gradually accelerating the tempo to a thrilling climax. This is no accident. Music is a language of emotions and choice of tempos is an important part of that emotion.

Common musical terms for tempo include the following, from slow to extremely fast:

Slow Tempos (40 bpm–80 bpm)
Grave = 40–50 bpm
Largo = 40–60 bpm
Lento = 50–62 bpm
Adagio = 66 bpm
Andante = 70–80 bpm

Medium Tempos (80 bpm–120 bpm)
Moderato = 80–110 bpm
Martial (march-like) = 110–132 bpm
Allegro = 124–140 bpm

Fast Tempos
Allegro = 132–140 bpm
Vivace = 140–170 bpm
Presto = 170–200 bpm
Prestissimo = 200–240 bpm

Music speeds up and slows down often, and there are musical terms for that as well. To gradually speed up, *accelerando;* to gradually slow down, *ralantando.* To take liberties with the beat, *rubato.* Certainly the tempo of a piece of music connotes certain emotional and kinesthetic feelings. Composers writing for cinema, television, and commercials must understand that tempo is an important piece in the attempt to create with music an artificial emotional force field.

The second part of style is the use of dynamics (loud, soft). Dynamics has to do with the choice of volume for a piece of music. Again, these choices are important in amplifying the other choices already made in writing a specific piece of music.

Loud volumes suggest power, anger, judgment, the power of nature (storms, earthquakes, massiveness), revenge, attack, etc. Kinesthetically, loud music suggests running, fighting, lifting, aggressive movements, overpowering movements, violence, etc. *Loud music with a sharp backbeat can trigger the fight-or-flight response and cause the listener to feel excited, agitated, and aggressive. Caution: use with care.*

Soft volume suggests peace, quiet, tranquility, stability, love, tenderness, nostalgia, remembrances, the gentleness and subtlety of nature, beauty, illness, death, etc. Kinesthetically, soft music suggests liquid, smooth movements, laying down, walking slowly, touching, stroking, holding, kissing, etc.

Sudden dynamic changes (called subito in music) also suggest emotions, feelings, and movement. Sudden soft to loud (pianissimo to fortissimo) suggests danger, surprise, spontaneity, a change of heart, attack, etc. Movement-wise soft to loud suggests a complete reversal of movement . . . smooth to rough, soothing to attack, peace to shock, etc. Sudden loud to soft (fortissimo to pianissimo) is also an attention-getter, suggesting emotional contrast: anger to forgiveness, attack to protect, power to fragility, etc.

Dynamic markings for soft sounds include: *pppp* (pianississisiaaimo), the softest sound possible; *ppp* (pianississimo), very, very soft; *pp* (pianissimo), very soft; *p* (piano), soft; *mp* (mezzopiano), moderately soft; and *p subito* (suddenly soft). *Crescendo* means to get gradually louder and louder. *Decrescendo* means to get gradually softer and softer. *Diminuendo* means to get gradually softer. *Sotto voce* means "half-voice," a very soft lullaby-level vocal sound.

One of the great criticisms about today's popular music is its lack of dynamic contrast. So much music today is loud and louder, to the point of pain and discomfort. It's like someone "shouting" all the time. Careful use of dynamics is one of the most important parts in making music. Like seasoning in food, dynamics bring out the best flavors of the melodies, harmonies, and rhythms.

The last part of style is called *articulation*. Articulation has to do with how long you hold a note—and whether or not you connect smoothly one note to another, or play or sing each note short with as much space between them as possible.

When a composer or arranger wishes a smooth, connected sound, he writes a long line above the notes he wishes to connect. This long tine is called a *slur*. When used, the notes should flow one to another with no break in-between, as smoothly as possible. Slurred music—with connected notes—suggests sensuality, love, tenderness, endearment, the beauty of nature, nostalgia, etc.

Normal articulation suggests a slight space between notes. No marking is indicated for this style, since it is the most common of the articulation styles. Normal spacing between notes suggests musical dialogue, walking, speaking, casual conversation.

Placing a small dot above each note indicates *staccato*. This tells the performer to play each note as short as possible, allowing as much space as possible between notes. Staccato suggests military bearing, stiffness, discipline, order, uptightness, mechanical movements (robotic), etc.

Articulation livens up a musical piece and brings the deeper meanings to life. A composer must make a careful choice in which articulation he wishes to use -because the wrong choice sends the wrong signal and can cancel out the intended meaning of the selected rhythm, form, melody, chord progression, or instruments used.

Chapter 28

Musical Instruments

The original musical instruments—and still the most popular and universal—are the human voice and the drum. Every musical instrument can trace its roots and sounds back to these two primal music–making sources. A great deal of the world's music—even today—is focused around these two sound–generators.

Over thousands of years, man developed several families of instruments. Besides the voice, other instruments are classified by how they are played. Percussion instruments are played by striking them. Some of the percussion instruments like the marimba, the kalimba (African finger piano), the xylophone, the bells, and the kettledrums (tympani), are tunable and capable of playing a melody. Most percussion instruments are not. There are probably more types of percussion instruments in the world than any other family of instruments.

Woodwind instruments are played by blowing air through them. In the case of most woodwinds (with the exception of the piccolo and flute), the air activates a reed that vibrates and forces the air through the instrument, where a combination of keys and pads along with increased or decreased air pressure, raises or lowers the pitch. Some woodwind instruments like the saxophone and clarinet have a single cane reed that vibrates. Others, like the oboe, bassoon, and English horn, have a double reed, which produces the sound.

Woodwinds are internally categorized by families. For instance, within the flute family are four instruments (from the highest to the lowest pitch): (1) the piccolo, (2) the flute, (3) the alto flute, and (4) the bass flute. The same is true for the saxophone and clarinet: there are soprano, alto, tenor, and bass versions of the same instruments. The double-reed woodwind instruments are also a family; i.e., the oboe (soprano), the English horn (alto), and the bassoon (tenor and bass).

Rare and seldom used woodwind instruments in regular performance include the family of recorders (a soft-sounding vertical blown instrument) in soprano, alto, tenor and bass versions. Other more recently popular ethnic woodwind instruments include the Irish penny whistle and the Japanese shagahatsi. There is a Polynesian nose flute—yes, blown by forcing air through one of your nostrils into the instrument—but I've never seen one played or heard a recording. Another exotic and very ethnic woodwind instrument is the Scottish and Irish bagpipes.

Brass instruments, because of their sharp, bright sound and their ability to be heard over long distances, have always been favored by military bands, as far back as the Romans legions. Like the woodwinds, brass instruments are played by blowing air through them, but instead of activating a reed the lips of the brass player (held in place by an oval mouthpiece) vibrate as the air escapes between them.

The bugle, a higher pitched brass instrument without valves, was used regularly by the military before WWII for signaling everything from when to get up to when to eat, when to go to bed, when to attack, and when to retreat. Who can forget the haunting strains of the bugle playing "Taps" at a military funeral? Other standard brass instruments, from small to large, include the trumpet, the flugelhorn, the cornet, the alto horn, the French horn, the baritone horn, the trombone, the bass trombone, and the tuba.

Jewish rabbis blow into a ram's horn on Jewish high holidays at certain times in the religious service. This exotic instrument goes back to the time of Abraham, over 2,000 B.C., and is probably the oldest continuously used brass instrument (although it is not made of brass, but of an animal horn) in use today.

The heart and soul of the symphony orchestra is the string section. From the highest pitched to the lowest: the violin, the viola, the cello, and the bass viola. For the most part, these string instruments are played by bowing. Another family of very popular string instruments is played by plucking the strings. From the highest pitched to the lowest are the ukulele, the mandolin, the lute, the Arabic oud, the Spanish guitar, and the Mexican guitarrone (bass guitar).

The oldest keyboard instrument is the organ. A huge organ, driven by steam, was used in Rome at the time of the Caesars to signal to the city when each chariot race was to begin at the Roman Hippodrome (race track). This primitive keyboard instrument had huge keys that were played by slaves striking the keys with a sledgehammer. The maximum number of different pitches was nine.

Later the early Christian church began organ construction and using organs in the church as early as the ninth century. Organ building became an art, and each new cathedral competed with the others to have the best organ and organist available. These early church organs were driven by air pumped by bellows, with strong individuals manning the bellows to provide the air for the organist, who then released the air through a note on his keyboard into one of the pipes—depending on the desired pitch—where the air vibrated in the chamber producing the desired sound.

Prior to the invention of the modern piano in 1728 by a Florentine keyboardist by the name of Christofori (financed by the Medicis), the most popular keyboard outside of the organ was the harpsichord, a piano–like keyboard that used a quill to pluck the string when the key was struck. The harpsichord was a popular instrument until the modern piano, but its inability to play beyond a soft piano as well as an inability to sustain pitch for very long caused those whose minds are always searching for something better, to come up with the piano.

The clavichord was a small, light portable keyboard with a very soft sound that resulted when a key was struck and a felt–tipped hammer struck a piece of metal, which proceeded to vibrate at a particular pitch. This instrument was popular and was called the "virginal" in England, because Queen Elizabeth played it, and could carry it from room to room because it was so light. Its limited size and soft sound soon made it also obsolete after the piano was invented.

The piano's full name is "Piano é Forte," meaning "soft and loud."

Keyboardists were looking for an instrument similar to the harpsichord that had a darker, more sustainable tone and a much wider range of dynamics. The early pianos had a huge problem holding pitch because of the several tons of torque placed on the wood frame when tuned.

It was not until the Steinway (originally Steinweg) Corporation invented and perfected the cast iron frame for the piano that the truly modern piano was born. This happened in the early 1800s, just in time for the Romantic movement in Western European music, which demanded a much grander and wider range of expression from all the instruments, including the piano.

Today some of the most popular musical instruments are electronically amplified: the guitar, bass, and electronic keyboards (synthesizer). One of the major breakthroughs was the ability through digital computer technology to duplicate through an electronic keyboard any musical sound. A true revolution was born. A sampling synthesizer can record, analyze, and then play through the entire range of the keyboard (88 keys and 5½ octaves) on any sound, natural or unnatural.

This has resulted in major works based upon whale sounds, animal growls, volcanic eruptions, automobile rumblings, etc. There is no limit. In addition, the most advanced (and expensive) of these sampling synthesizers can imitate traditional orchestral sounds to such an accurate degree that only a trained expert can tell the difference. Most of the supposedly "large" orchestral backgrounds you hear behind certain television shows like "Star Trek" are really sampling synthesizers, well played, mixed, and presented as "real."

There is a school of electronic composers that write music for computer-produced synthesizer sounds as serious "art" music. Some of the more commercial versions of this, like Vangelis' musical score to *Chariots of Fire* (film) and Tomita's resetting of Gustav Holst's *The Planets,* and other classical works, have become widely popular.

Summary

Regardless of the family of instruments, there are still only two basic musical sounds—that of the drum and that of the human voice. Everything after has been nothing but a variation on these two original sounds. Still, composers are constantly looking for new ways to express themselves. The discovery and perfection of the sampling synthesizer has opened a vast new library of unlimited potential of musical sounds to the ever-searching, ever-innovative serious composer of tomorrow.

The Future

Chapter 29

The Future of Music

Music will play a much greater role in the life of each of us in the future. Research and recent studies, and books like this one, will help make the public more aware of the amazing and powerful effect of music on the body, the mind, the soul, the culture, and the civilization that we have developed.

In the not-too-distant future we will wake up to music that is carefully programmed to stimulate our respiratory and circulatory systems, calm our endocrine gland systems, quiet our digestion systems, and stimulate our brains through adjusting our brain to the correct waves—alpha, beta, theta, etc. We will have discovered that some types of music stimulate digestion and are okay to play in the background softly while eating, while other types of music can actually interfere with the digestive process. We will eat our meals in silence or listen to "breakfast" music at breakfast, "lunch" music at noon, and "dinner" music with our evening meal. Each member of the family will have special music prescribed for the physical and emotional needs by a professional music therapist working with the families general practitioner and endocrinologist.

When not engaged in highly concentrative work we will avoid chaos by listening with one-ear headsets that allow us to communicate and hear what is being said and at the same time still listen to our prescribed list of daily tunes and musical styles that we will need to balance physical and mental health. After a hard day at the office or on the freeway we will reach for our sound system when we get home and tune in soothing music. We may have a cocktail or glass of wine, but it will be for enjoyment, not a necessity to calm jangled nerves. The turf wars and arguments between generations will cease.

We will learn that teenagers have different musical needs than their parents or grandparents. Sure, there will be some music the entire family can and should share and enjoy, but for the most part, we will stay in our own room musically. Also, the customized programming will change as we grow older or discover we have special needs or physical conditions that need to be treated with music.

Music therapy will continue to grow until treatment for many chronic and even terminal illnesses will involve the use of music. Music's ability to affect positively or negatively cell growth will be capitalized on and developed into treatment regimens. Music will be combined with color and light and even aromas to help stimulate positive endorphins in the body that aid in healing. I believe that sound, not necessarily music, will be used to destroy cancer cells and other potentially deadly threats to the body and the mind.

Babies in the womb will listen to prescribed music via their pregnant mothers—music of a type that will calm and quiet the baby, stimulate growth, and ensure healthy development of cells within the fetus. Music, diet, and exercise will change the way we treat pregnancies and increase the chances of giving birth to mentally and physically healthy babies.

Music will be used to treat addictions: addictions to food, alcohol, drugs, sex, and tobacco in particular. The pleasure centers in the brain that are associated with the above can be artificially stimulated by music, thereby developing a positive addiction to music and dropping a negative one in the process.

One of the most dramatic discoveries that will change our listening habits forever will be the discovery that music itself can become a dangerous drug, demanding treatment for withdrawal. The undiscovered addiction to loud music has caused more damage in the latter part of the 20th century and early part of the 21st century to our young people than alcohol, smoking, or recreational drugs put together. One of the reasons it has caused so much harm is because its negative effects—physically and psychologically—were ignored by unscrupulous record, film, and television producers because they were making millions of dollars. As a result, we have produced a generation of partially dysfunctional citizens whose nervous and immune systems suffered premature burnout along with serious premature hearing loss.

One of the greatest areas of continuous discovery in regard to the power of music is in the area of learning. We already know that certain styles of music played quietly in the background in a classroom with students studying language, math, history, etc., can stimulate retention beyond our wildest dreams and dramatically speed up the learning process. This type of learning is called "Suggestology" or "superlearning." Why the professional educational world has resisted its adoption into our public school classrooms is unfortunate.

We discussed that the brain of a child goes through incredible changes between the ages of three and six years old and again at puberty, roughly 13 to 17 years of age. The type of music listened to at these times can have a dramatic effect in stimulating or repressing brain development in critical areas. Our society will be shocked when they begin to realize the damage caused up till now in allowing destructive musical styles to be openly purchased and listened to by children, particularly in these age categories. Chronic and widespread stunted brain development from listening to often-too-loud damaging music will come as a shock to our society and it will result in the demise of MTV and rock as a basic music style. The lawsuits against record companies and artists by angry parents and dysfunctional adults will put them out of business. I can hardly wait for that day to arrive! As a teacher, I have seen too often up close and personal the damage this drug music called "rock" can produce.

Music backgrounds in radio, television, and films will be carefully monitored. Any attempts to use music to artificially stimulate the "fight-or-flight" response to enhance the drama will be declared illegal.

Certain styles of music, particularly when played at 90 dB or louder, are so harmful to the body and the mind they will be declared illegal. Children both at home and at school will be taught why these musical styles are dangerous and why they can cause permanent physical, mental, and emotional harm. Students will learn early on in school and at home the delicate nature of the human hearing process. Just as we learned that strobe lights can produce seizures in epileptic patients, certain styles of music can produce classic negative behavioral patterns, particularly with young adolescents with classic negative emotional tendencies.

Can music cause someone to commit murder? The answer is "no," unless that person *already* has dangerous tendencies in that direction. Music is not the emotional bomb that goes off, but it can be the match that lights the fuse. Once the general public clearly understands this, unscrupulous record companies and film and television producers that cater to this kind of explosive music and gratuitous violence will be driven out of business by combination of punitive lawsuits and local, regional, and federal intervention.

Juvenile delinquents and young criminals will be weaned from negative musical styles and will be given positive musical styles that will help heal their bodies and minds and curb their unnatural aggression. They will be taught in penal institutions that indiscriminate listening to rock/pop music can trigger physical and emotional behavior that is difficult if not impossible to control.

In school all language and math classes will be taught with a soft, classical music background (Bach, Mozart, etc.). When information is combined with music, retention is transferred from the left–brain (short–term memory) to the right–brain (long–term memory). Third–world tribal societies have known this for centuries. Their entire history and identity is preserved through music. We have discovered the wisdom of our ancestors and we will reintroduce music as a major learning tool.

Athletes will learn to use music to positively enhance performance, increase motivation, and lower pain levels. Music will be used as a mild anesthetic in hospitals and dentist offices, and will be piped into operating and recovery rooms for surgical patients. Both the patient and the team of doctors will benefit from the use of carefully selected music being played in the surgical theater. The music will enhance the concentration and physical coordination of the surgeon and increase the energy and concentration of all involved. Terminally ill patients will find carefully selected music will decrease their chronic pain, relax their bodies and minds, calm their fears of death, and generally promote a humane and loving way to leave the planet. Prescribed music will help grieving families cope with the loss of a loved one.

Amazing results will continue to take place in the use of music to enhance growth and yield in agriculture. Music will be played from loudspeakers on top of fence posts across cornfields, vineyards, orchards, and other types of agriculture. Cows will listen to music while being milked; chickens will lay eggs to music; and animals entering a slaughterhouse will be calmed and sedated by music. Hydroponic farming (plants grown in a liquid chemical mixture of nutrients instead of soil) will allow nations with a limited quantity of quality soil for growing to survive.

Military and law-enforcement agencies will use music to calm prisoners, enhance interrogation techniques, and change behavioral patterns. Sound batons approximately the size of a large flashlight can be pointed at rioters, a prisoner, or an enemy soldier and the high-frequency sound produced and projected by the baton can be so painful the individual will immediately drop to their knees in pain, totally incapacitated. The projected cone of sound can be narrowed to one individual or enlarged to encase a small group.

Sound weapons will use low-frequency vibrations that can be sent through the earth to distant locations. The low-frequency vibrations will incapacitate any military personnel in the area. Low frequency sound waves are incredibly durable and strong and can cause everything from mild nausea to death.

Sonic cannons will be perfected by the military. A sonic cannon pointed at an enemy target will emit a powerful, explosive sound wave that will be projected a long distance via a laser beam and hit a target on the ground or in the sky and incapacitate or destroy it. Eventually explosives as we know them will no longer be used in war.

Adding music to enhance outdoor entertainment performances, like the dancing waters at the famous Bellagio Hotel in Las Vegas,

Nevada,will become a standard practice. Music will be coordinated with movement by a super–fast computer. Color, like sound, is composed of high–frequency vibrations. *Someday, we will see as well as hear a Beethoven symphony!*

Someday, every note played by an orchestra will be translated by computers into color, and the colors and patterns produced will be projected on a large screen behind the stage. Can you imagine the lift this will give live performances? Lines will form around classical, jazz, and ethnic ensemble box offices demanding tickets to this new and exciting addition to the experience of going to a concert.

Actually the rock 'n roll world was experimenting with the combining of color with sound at Fillmore West in San Francisco in the 1960s and 1970s. There was no way to directly link the music to the color patterns being projected behind the bands. This early experiment was but a prelude to the future, a breakthrough tying sound to color that will revolutionize the performing arts.

Ethnomusicology will receive much more attention if only for the recent discovery that many older and wiser societies had learned how to use music more carefully in their culture. A scientific as well as a musical curiosity will bring many musicologists and anthropologists to study and listen to the music of older civilizations.

Quiet, reverent music will return to worship in our churches. They will stop being centers of entertainment and will return to the important role of supporting worship of a just and holy God. Music for worship will be carefully selected. Lyrics will be screened for scriptural accuracy and for proper sentiment and respect. The experiment to blend secular music with sacred will have failed, failing to enhance either worship or entertainment. Most secular music in worship centers today is nothing but a watered–down imitation of popular secular music styles. By combining the two, we discovered you weaken both the worship process and the music. There is music suitable for worship and it is called "sacred." There is music that is suitable (although usually flat and uninspired) that is called "secular." They shall forever remain separate, particularly after discovering that a great deal of the secular music now being played in our churches is distracting and inappropriate.

Summary

Today we have discovered both the healing potential and the potential to cause harm through music. However, the future is bright. Because music is sound, and sound is vibration, and we are vibration, there is an even stronger relationship between music and matter. After all, the Bible, the Holy Word of God, opens in Genesis describing creation and tells us that the God of the universe "spoke" the world into being . . . matter was created through vibration.

Scientists at UCLA in Los Angeles have discovered that when certain sound frequencies were played over a Plexiglas tank full of water in a dark room, the sounds would "disturb" the water and produce a fatal light, or glow. Are we that close to discovering the secret of the universe through music and sound?

Bibliography

Aiello, Rita & Sloboada, John. *Musical Perceptions.* Oxford University Press, 1994.

Aitkin, Lindsay. *The Auditory Complex: Structural and Functional Bases of Auditory Perception.* Chapman & Hall, 1990.

Andrews, John C. *Music in the Early Christian Church.* Vol. 4, in *New Grove Dictionary of Music and Musicians,* edited by Stanley Sadie, 363-364. 1980.

Backus, John. *The Acoustical Foundations in Music.* W. W. Norton, 1977.

Baker, Paul. *Why Should the Devil Have All the Good Music?* Waco, TX: Word Books, 1979.

Barrier, Julie. "Contemporary Worship Trends." *International Resource Book for Church and School Musicians,* December 2000.

Begly, Sharon. "Your Child's Brain." *Newsweek,* February 19, 1996.

Benson, Carl, ed. *The Bob Dylan Companion.* Schirmer Books, 1998.

Berry, Wallace. *Structural Functions in Music.* Dover Publishing, 1987.

Best, Harold. *Music and the Church: A Theology of Church Music.*

Bjorkvold, John–Roar. *Man Is Musical: Universal of Child Culture in the U.S., Norway, and the Soviet Union.*

Booth, Stanley. *Keith.* New York City, NY: St. Martin's Press, 1995.

Brewer, Jane F. "Healing Sounds." *Complementary Therapies in Nursing & Midwifery: An International Journal* 4, no. 1 (April 1998).

Broadbent, E. H. *Pilgrim Church.* Grand Rapids, MI: Gospel Folio Press, 1933, rev. 1999.

Broughton, Simon, Mark Ellingham, David Muddymand, & Richard Trillo. *The Rough Guide to World Music.* London: Penguin Books, 1994.

Camp, Steve. "A Call for Reformation in the Contemporary Christian Music Industry." October 31, 1997.

Campbell, Don. *The Mozart Effect.* Avon, 1997.

Christians and Popular Culture. *All God's Children and Blue Suede Shoes.* Westchester, IL: Crossway Books, 1989.

Colson, Chuck. *The Body.* Dallas, TX: Word Publishing, 1992.

Dejtsch, Diana, ed. *The Psychology of Music.* 1999.

Edwards, Jonathan. *Sinners in the Hands of an Angry God.* New Kensington, PA: Whitaker House, 1997.

Graham, Billy. *Just As I Am.* New York City, NY: Harper/Collins, 1997.

Green, Melody & Hazard, David. *No Compromise.* Nashville, TN: Sparrow Press, 1989.

Hanegraaff, Hank. *Counterfeit Revival.* Dallas, TX: Word Publishing, 1997.

Hayford, Jack W. *Worship His Majesty.* Waco, TX: Word Books, 1987.

Hodges, Donald. *Handbook of Music Psychology.* 1996.

Howard, David. *Acoustics and Psychoneurotics.* Focal Press, 1990.

Joseph, Mark. *Rock and Roll Rebellion.* Nashville, TN: Broadman & Holman, 1999.

Jourdain, Robert. *Music, the Brain and Ecstasy.* 1997.

Juslin, Patrick & Sloboada, John, ed. *Music and Emotion.* 2001.

Lane, Deforia. *Music as Medicine.* Zondervan, 1994.

Learning to Worship as a Way of Life. Minneapolis, MN: Bethany House, 1984.

Lewis, C. S. *The Business of Heaven.* New York City, NY: Harvest House, 1984.

Liesch, Barry. *The New Worship.* Grand Rapids, MI: Baker Books, 1996.

Lucarini, Dan. *Why I Left the Contemporary Church Movement.* Evangelical Press, 2002.

"Making Music Makes You Smarter." Carlsbad, CA: NAMM.

Manning, Jacqueline. "Music Therapy." *British Journal of Theatre Nursing* 7, no. 3 (June 1997).

Medved, Michael. *Hollywood vs. America.* New York City, NY: Harper/Collins, 1992.

Meyer, Leonard. *Emotion and Meaning in Music.*

Miles, Elizabeth. *Tune Your Brain Using Music to Manage Your Mind, Body, and Moods.* Berkeley Publishing Group, 1997.

Morgenthaler, Sally. *Worship Evangelism.* Grand Rapids, MI: Zondervan, 1995.

Music Perception. www.ucpress.edu/journals/mp/.

Music Through the Eyes of Faith. San Francisco, CA: Harper & Collins, 1993.

Musica Research Notes. "Brain Anatomy and Music." Spring 1999.

Musica Research Notes. "The Mozart Effect: A Small Part of the Big Picture." Winter 2000.

Nobel, David. *Hypnotism and the Beatles: The Legacy of John Lennon.*

—. *Rhythm, Riots, and Revolution.*

Osbeck, Kenneth W. *101 Hymns Stories.* Grand Rapids, MI: Kregel Publications, 1982.

—. *101 More Stories.* Grand Rapids, MI: Kregel Publications, 1984.

Peacock, Charlie. *At the Crossroads: An Insider's Look at the Past, Present, and Future of Contemporary Christian Music.* Nashville, TN: Broadman & Holman, 1999.

Peretz, Isabelle, ed. *The Cognitive Neuroscience of Music.* 2003.

Petrie, Phil. "The History of Gospel Music." *CCM Magazine*, February 1996.

Psychology of Music. www.sempre.org.uk/journal/index.html.

Psychomusicology. www.c,rf/fsi/edi-psychmus/.

Quest Books. *Music Physician (For Times to Come).* 1991.

Rabey, Steve. "A Nobel Cause: The Constant Crusader Shares His Rhetoric on Rock." *CCM Magazine*, May 1986: 23–25.

—. "Silver Anniversary: Maranatha!" *CCM Magazine*, November 1996.

Religious Responses to Media and Pop Culture. 1998.

Robinson, Jennifer. *Music and Meaning.* Cornell University Press, 1997.

Rolling Stone Album Guide. New York City, NY: Random House, 1992.

Rossing, Thomas. *The Science of Sound.* Addison-Wesley Publishers, 1990.

Rykov, Mary, MA, MTA, & Deborah Salmon, MA, MTA, MCT. "Bibliography for Music Therapy." *The American Journal of Hospice and Palliative Care* 15, no. 3 (May/June 1998).

"Scientific Studies Have Proven That Music Participation Enhances Vital Intellectual Skills in Children." NAMM / Iowa Alliance for Arts Education.

Sloboada, John. *Music Mind.* 1985.

Storr, Anthony. *Music and the Mind.* Ballantine Books, 1992.

Suzuki, Shinichi. *Nurtured by Love: A New Approach to Education.* Exposition Press, 1969.

The Economist. "The Biology of Music."

The Free Press. *The Hole In Our Soul: The Loss of Beauty and Meaning in American Popular Music.* New York City, NY, 1994.

Tozer, A. W. *Whatever Happened to Worship?* Edited by Gerald B. Smith. Camp Hill, PA: Christian Publications, 1985.

Turner, Steve. *Hungry for Heaven.* Downer's Grove, IL: Intravarsity Press, 1995.

Weiss, Joanna. "The So-Called Mozart Effect May Be Just a Dream." *Boston Globe.*

Weiss, Rick. "Music Therapy." Silver Springs, MD.

Wells, David F. *God in the Wasteland.* Grand Rapids, MI: Wm. B. Eerdmans, 1994.

Westley, Marian. "Music Is Good Medicine." *Newsweek*, September 21, 1998: 103–104.

Wheaton, Dr. Jack. *All That Jazz: A History of Afro-American Music.* Scarecrow Press.

—. "Do's and Don'ts in Hiring Pros for Church Programs." *International Resource Book for Church and School Musicians*, December 2000.

—. *Rock and Revolution.* JCW Productions, 1980.

—. *Technological and Sociological Influences on Jazz as an Art-Form in America.* University of Michigan Press, 1976.

About the Author

Dr. Jack Wheaton is a man of many talents. He is a composer, conductor, pianist, educator, writer, and lecturer. He has written several books, including *All That Jazz: A History of Afro–American Music,* and *Crisis in Christian Music.* He has recorded ten commercial CDs, and has scored the musical soundtracks to five Hollywood films, plus numerous documentaries. He won an Emmy Award for conducting the Stan Kenton Collegiate Orchestra in an ABC–TV music special from the Hollywood Palace in Hollywood, California. He, along with a colleague, selected pianists for the Gershwin segment ("Rhapsody in Blue") of the Opening Ceremonies of the 1984 Olympics in Los Angeles, as well as the Superbowl half–time show held in San Diego in 1988. He also conducted, composed, and arranged music for eight years for the Monterey Jazz Festival High School All–Star Ensemble. Dr. Wheaton has conducted the Rome Opera Orchestra, the Downey Symphony, the Denver Municipal Band, and the Kenton All–Star Band.

Dr. Wheaton is former president and an original founder of the highly successful and rapidly growing International Association of Jazz Educators, one of the most universally popular music education organizations in the world. He was Administrative Director of Jazz Studies at the University of Southern California for ten years, and was instrumental in helping to attract the Thelonius Monk Institute to the Campus while there.

Most recently, Dr. Wheaton completed six years as president of the American Federation of Musicians in San Diego, California. He is currently the Steinway Piano consultant for schools, colleges, churches, and private institutions for Southern California, as well as the leader of the San Diego Jazz Quartet.